The American Chess Player's Handbook: Teaching The Rudiments Of The Game, And Giving An Analysis Of All The Recognized Openings

Howard Staunton

In the interest of creating a more extensive selection of rare historical book reprints, we have chosen to reproduce this title even though it may possibly have occasional imperfections such as missing and blurred pages, missing text, poor pictures, markings, dark backgrounds and other reproduction issues beyond our control. Because this work is culturally important, we have made it available as a part of our commitment to protecting, preserving and promoting the world's literature. Thank you for your understanding.

THE AMERICAN
CHESS PLAYER'S
HANDBOOK

TEACHING THE RUDIMENTS OF THE GAME, AND
GIVING AN ANALYSIS OF ALL THE
RECOGNIZED OPENINGS

ILLUSTRATED BY

APPROPRIATE GAMES ACTUALLY PLAYED

BY MORPHY, HARRWITZ, ANDERSSEN, STAUNTON, EVANS,
MONTGOMERY, MEEK AND OTHERS

INCLUDING

LASKER, STEINITZ, SCHLECHTER, PILLSBURY,
MARSHALL, TARRASCH, CAPABLANCA,
ALECHINE AND OTHER RECENT
PLAYERS

REVISED EDITION

Based on the work of Staunton and Modern Authorities

PHILADELPHIA
THE JOHN C. WINSTON CO.
1921

Copyright, 1917,
THE JOHN C. WINSTON CO.
Copyright, 1910-1914, The John C. Winston Co.
MADE IN U. S. A.

CHESS BOARD
Showing the men properly set up to commence play

PREFACE TO NEW REVISED EDITION.

THE following work is designed for those who are learning the noble game of Chess.

Many persons have been confused and discouraged at the very outset of the study by the great variety and the delicate distinctions of the openings; and this has constituted a fault in many otherwise excellent manuals for the learner.

The chief aim of the Editor of these pages has been to avoid this fault, by simplifying the openings, and by giving to the student chiefly such moves as are recognized to be the best, both in attack and defence. By playing over carefully the illustrative games, the learner will also see, at each opening, the variations made by experienced players in accordance with circumstances. As great a variety of actually played games has been given as was possible in a work of such limited scope. To this end the games of the distinguished players of different nations have been introduced, classified according to the different openings; and thus the reader will find the combined genius and skill of the old heroes like Philidor, Morphy, Staunton, Anderssen, Harrwitz, Evans, Montgomery and Cochrane, together with such recent masters as Lasker, Capablanca, Schlechter, Pillsbury, Marshall, Tarrasch, Janowsky, Alechine, and many other players of world-wide celebrity. The basis of this work is Staunton's "Chess Player's Handbook;" but other standard books have been drawn upon to fit it to be a manual for the beginner of to-day.

In order to insure perfect accuracy, all the lessons and games have been carefully gone over on the board after being put in type.

NAMES OF PLAYERS.

ALECHINE, 83, 110, 206.
ANDERSSEN, 91, 93, 165, 207, 212, 214.
BIERWIRTH, 200.
BLEDOW, 132, 140.
BOUCHER, 57.
BUCKLE, 86.
CAPABLANCA, 66, 98, 178.
CAPDEBO, 79.
CHENEY, 85.
CLEMENTS, 204.
COCHRANE, 72, 111, 125, 166.
DANIELS, 126.
DER LAZA, 96, 140, 141, 159.
DESCHAPELLES, 111.
DESLOGES, 180.
EVANS, 114, 135, 136, 166.
GHULAM CASSIM, 161.
GUNSBERG, 178.
HARRWITZ, 58, 59, 79, 86, 113, 210, 211.
HENDERSON, 114.
HILLEL, 93.
HORWITZ, 80, 114, 132.
JAENISCH, 73.
JANOWSKY, 190.
JONES, Dr., 208.
KIESERITZKY, 180.
KIPPING, 165.
LA BOURDONNAIS, 124, 161, 177.
LASKER, 98, 99, 110, 199, 206.
LEWIS, Dr., 204.
LEWIS, Mr., 158.
McADAM, 184.
McCABE, 80.

McDONNELL, 124, 161, 177.
MARACHE, 94.
MARSHALL, 66, 190.
MEEK, 110.
MONTGOMERY, 80, 184, 201, 206, 208.
MORPHY, 57, 58, 59, 60, 65, 91, 94, 200, 203, 207, 210, 211, 212, 214.
NEW YORK, 108, 109, 202.
PERIGAL, 178.
PETROFF, 73.
PHILADELPHIA, 108, 109, 202.
PHILIDOR, 60.
PILLSBURY, 67, 188.
PINDAR, 201.
POPERT, 85, 122, 141.
POTIER, 65.
PRETI, 203.
ROUSSEAU, 131.
SCHLECHTER, 188.
SCHULTEN, 132.
SPIELMANN, 209.
ST. AMANT, 84, 136, 137.
STANLEY, 131.
STAUNTON, 72, 80, 84, 113, 122, 125, 162, 179.
STEINITZ, 99, 213.
SZEN, 159.
TARRASCH, 83, 199.
TARTAKOWER, 209.
TCHIGORIN, 67.
THOMPSON, 206.
VON BILGUER, 132.
WALKER, 126, 137.
ZUKERTORT, 213.

CONTENTS.

CHAPTER I. INTRODUCTION.. Page 7
    The Chess-Board and Men—Moves and Powers of the Pieces and Pawns—Notation Used to Describe their Movements—Technical Terms of Chess—Illustrations of Technical Terms—Relative Value of the Chess Forces—The Chess Code, or, Laws of the Game—General Rules and Observations—Maxims and Advice for an Inexperienced Player—Preliminary Game.

II. KING'S KNIGHT'S OPENING..51-115
    Damiano Gambit, 52; Philidor's Defence, 54; Petroff's Defence, 61; Counter Gambit in the Knight's Opening, 68; The Giuoco Piano, 74; Captain Evans's Gambit, 88; The Two Knights' Defence, 95; The Knight's Game of Ruy Lopez, 97; The Queen's Pawn Game, or Scotch Gambit, 101; The Queen's Bishop's Pawn Game in the King's Knight's Opening, 116.

III. THE KING'S BISHOP'S OPENING.......................................116-137
    The Two Kings' Bishops' Game, 116; McDonnell's Double Gambit, 120; The Lopez Gambit, 121; The King's Knight's Defence in King's Bishop's Opening, 127; Counter Gambit in the King's Bishop's Opening, 128; The Queen's Bishop's Pawn's Defence in the King's Bishop's Opening, 130; Queen's Bishop's Pawn's Opening, 134.

IV. THE KING'S GAMBIT..138-184
    The King's Gambit proper, or King's Knight's Gambit, 138; The Cunningham Gambit, 142; The Salvio Gambit, 144; The Cochrane

Gambit, 146; The Muzio Gambit, 152; The Allgaier Gambit, 162; The King's Rook's Pawn Gambit, 164; The King's Bishop's Gambit, 166; The Gambit Declined, 180.

V. THE QUEEN'S GAMBIT..................................185-191

    The Gambit refused, 186.

VI. IRREGULAR OPENINGS..................................192-214

    The French Game, 192; The Sicilian Game, 193; The Wing Gambit, 194; The Centre Counter Gambit, 195; The Fianchetto, 196; Steinitz Gambit, 213.

VII. ENDINGS OF GAMES 215

    CHESS PROBLEMS 248

THE CHESS HANDBOOK.

CHAPTER I.

INTRODUCTION.

DESCRIPTION OF THE CHESS-BOARD AND MEN—ARRANGEMENT OF THE MEN—THE KING—THE QUEEN—THE ROOKS OR CASTLES—THE BISHOPS—THE KNIGHTS—AND THE PAWNS—THEIR MOVEMENTS, POWERS, METHOD OF CAPTURING AN ADVERSE MAN, ETC.

DESCRIPTION OF THE CHESS-BOARD AND MEN.

THE game of Chess is played by two persons, each having at command a little army of sixteen men, upon a board divided into sixty-four squares. The squares are usually colored white and black, or red and white, alternately; and custom has made it an indispensable regulation, that the board shall be so placed that each player has a white square at his right-hand corner.

The following diagram represents the board with all the men arranged in proper order for the commencement of a game:—

8 CHESS HANDBOOK.

No. 1.

Each player, it will be observed, has eight superior Pieces or officers, and eight minor ones which are called Pawns; and, for the purpose of distinction, the Pieces and Pawns of one party are of a different color from those of the other.

A King	♔ ♚
A Queen	♕ ♛
Two Rooks, or Castles . . . . (as they are indiscriminately called)	♖ ♜
Two Bishops	♗ ♝
Two Knights . . .	♘ ♞

INTRODUCTION. 9

And each of these Pieces has his Pawn or Foot-soldier . . . . .
making in all an array of sixteen men on each side.

On beginning a game, these Pieces and Pawns are disposed in the manner shown on the foregoing diagram. The King and Queen occupy the centre squares of the first or "royal" line, as it is called, and each has for its supporters a Bishop, a Knight, and a Rook, while before the whole stand the Pawns or Foot-soldiers in a row. (To prevent a common error among young players, of misplacing the King and Queen on commencing a game, it is well to bear in mind that at the outset each Queen stands on her own color. The Pieces on the King's side of the board are called the King's, as King's Bishop, King's Knight, King's Rook; and the Pawns directly in front of them, the King's Pawn, King's Bishop's Pawn, King's Knight's Pawn, and King's Rook's Pawn. The Pieces on the Queen's side are, in like manner, called the Queen's Bishop, Queen's Knight, and Queen's Rook; and the Pawns before them, Queen's Bishop's Pawn, Queen's Knight's Pawn, and Queen's Rook's Pawn.

MOVEMENT OF THE PIECES AND PAWNS, AND MODE OF CAPTURING AN ADVERSE MAN.

A knowledge of the moves peculiar to these several men is so difficult to describe in writing, and so comparatively easy to acquire over the chess-board, from any competent person, that the learner is strongly recommended to avail himself of the latter means when practicable: for the use, however, of those who have no chess-playing acquaintance at command, the subjoined description will, it is hoped, suffice.

The "Pieces," by which title the eight superior officers are technically designated, in contradistinction to the "Pawns," all take in the same direction in which they move. This act consists in removing the adverse Piece or Pawn from the board, and placing the captor on the square the former occupied To make this clear, we will begin with the King, and show his mode of moving and of capturing an adverse man.

The King.

The King can move one square only at a time (except in "Castling," which will be explained hereafter), but he can make this move in any direction, forwards, backwards, laterally, or diagonally. He can take any one of the adversary's men which stands on an adjoining square to that he occupies, provided such man is left unprotected, and he has the peculiar privilege of being himself exempt from capture. He is not permitted, however, to move into check, that is, on to any square which is guarded by a Piece or Pawn of the enemy, nor can he, under any circumstance, be played to an adjacent square to that on which the rival King is stationed. Like most of the other Pieces, his power is greatest in the middle of the board, where, without obstruction, he has the choice of eight

No. 2.

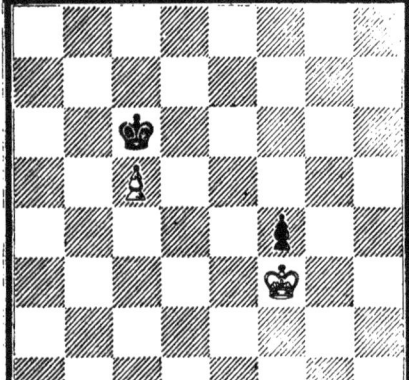

different squares. At the sides, he may play to any one of five, but when in the angles of the board, three squares only are at his command.

Supposing diagram No. 2 to show the position of the men towards the conclusion of a game, and it being either party's turn to play, he could take the adverse Pawn from the board, and place his King on the square it occupied; and, by doing so, the King would not depart from the order of his march, which, as we have before said, permits him to move *one step* in every direction. In each of these instances we have placed the Pawn in *front* of the King, but he would be equally entitled to take it were it standing on any other part of the eight squares immediately surrounding him, *always provided it was not sustained or guarded by some other Piece or Pawn.*

 THE QUEEN.

The Queen is by much the most powerful of the forces

No. 3.

12   CHESS HANDBOOK.

She has the advantage of moving as a Rook, in straight lines, forwards, backwards, and sideways, to the extent of the board in all directions, and as a Bishop, diagonally, with the same range. To comprehend her scope of action, place her alone in the centre of the board; it will then be seen that she has the command of no less than twenty-seven squares, besides the one she stands on. (Diagram No. 3.)

Thus placed in the middle of the board, the range of the Queen is immense. She has here the option of taking any one of eight men at the extremity of the board, on the squares respectively numbered 1, 2, 3, 4, 5, 6, 7, and 8, should her line of march be unobstructed; and if these men were nearer, on any of the intermediate squares, she would be equally enabled to take any one of them at her choice. Like all the other Pieces and Pawns, she effects the capture by removing the man from the board and stationing herself on the vacated square.

THE ROOK.

No. 4.

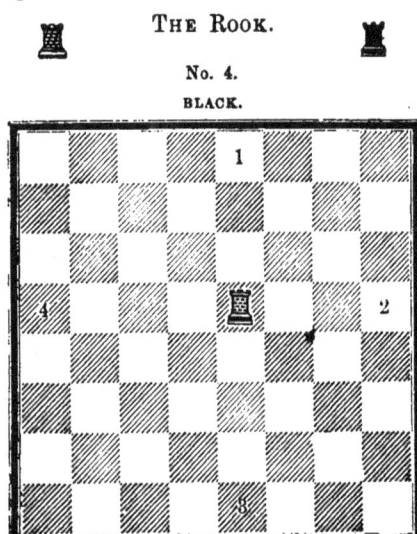

INTRODUCTION.

The Rook, or Castle, is next in power to the Queen. He moves in a straight line, forwards, backwards, or sideways, having a uniform range, on a clear board, of fourteen squares, exclusive of the one he occupies.

The Rook has the same power in taking as the Queen, forwards, backwards, and sideways, but he cannot, like her, take any man diagonally.

For example, place the Rook in the centre of the board, and an opposing man on each of the squares numbered, and the Rook has the power of taking any one of the four; and he has the same power if the Pieces are one or two squares closer to him, or immediately surrounding him, in the direction indicated by the four figures. (See Diagram No. 4.)

THE BISHOP.

The Bishop moves diagonally forwards or backwards, to the extent of the Board. It follows, therefore, that

No. 5.

he travels throughout the game only on squares of the same color as the one on which he stands when the game begins, and that each player has a Bishop running on white squares, and one on black squares. When placed on a centre square of a clear board, he will be found to have a range of thirteen squares.

The Bishop takes, as he moves, diagonally, either forwards or backwards, his range extending, on unobstructed squares, to the extent of the diagonal line on which he travels. (See Diagram No. 5.)

 THE KNIGHT.

The action of the Knight is peculiar, and not easy to describe. He is the only one of the Pieces which has the privilege of leaping over another man. The movements of the others are all dependent on their freedom from obstruction by their own and the enemy's men. For example, when the forces are duly ranged in order of

No. 6.

BLACK.

WHITE.

battle before the commencement of the game, the Knight is the only one of the eight capital Pieces which can be played before the Pawns are moved—King, Queen, Bishop, and Rook are all hemmed in by the rank of Pawns, which they cannot overleap; but the Knight, having the liberty of springing over the heads of other men, can be brought into the field at once. His move is one square *in a straight line*, and *one in an oblique direction;* or it may be perhaps better understood by saying that he moves two squares *in a straight line*, and *one in a side direction.*

His power and method of taking an opponent's man will be seen from the diagram (No. 6) on page 14.

In this situation, in the centre of the board, he would have the power of taking any one of the men stationed on the squares numbered, by removing the man and placing himself on the vacant square.

The Pawn.

The Pawn moves only one square at a time, and that *straight forward*, except in the act of capturing, when it takes one step diagonally to the right or left file on to the square occupied by the man taken, and continues on that file until it captures another man. It may, however, for its *first* move advance *two* steps, *provided no hostile Pawn commands the first square over which he leaps*, for, in that case, the adverse Pawn has the option of taking him in his passage, *as if he had moved one step only.* A Pawn is the only one of the forces *which goes out of his direction to capture*, and which has not the advantage of moving backwards; but it has one remarkable privilege, by which, on occasions, it becomes invaluable, *whenever it reaches the extreme square of the file on which it travels, it is invested with the title and assumes the power of any superior Piece, except the King, which the player chooses.* From this circumstance it frequently happens that one party, by skilful management of his

Pawns, contrives to have two, and sometimes even three Queens on the board at once, a combination of force which of course is irresistible.

As we before observed, the Pawn is the only man which captures in a direction different from his line of march. Suppose, at the opening of the game, White begins by playing King's Pawn to King's fourth square (see the article on Notation), Black may reply in the same manner with King's Pawn to King's fourth square, and neither Pawn can do more than remain an obstruction to the onward march of the other, but if Black answer instead with King's Bishop's Pawn to Bishop's fourth, or as in the

No. 7.

BLACK.

WHITE.

diagram, with Queen's Pawn to Queen's fourth, then White, if he choose, may take the adverse Pawn from the board and place his own in its stead

THE NOTATION ADOPTED TO DESCRIBE THE MOVES OF THE MEN.

THERE is no portion of an elementary work on Chess of so much importance to the learner, and none which requires more resolute mastering than this.

The notation may be called the language of the game and a knowledge of it is absolutely indispensable to every one who is himself ambitious of excelling, or who is desirous of appreciating the excellencies of other players.

Having marshalled the men in battle order, as shown in the first diagram, you will observe that each party has two *ranks* of men, on the first of which stand the superior Pieces, and on the next the eight Pawns. The eight squares which compose the first rank are each distinguished by the name of the Piece which occupies it when the men are first arranged. There are, therefore, the King's square, the King's Bishop's square, King's Knight's square, and King's Rook's square, and in like manner, the Queen's square, Queen's Bishop's square, Queen's Knight's and Queen's Rook's squares. The *files*, that is, the row of squares running from top to bottom of the board, are also named by the Pieces occupying the first square in each *file*. Thus each of the superior officers has a file or row of eight squares running from his end of the board to the corresponding Piece of the enemy, and every one of these eight squares takes its name from such officer.

Bear in mind that White names every square on the board, in accordance with its relative position to one of *his* eight Pieces, and that Black does the same. Hence it follows that Black's *first* squares are White's *eighth*, and *vice versâ*.

Before proceeding further, it will be desirable for the student to familiarize himself with the respective moves of the Pieces, names of the squares, &c. A very little practice will enable him to do so, especially with the aid of any friend acquainted with them. He should, in the first place, accustom himself to the setting up the men in order of battle; after a few repetitions of the process, and comparing their position with diagram No. 1, he will soon have no difficulty whatever in arranging them correctly without referring to the book. It will then be well to clear the board of all but a single Piece, and practise with that until perfect in its movements; another, and then another, may be added, until the action of every one is as familiar as the alphabet.

Suppose, as a first exercise, you begin by placing your Queen on her square (*i. e.*, her first square), then play her to Q's 5th square, then (diagonally, observe) to Q Rook's 8th square, then to King's Rook's 8th square, then to Q. R's square, and then home again to her square. It is proper to mention that the directions for moving a Piece are not usually printed in full, and that, according to the modern abbreviations in the present and other chess-books, these several instructions would be given thus :—

1. Q. to her sq.
2. Q. to her 5th.
3. Q. to her R's 8th
4. Q. to K. R's 8th.
5. Q. to her R's sq.
6. Q. to her sq.

As a next exercise, put the Queen's Bishop on his square, beside the Queen, and play him as follows :—

1. Q. B. to K. R's 6th.
2. Q. B. to K. B's 8th.
3. Q. B. to Q. R's 3d.
4. Q. B. to his sq.

To these two Pieces now add the Queen's Knight, or his own square, and play as follows :—

1. Q. Kt. to Q's 2d.
2. Q. Kt. to K's 4th.
3. Q. Kt. to K. B's 6th.
4. Q. Kt. to K's 8th.
5. Q. Kt. to Q. B's 7th.
6. Q. Kt. to Q. Kt.'s 5th.
7. Q. Kt. to Q. B's 3d.
8. Q. Kt. to his sq.

By taking all the Pieces in succession thus, you will speedily obtain sufficient knowledge of their movements to commence the opening of a game; but before attempt ing this, it is needful for you to be acquainted with the technical terms in use among chess-players, and the code of laws which governs the game.

TECHNICAL TERMS IN USE AMONG CHESS-PLAYERS.

Castling.—Although, as a general rule, the move of the King is restricted to one square at a time, he has the privilege, under certain conditions, once in the game, of moving in conjunction with either of the Rooks two squares. This peculiar movement is called *Castling*, and is performed in the following manner:—If a player wishes to castle on his King's side of the board, he moves the King to K. Kt.'s sq., and then places the K's Rook on K. B's square. If he castle on the Queen's side, he plays his King to Q. B's sq., and Q's Rook to Q's sq. The object of this compound move is to place the royal Piece in safety, and at the same time bring the Rook from the corner square into better play.

The conditions under which a player is permitted to castle are:—1st. The King must not be in check. 2d. The King must not have moved. 3d. The Rook must not have moved. 4th. The King must not pass over or on to any square attacked by an enemy's man. And 5th. There must be no Piece, either of his own or the adversary's, between the King and the Rook.

In exemplification of the importance of castling, to escape from an attack, and to retort one on the adversary, see, presently, the diagram No. 8 (p. 24).

Check and Checkmate.—The King is said to be in *check* when he is attacked by any Piece or Pawn, for it being a fundamental law of chess that the King can never be taken, whenever any direct attack upon him is made, he must be warned of his danger by the cry of *check*, and the player is then compelled either to remove his King *out* of *check*, or parry the check by interposing a man between the King and the attacking Piece, or capture the checking man.

When he can do none of these three things, he is *check-*

mated, and the game won by the other side. (See diagrams Nos. 9 and 10.) When the King is directly attacked by the Piece played, it is a *simple* check; but when the Piece moved does not itself give check, but unmasks another which does, it is called a *discovered check*. (See diagram No. 8.) The third species of check is named the *double check*, where the King is attacked both by the Piece moved and the one discovered. The fourth description is called *perpetual check*, a case which arises when a player has two or more squares on which he can give check, and his opponent can only parry one check by affording an opportunity for another. If the first player then persists in the repetition of these particular checks, the game must be abandoned as drawn (See diagram No. 11).

Doubled Pawn.—When two Pawns of the same color are on the same file, the front one is called a *doubled pawn*.

Drawn Game.—When neither party can give checkmate, the game is drawn. This may arise from several causes, as :—1st. *Perpetual check.* 2d. Where there is not sufficient force to effect a mate, as a King and a Knight only, or a King and two Knights, &c., &c. 3d. Where one party has force sufficient, but is ignorant of the proper mode of applying it, and thus fails to checkmate his helpless adversary within the fifty moves prescribed by the " Code ". 4th. Where both parties persist in repeating the same move from fear of each other. 5th. Where both parties are left with the same force at the end, as a Queen against a Queen, a Rook against a Rook, and the like, when, except in particular cases, the game should be resigned as a drawn battle. And 6th. When one of the Kings is *stalemated*.

En Prise.—When a Piece or Pawn is in a situation to be taken by the enemy, it is said to be *en prise*. To put a piece *en prise*, is to play it so that it may be captured.

The Exchange.—When a player gains a Rook for a Bishop or a Knight, it is termed *winning the exchange*.

False Move.—Any illegal move, such as castling when the King has been moved or is in check, moving a Rook diagonally, or a Bishop like a Knight, is called a false or an "impossible" move.

Fool's Mate.—This is the simplest of all checkmates being accomplished in two moves in the following manner:—

WHITE.	BLACK.
1. K. Kt. P. to K. Kt.'s 4th.	1. K. P. to K's 4th.
2. K. B. P. to K. B's 4th.	2. Q. to K. R's 5th, checkmate.

It cannot possibly be given by the first player.

Forced Move.—When a player has one only legal move at command, it is said to be a *forced move.*

Gambit.—This word is derived from an Italian phrase in wrestling, and signifies a movement by which the adversary is tripped up. In chess, this is attempted by the first player putting a Pawn *en prise* of the enemy early in the game, by which he is enabled more rapidly and effectually to develope his superior Pieces. There are several gambits, but the most important, and one which includes many others, is the King's gambit, commenced as follows:—

WHITE.	BLACK.
1. K. P. to K's 4th.	1. K. P. to K's 4th.
2. K. B. P. to B's 4th.	2. P. takes K. B. P.

The Pawn offered by the first player here at his second move is called the Gambit Pawn, and when taken by the adversary the opening becomes a gambit.

The varieties of the gambits are often designated by the names of the players who invented or first brought them into vogue—as the *Muzio* gambit, the *Salvio* gambit, the *Allgaier* gambit, the *Lopez* gambit; while others obtain their names from the opening moves of the first player, as the King's Bishop's gambit, which begins thus:—

WHITE.	BLACK.
1. K. P. to K's 4th.	1. K. P. to K's 4th.
2. K. B. P. to B's 4th.	2. P. takes P.
3. K. B to Q. B's 4th.	

and is so called because the K's Bishop is played out at the 3d move instead of the K's Knight.

There is also the Queen's gambit, of which the opening moves are—

WHITE.	BLACK.
1. Q. P. to Q's 4th.	1. Q. P. to Q's 4th.
2. Q. B. P. to B's 4th.	2. P. takes P.

The gambits are the most brilliant and animated of all the openings, full of hair-breadth 'scapes and perilous vicissitudes, but affording an infinitude of beautiful and daring combinations.

"*Giuoco Piano*," a solid and instructive modification of the King's Knight's game, is safe and for drawing games generally practised by the leading players. The opening moves are:

WHITE.	BLACK.
1. P. to K's 4th.	1. P. to K's 4th.
2. K. Kt. to B's 3d.	2. Q. Kt. to B's 3d.
3. K. B. to Q. B's 4th.	3. K. B. to Q. B's 4th.

To Interpose.—When the King is checked, or any valuable Piece in danger from the attack of an enemy, you are said to *interpose* a man when you play it between the attacked and attacking Piece.

Isolated Pawn.—A Pawn which stands alone, without the support and protection of other Pawns, is termed an *isolated* Pawn.

J'adoube.—A French expression, signifying "I arrange," or "I replace," which is used by a player when he touches a man merely to adjust its position on the board, without intending to play it. (See the 7th law.)

Minor Pieces.—The Bishop and Knight, in contradistinction to the Queen and Rook, are called *Minor Pieces*.

The Opposition.—A player is said to have the opposition when he can place his King directly in front of the adverse King, with only one square between them. This is often an important advantage in ending games.

Party.—From the French *partie*. Frequently used by modern writers instead of the word "game."

Passed Pawn.—A Pawn is said to be a *passed* one

when the adversary has no Pawn to obstruct its march on the same file, or on either of the next files to the right or left.

Pion Coiffé, or Marked Pawn.—This is a description of odds but rarely given, and only when there is a vast disparity between the skill of the players. It consists in one party placing a *cap* or ring on one of his Pawns, and undertaking to checkmate his opponent with that particular Pawn. He is not allowed to *Queen* the Pawn, and if he loses it, or happens to checkmate his opponent with any other man, he forfeits the game. The Pawn usually *capped* is the King's Knight's, because it can be more readily and effectually surrounded by protecting Pieces.

To Queen a Pawn, or to advance a Pawn to Queen.— When a player has contrived to advance a Pawn to the eighth or last square of the file, it assumes the rank and power of a Queen, or of any other Piece he chooses, and he is then said to have *queened* his Pawn. (See the 21st law.)

Scholar's Mate.—A checkmate occasionally given at the opening of a game by a practised player to one but little tutored in the science. The following are the moves:—

WHITE.	BLACK.
1. P. to K's 4th.	1. P. to K's 4th.
2. K. B. to Q. B's 4th.	2. K. B. to Q. B's 4th.
3. Q. to K. R's 5th.	3. Q. P. one.
4. Q. takes K. B. P., giving checkmate.	

Smothered Mate.—A checkmate which is sometimes given by the Knight when the adverse King is hemmed in, or *smothered*, by his own forces. (See diagram No. 12.)

Stalemate.—When one party has his King so circumstanced that, not being at the moment in check, he cannot play him without going into check, and at the same time has no other Piece or Pawn to move instead, he is said to be *stalemated*, and the game is considered drawn. (See diagram No. 13.)

Taking a Pawn en Passant, or in Passing.—It has been shown before, in speaking of the action of the Pawn, that he is limited in his march to one square forward at a time when not capturing, and one square forward diagonally, either to the right or left, when he takes an adversary. but that he has the privilege, on being first played in the game, to advance two squares, unless in so doing he pass a square which is attacked by a hostile Pawn; in which case the opponent may, at his option, permit him to make the two steps forward, and there remain, or may capture him in his passage in the same way as if he had moved but one step.

ILLUSTRATIONS OF TECHNICAL TERMS.

The Operation of " Castling ;" and " Discovered Check "

No. 8.

BLACK.

WHITE.

In this situation the white King is threatened with what is called "a discovered check," that is, his opponent. by removing the Bishop, would *discover* check from the Queen a proceeding in the present instance, which would speedily involve the loss of the game to White. Not being at the moment in check, however, and having moved neither King nor Rook, and there being no *intervening* Piece between the King and his own Rook, White is enabled to castle, giving check to the adverse King at the same time, and win the game easily, for Black has no square to which he can move his King without going into check, and is consequently obliged to interpose his Q. at K. B's second, or K. B's third square, in either case being checkmated in two more moves, as you will soon be able to see.

Checkmate.

No. 9.

BLACK.

WHITE.

The above position represents the appearance of the forces on each side towards the end of a game, and will assist to explain the application of two or three of the technical terms described in the present section, as well as to exhibit the King in a situation of checkmate. You already understand that the moves at chess are played by each party alternately; in this case it is White's turn to play, and he will checkmate his antagonist in two moves. Place the chess-men on your board exactly in the order they stand in the diagram; having done this, suppose yourself to be playing the White men, and take the Black King's Pawn with your Queen, in the manner before shown, *i. e.*, by taking the Pawn from the board and stationing your Queen on the square it occupied. By this act, you not only take his Pawn, but you attack his King, and must apprise him of his danger by calling "*check*." He has now two ways only of parrying this check. It is clear he cannot move his King, because the only two squares to which he could move without going into check are occupied by his own men; he is forced then either to take the Queen with his K. B.'s Pawn, or to interpose the Bishop at King's second square. If he take the Queen with his K. B's Pawn, you must reply by playing your King's Bishop (which you will know by the color of the diagonal on which he travels) to K. Kt.'s sixth square, crying "check." Examine the position attentively, and you will find that Black has no square to which he can move his King, the only vacant one being attacked by your Queen's Bishop, that he has nothing wherewith to take the Bishop that has given check, and neither Piece nor Pawn with which to interpose between it and his King, and that consequently, he is not only checked, but *checkmated*. In like manner, if, at his first move, instead of capturing your Queen, he interpose his Bishop at King's second square, you immediately take the Bishop with your Queen, who is protected by her Bishop, and say "checkmate."*

Perpetual Check.

The diagram on page 28 will enable you to understand what is meant by *perpetual check* as well as the most

---

* We append a diagram here, showing a position which has frequently been misapprehended by unpractised players.

By inspecting the diagram it will be seen that the White King 's in check of the Black Queen. By the simple move of the White

elaborate arrangement of the men could do. Place the men on your chess-board according to the diagram, suppose yourself to be playing the white Pieces, and that it is your turn to move. Your adversary, you will observe, has the advantage in point of force, but this is counterbalanced by the situation, which enables you to draw the game. To do this, you must first play your Queen to one of the three squares where she will check the King, *i. e.*, to K's 4th, Q's 5th, or Q. B's 6th; it is indifferent which, say, therefore, Q. to K's 4th (check). Black has no option, his King cannot move, he must interpose his Queen. If now you were to take the Queen you would lose the game, on account of his two Pawns; but instead of doing so,

---

Rook to K. Kt.'s 5th square, checking the Black King, and at the same time discovering check by the White Queen, Black is check-mated, although having by far the strongest force of men. We give the position to show that any Piece or Pawn, although employed in covering a check of its own King, has nevertheless the power to check the adverse King.

No. 10.

BLACK

WHITE.

No. 11.

BLACK.

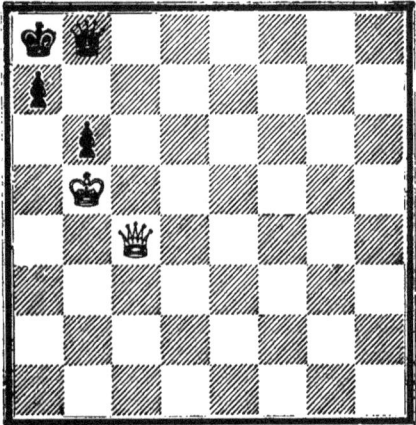

WHITE.

you play the Queen to King's 8th sq., giving check. The black Queen must again interpose; you repeat the check at K's 4th, Black can only parry it with his Queen, and you may persist in giving the same two checks, *ad infinitum*. In such cases, the game is resigned as " drawn by *perpetual check*."

Smothered Mate.

This is a familiar example of *smothered mate*, which you will find can be effected by no other Piece than the Knight. White first move is, Queen to her 5th square checking. Black is obliged to retreat his King to the R's sq., because, were he to play him to his B's sq., the Q would checkmate at once. Upon the King retiring, White gives check with his Kt. at K. B's 7th; this brings the King back again to Knight's sq., and affords to White an opportunity of giving *double check*, which he does by moving the Knight to K. Rook's 6th, checking with both

No. 12.
BLACK.

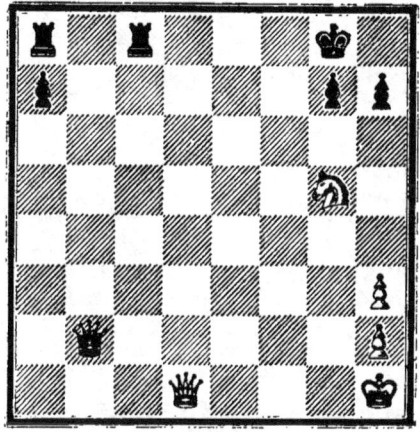

WHITE.

Q. and Knight; as before, the King must go to Rook's sq.; and now follows a beautiful move—White plays his Queen down to K. Kt.'s 8th (next square to the Black King), giving check; the King cannot take on account of the Knight; he is compelled, therefore, to capture with his Rook, and the Knight then gives the *smothered mate* at K. B.'s 7th square.

Stalemate. (See Diagram on page 30.)

Here you observe that White has the great advantage of a Queen against a Rook; but with all this, and the move to boot, it is impossible for him to do more than draw the game. It is evident that he cannot move his Queen from the front of his King on account of exposing him to check with the Rook. If he move his King, Black takes the Queen, and the game is drawn. And lastly, if he take the Rook with his Queen, he places the adverse King in the position before described of *stalemate*.

No. 13.

BLACK.

WHITE.

ON THE RELATIVE VALUE OF THE CHESS FORCES.

An attempt to establish a scale of powers whereby the relative values of the several men could be estimated with mathematical exactitude, although it has frequently engaged the attention of scientific minds, appears to be an expenditure of ingenuity and research upon an unattainable object. So ever varying, so much dependent on the mutations of *position* which every move occasions, and on the augmented power which it acquires when combined with other forces, is the proportionate worth of this with that particular man, that it would seem to be beyond the reach of computation to devise a formula by which it can be reckoned with precision. But still an approximation to correctness has been made, and the result arrived at gives the following as the ultimate respective values :—

Pawn . . . . . = 1.00
Knight . . . . = 3.05
Bishop . . . . = 3.50
Rook . . . . . = 5.48
Queen . . . . . = 9.94

The King, from the nature of the game, which does not admit of his being exchanged or captured, is invaluable, and he is not, therefore, included in the calculations.

The Pawn, it is seen, is the least valuable of all the men, the Knight being worth at least three Pawns.

The Bishops and Knights are practically considered of equal value, although there is a difference in the estimate here given.

A Rook is of the value of five Pawns and a fraction, and may be exchanged for a minor Piece and two Pawns. Two Rooks may be exchanged for three minor Pieces.

The Queen is usually reckoned equal, in average situations, to two Rooks and a Pawn, but towards the end of a game she is hardly so valuable as two Rooks.

These comparative values may be of service to the student in general cases of exchanging men, but he will find in practice the relative worth of his soldiers is modified by so many circumstances of time, opportunity, and position, that nothing but experience can ever teach him to determine accurately in every case "which to give up and which to keep."

THE CHESS CODE.
OR, LAWS OF THE GAME.
DEFINITIONS OF TERMS USED.

Whenever the word "*Umpire*" is used herein, it stands for any Committee having charge of Matches or Tournaments, with power to determine questions of chess-law and rules; or for any duly appointed Referee, or Umpire; for the bystanders, when properly appealed to; or for any person, present or absent, to whom may be referred any disputed questions; or for any other authority whomsoever having power to determine such questions.

When the word "*move*" is used it is understood to mean a legal move or a move to be legally made according to these laws.

When the word "*man*" or "*men*" is used, it is understood that it embraces both Pieces and Pawns.

THE CHESS-BOARD AND MEN.

The Chess-board must be placed with a white square at the right-hand corner.

If the Chess-board be wrongly placed, or if there is a deficiency in number, or a misplacement of the men, at the beginning of the game, the game shall be annulled, provided the error is discovered before the second player makes four moves.

FIRST MOVE AND COLOR.

The right of first move must be determined by lot.

The right of first move shall alternate, whether the game be won, lost or drawn.

Whenever a game shall be annulled, the party having the move in that game shall have it in the next game. An annulled game must be considered, in every respect, the same as if it had never been begun.

CONCESSIONS.

The concession of an indulgence by one player does not give him the right of a similar or other indulgence from his opponent.

ERRORS.

If, during the course of the game, it be discovered that any error or illegality has been committed in the moves of the pieces, the moves must be retraced, and the necessary correction made, without penalty.

If the moves cannot be correctly retraced the game must be annulled.

If a man be dropped from the board and moves made during its absence, such moves must be retraced and the man restored. If this cannot be done, to the satisfaction of the Umpire, the game must be annulled.

CASTLING.

The King can be Castled only:—

When neither the King nor the Castling Rook has been moved, and

Where the King is not in check, and

Where all the squares between the King and Rook are unoccupied, and

Where no hostile man attacks the square on which the King is to be placed, or the square he crosses.

In Castling, the King must be moved first, or before the Rook is quitted. If the Rook be quitted before the King is touched, the opposing player may demand that the move of the Rook shall stand without the Castling being completed.

The penalty of moving the King prohibits Castling.

EN PASSANT.

Taking the Pawn "*en passant,*" when the only possible move, is compulsory.

PROMOTING THE PAWN.

A Pawn reaching the eighth square must be at once exchanged for any piece of its own color (except the King) that the player of the Pawn may elect.

INTRODUCTION. 33

CHECK.

No penalty can be enforced for an offence committed against these rules in consequence of a false announcement of "check." When check is given it is not obligatory to announce the check.

"J'ADOUBE."

"J'adoube," "I adjust," or words to that effect, cannot protect a player from any of the penalties imposed by these laws, unless the man or men touched, obviously *need* adjustment, and unless such notification be distinctly uttered *before* the man, or men, be touched, and only the player whose turn it is to move is allowed so to adjust.

The hand having once quitted the man, but for an instant, he move must stand.

Men overturned or displaced accidentally may be replaced by either player, without notice.

A wilful displacement, or overturning of any of the men, forfeits the game.

PENALTIES.

Penalties can be enforced only at the time an offence is committed, and before any move is made thereafter.

A player touching one of his men, when it is his turn to play, must move it. If it cannot be moved he must move his King. If the King cannot move, the offender must move a man selected by his opponent.

For playing two moves in succession the adversary may elect which move shall stand.

For touching an adversary's man, when it cannot be captured, the offender must move his King. If the King cannot move, the offender must move a man selected by his opponent. But if the man touched can be legally taken, it must be captured.

For playing a man to a square to which it cannot be legally moved, the adversary, at his option, may require him to move the man legally, or to move the King. If the latter penalty be exacted, and the King cannot legally be moved, the offender must move any piece designated by the opposing player.

For illegally capturing an adversary's man, the offender must move his King, or legally capture the man, as his opponent may elect. If neither is possible, the offender must move a man selected by his opponent.

For attempting to Castle illegally, the player doing so, must move either the King or Rook, as his adversary may dictate.

For touching more than one of the player's own men, he must move either man that his opponent may name.

For touching more than one of the adversary's men, the offender must capture the one named by his opponent, or if *either* cannot be captured, he may be required to move the King or capture the man which can be taken, at the a 'versary's option; or, if *neither* can be captured, then the King must be moved.

A player moving into check may be required, by the opposing player, either to move the King elsewhere, or to move some other piece designated by the opposing player.

For discovering check on his own King, the player must either legally move the man touched, or move the King a his adversary's option. In case neither move can be made he must move a piece designated by his adversary.

While in check, for touching or moving a man which does not cover the check, the player may be required to recover with another piece, or move the King, as the opposing player may elect.

ADJOURNED GAME.

Upon a game being adjourned, the player whose turn it is to move shall seal his move. Sealing a move consists in writing it legibly on a piece of paper which shall remain in the keeping of a third party during the adjournment.

Upon the resumption of an adjourned game the position existing at the time of adjournment shall be set up and the sealed move made on the board.

If the position existing at the time of adjournment cannot be ascertained the game shall be annulled.

If upon opening a sealed move the record cannot be interpreted as expressing a legal move, the offending player may be required to move his King, or, if the King cannot legally be moved, a piece designated by his opponent. If the record can be interpreted as expressing either of two moves, the offender shall make the one selected by his opponent.

DRAWN GAMES.

A game is drawn—
 (a) When the players agree to treat it as drawn.
 (b) Upon the proof by either player that fifty moves have been made on each side without a piece being captured.
 (c) When either player claims a draw upon his turn to play, and proves that the existing position has occurred at least twice before during the game.
 (d) When either player claims a draw and demonstrates that he can subject the opposing King to an endless series of checks.
 (e) When a stale-mate occurs.

TIME LIMIT.

The penalty for exceeding the time limit is the forfeiture of the game.

It shall be the duty of each player, as soon as his move be made, to stop his own register of time and start that of his opponent, whether the time be taken by clocks, sand-glass, or otherwise. No complaint respecting an adversary's time can be considered, unless this rule be strictly complied with. But nothing herein is intended to affect the penalty for exceeding the time limit as registered.

ABANDONING THE GAME.

If either player abandon the game by quitting the table in anger, or in an otherwise offensive manner; or by momentarily resigning the game; or refuses to abide by the decision of the Umpire, the game must be scored against him.

If a player absent himself from the table, or manifestly ceases to consider his game, when it is his turn to move, the time so consumed shall, in every case, be registered against him.

DISTURBANCE.

Any player wilfully disturbing his adversary shall be admonished; and if such disturbance be repeated, the game shall be declared lost by the player so offending, provided the player disturbed then appeals, to the Umpire.

THE UMPIRE.

It is the duty of the Umpire to determine all questions submitted to him according to these laws, when they apply, and according to his best judgment when they do not apply.

No deviation from these laws can be permitted by an Umpire, even by mutual or general consent of the players, after a match or tournament shall have been commenced.

The decision of the Umpire is final, and binds both and all the players.

RULES FOR PLAYING THE GAME AT ODDS.

I. In games where one player gives the odds of a piece, or "the exchange," or allows his opponent to count drawn games as won, or agrees to check-mate with a particular man, or on a particular square, he has the right to choose the men, and to move first, unless an arrangement to the contrary is agreed to between the combatants.

II. When the odds of Pawn and one move, or Pawn and more than one move, are given, the Pawn given must be the King's Bishop's Pawn when not otherwise previously agreed on.

III. When the odds of two or more moves are given, the player receiving the odds shall begin the game with these moves, but may not, in making them, advance any piece beyond his fourth rank.

IV. When a player gives the odds of a Rook he may move his King as though to castle with the Rook given, provided the square of the missing Rook has been unoccupied throughout the game, and provided the ordinary conditions as to squares and the King are complied with.

V. When the odds of a Pawn, Knight, Bishop, or Rook, are given, it is understood that the King's Bishop's Pawn, or the Queen's Knight, Queen's Bishop or Queen's Rook, is intended unless special agreement to the contrary is made.

GENERAL RULES AND OBSERVATIONS.

Concerning the King.—It is mostly advisable to castle the King pretty early in the game, and to do so on the King's side, because he is less subject to an attack, and better able to repel one on that side than the other.

Be fearful, when castled on the King's side, of permitting an adverse Knight to gain safe possession of your King's Bishop's 4th square, and remember that it is seldom prudent in an inexperienced player to advance the Pawns on the side his King has castled.

Be cautious of playing your Queen in front of your King and in subjecting yourself to a *discovered check.* It is better when check is given to your King to interpose a man that attacks the checking Piece than with one that does not. Beware of giving useless checks to your adversary's King, but when, by checking, you can oblige him to move, and thus deprive him of the right to castle, it is generally good play to do so. It is sometimes useful to give a series of checks, and even sacrifice a Piece, to force the King into the middle of the board, where he may be subjected to the attacks of your other men.

Do not in all cases take an enemy's Pawn which stands before your King,—it may serve sometimes as a protection to him; and bear in mind that towards the termination of a game, especially when the superior Pieces have been taken off the field, the King should be made to compensate for his previous inactivity, by being busily engaged. The fate of the game is then dependent for the most part on the skill displayed in the management of the King.

Concerning the Queen.—The Queen is so powerful and important a Piece at chess that she should rarely be employed to defend or attack any point if you can do it as well with a subordinate.

It is not good to play the Queen out in the game at the beginning, because she can be attacked by inferior Pieces, and is compelled to retire with the loss of many moves.

Be careful, too, when about to capture a distant Pawn or Piece, that you do not remove your Queen too far from the immediate point of action. A skilful player will often permit you to win a Pawn with the Queen, that he may prevent her returning in time to rescue your King from his attack. The power of the Queen is wonderfully greater when she is aided and protected by other Pieces than when she goes forth unsupported; it is generally injudicious, therefore, to make an attack with her unless in combination with some other of your forces.

Concerning the Rook.—The Rook is a most important officer, yet few players even amongst the best avail themselves sufficiently of his power. He has seldom much scope for action in the early part of the engagement, but when the field is thinned no time should be lost in bringing him into action. You should then endeavor to *double* your Rooks, that is, to place them one before the other on the same file: in this situation, mutually sustaining one another, their potency on a clear field is equal to the Queen's.

It is usually good play to get command of an open file,

that is to say, a file which is occupied by no other man, by stationing a Rook at one end of it. When you have thus gained possession of the file, should your opponent try to dispossess you of it, by playing one of his Rooks on the same file, it is frequently better to defend with your other Rook than to take his or remove your own. You will often embarrass your adversary, too, if you can nanage to post a Rook on his second rank, say at your King's 7th or Queen's 7th square. In this position he generally makes an attack on the Pawns unmoved, and compels the enemy to lose time in defending them, while you can bring more forces into action.

One of the strongest reasons for playing out your Pieces early in the battle, is, that while at home they are not only themselves inactive, but they utterly retard the movements of your Rooks. In an unskilfully developed game it is a common occurrence to see the victory won before the defeated player's Rooks have ever moved.

Concerning the Bishop.—When the game is opened by each party with King's Pawn to King's 4th square, the *King's Bishop* is somewhat superior to the *Queen's*, because it can be sooner brought into play, and may be made to bear immediately on the King's weak point, his Bishop's Pawn. It is desirable therefore generally to exchange your Queen's Bishop or Queen's Knight for the adversary's King's Bishop. The King's Bishop should rarely or never be played to the Queen's 3d square before the Queen's Pawn is moved. His best position, as we have remarked above, is to Queen's Bishop's 4th square, where he attacks the opponent's King's Bishop's Pawn. If your antagonist then challenges an exchange of Bishops by moving his Queen's Bishop to King's 3d square, it is not always prudent to accept it, because although you may double the Pawns on his King's file, you at the same time afford him an open range for his King's Rook when he has castled. The best play in such a case is, therefore, to retreat your King's Bishop to *Queen's Knight's 3d square.*

Be careful, as a general rule, in an open game, not to

move your Queen's Pawn *one* square *before* you bring out the King's Bishop, as by so doing you leave him but the *King's 2d square* on which to move, and there his position is defensive rather than attacking.

It strong in Pawns towards the conclusion of the game, endeavor to get rid of the enemy's Bishops, because they can impede the march of your Pawns more readily than either the Rooks or Knights.

When the other men are exchanged off, and you remain with a Bishop and two or three Pawns, it is often proper to keep your Pawns on squares of a different color from those on which your Bishop travels, as he can then prevent the opposing King from approaching them. If, however, you have the worst of the game, it is mostly better then to keep them on the same color as the Bishop, that he may defend them.

Supposing you have *Pawns only* at the end of a game, and the adversary has a Bishop, it is generally advisable to move the Pawns as soon as possible to squares of a different color from the diagonals on which he moves.

Do not indiscriminately exchange your Bishops for Knights, or *vice versâ.* Two Bishops at the finish of a game are stronger than two Knights, and one Knight generally more useful than a single Bishop.

Concerning the Knight.—The Knight is at once the most striking and most beautiful of all the Pieces. The singularity of its evolutions, by which it is enabled to overleap the other men and wind its way into the penetralia of the adverse ranks, and if attacked leap back again within the boundary of its own, has rendered it the favorite Piece of leading players in every country.

The assault of the Knight is more subtle and dangerous than that of any other Piece, because he attacks without putting himself *en prise,* and his attack can never be resisted by the interposition of another man.

At the commencement of a game, the best place for the King's Knight is at *K. B's 3d sq.;* it there attacks your adversary's K's Pawn, if it has been moved two squares, and offers no impediment to the playing out your

INTRODUCTION.

King's Bishop, and prevents the adversary from placing his Queen on your King Rook's 4th sq., where she would often be a source of restraint and danger to your King. Many persons prefer playing the K. Kt. to K's $2d$ at the second move, from the mistaken notion that the K. B's P. should be moved before the Knight is played to B's 3d; this is an error, and generally leads to a very bad game.

When you have brought out your Q. Kt. to B's $3d$, it is frequently advisable, at a proper opportunity, to get him round by K's $2d$ sq. to the K. Kt's $3d$, where he exercises a very important influence, by threatening, whenever the square is left unguarded, to post himself on K. B's $5th$.

A Knight with three or four Pawns, at the end of a game, has an advantage over a Bishop with an equal number of Pawns, because he can leap from white to black, and thus attack the Pawns on either colored squares, whereas the Bishop can attack them only when they move on squares of the color of his diagonals. In similar circumstances, however, he is not so useful in defending as a Bishop or a Rook, since if forced to remove he ceases to defend, while the Rook or Bishop may retreat and still protect.

Concerning the Pawns.—Struck by the scope and power of the higher Pieces, young players commonly overlook the homely Pawns, or deem them scarcely worthy of regard, and are amazed to learn that the combinations of these simple elements are among the most refined and arduous studies of the science. Yet such is the fact, and without a thorough comprehension of their quiet but remarkable predominance in almost every circumstance of the game, it is impossible for any one to attain a high degree of excellence.

It is generally advantageous for your Pawns to occupy the middle of the board, because when there they greatly retard the movements of the opposing forces. The King's Pawn and Queen's Pawn, at their fourth squares, are well posted, but it is not easy to maintain them in that position, and if you are driven to advance one of them, the powe.

of both is much diminished. It is well, therefore, not to be too eager to establish two Pawns abreast in the centre until you are fully able to sustain them there.

When you have two Pawns abreast, the King and Queen's, for instance, at their fourth squares, should the adversary attack one of them with a Pawn, it is occasionally better to advance the Pawn that is attacked another step, than to take the Pawn.

The Pawns, however, should seldom be far advanced, unless they can be properly sustained by the Pieces. Pawns at their fourth squares are therefore mostly more powerful than at their sixth.

The King's Bishop's Pawn having no support but that of the King, is usually the point to which the first attack is directed, and more than ordinary care should be taken to preserve it. It is rarely good play to move the King's Bishop's Pawn to Bishop's 3d early in the game.

As a general rule, it is not advisable to move King's Knight's Pawn or Queen's Knight's Pawn early in the game. The former played to K. Kt's 3d square will often allow your adversary to play his Queen's Bishop to your King's Rook's 3d square, a dangerous move when you have castled on King's side.

After castling, it is generally proper not to move the Knight's Pawn that is before your King, until you are obliged.

In a diagonal line of Pawns you should endeavor to preserve the Pawn at the head of them. Pawns, when united, have great strength; but when separated, their power is sensibly lessened.

A passed Pawn is mostly serviceable when supported by another Pawn.

A doubled Pawn is not in all cases a disadvantage, especially if it is united with other Pawns. The worst kind of doubled Pawn is one on a Rook's file; while the most advantageous is the King's Bishop's Pawn doubled on the King's file, because it strengthens your middle Pawns and opens a file for your King's Rook.

The Pawn being less important than a Piece, it is usu

ally better to defend with it than with a Piece. For the same reason it is likewise better to protect a Pawn with a Pawn than with a Piece. No Piece can interpose between the attack of a Pawn, it can therefore frequently check the King with great advantage.

Be cautious generally of advancing the Pawns far on either side, till you see on which your opponent castles; and remember, when approaching the end of a game, where you have Pawns, or even a Pawn, against a minor Piece, that *you may win*, but that your opponent, except in very rare cases, cannot, and that two Pawns in any situation can *protect themselves* against the adverse King.

MAXIMS AND ADVICE FOR AN INEXPERIENCED PLAYER.

THERE is nothing that will improve you so much as playing with good players; never refuse, therefore, when any one offers you odds, to accept them: you cannot expect a proficient to feel much interest in playing with you upon *even* terms, and as you are sure to derive both amusement and instruction from him, it is but fair that he should name the conditions. It will soon happen that you yourself will be able to give odds to many amateurs whom you meet; when this is the case, avoid, if possible, playing them *even*, or you are likely to acquire an indolent, neglectful habit of play, which it will be very difficult to throw off.

Never permit your hand to hover over the board, or indeed to approach it, until you have completely made up your mind what Piece to move; a contrary habit begets a feeling of indecision that is fatal to success. Play invariably according to the laws of the game, neither taking back a move yourself, nor allowing your opponent to recall one. Do not exhibit impatience when your adversary is long in making his move. His slowness is a tacit compliment to your skill, and enables you to play with proportionate quickness, because while he is meditating on his next step you can take advantage of the time to consider what shall be your rejoinder; besides, it is absolutely necessary for every one desirous of excelling at chess to play slowly. A fine player examines occasionally from five to twenty or more moves on each side: can this be done in a moment? It is easy enough to play quick against inferior play; but against equal and very good play one cannot play quick without losing.

Learn to play indifferently either with the white or black men. Do not play too many games at a sitting—and never suffer the loss of a game to occasion you much disquietude. Think of how many thousand games a Philidor must have lost before he attained his highest excellence; besides, the loss of one well-fought game with a fine practitioner will do more towards your improvement than the gain of ten light skirmishes with weaker players than yourself. Endeavor to play all your Pieces equally well. Many young players have a predilection for a particular Piece, as the Knight or the Queen, and lose both time and position in trying to prevent exchanges of their favorite. In opening your game, endeavor to bring your superior officers into action speedily, but avoid all premature attacks. Take care not to play a Piece to a square where it impedes the action of another, and beware of venturing an unsupported Piece in the adversary's game.

If subjected to a violent attack, you may often disconcert your opponent by compelling the exchange of two or three Pieces. When, however, you are about to exchange officers, you must calculate not only their ordinary value, but their peculiar worth in the situation in question; for example, a Rook is generally more valuable than a Knight or a Bishop; but it will happen, that by exchanging a Rook for one of the latter you may greatly improve your game.

It is mostly good play to exchange the Pieces off when you are superior in power, so that when you have the odds of a Piece given to you by a finished player, you should endeavor to exchange as often as you can consistently with safety.

When an exchange of two or more Pieces appears in

evitable, look closely to see whether it is better for you to take first or to compel your opponent to do so. When one of the enemy is *completely* in your power, do not be too eager to make the capture—there may perhaps be a move of importance which you can make before you take him. Beware also of snatching hastily a proffered man, it may be only given as a bait to catch a more important advantage from you.

If at the end of a game you remain with Pawns against a Knight and find it difficult to evade his repeated checks, recollect that by placing your King on the same diagonal as the Knight, with but one intervening square between them, you cannot again be checked under three moves.

When you have lost a game which has cost you great attention, it is a good practice to play it over afterwards in private, and endeavor to discover where the error occurred through which your opponent gained his first advantage. This custom will improve both your memory and your play.

ON THE SEVERAL OPENINGS OR BEGINNINGS OF GAMES.

BEFORE proceeding to the consideration of the various methods of commencing the game, it is advisable for you to recur to the preceding sections, which treat of the arrangement of the men—the moves of the men—their relative powers—the technical terms in use among players—and the laws of the game. When you have familiarized yourself with these, it will be time for you to direct your attention to that most important feature in the game of chess—the art of opening the game.

There are several modes of beginning the game, but the following are the principal:—

1st. Each player begins by moving his *King's Pawn to King's 4th square*, and the first player then moves *King's Knight to King's Bishop's 3d square*. This is called the *King's Knight's opening*.

2d. Each player commences by moving his *King's Pawn to King's 4th square*, and then he who has the first move plays *King's Bishop to Queen's Bishop's 4th square.* This is known as the *King's Bishop's opening.*

3d. Each player opens with *King's Pawn to King's 4th square,* and the first plays *Queen's Bishop's Pawn to Bishop's 3d square.* This is termed the *Queen's Bishop's Pawn's opening.*

4th. Each player begins with *King's Pawn to King's 4th square,* and the first follows with *King's Bishop's Pawn to Bishop's 4th square.* This is called the *King's gambit.*

Of these four openings on *the King's side* there are many modifications, of which each has its appropriate appellation; there are also several openings begun on the Queen's side, but the four above-named are those most generally practised, and with them you should be thoroughly conversant before advancing further.

PRELIMINARY GAME.

PREPARATORY to the investigation of the several openings treated of in the following chapters, it may not be uninstructive to give a short game which shall exhibit the application of some technical phrases in use at chess, and at the same time show a few of the most prominent errors into which an inexperienced player is likely to fall.

In this game, as in all the analyses which follow, the reader will be supposed to play the White Pieces and to have the first move, although, as it has been before remarked, it is advisable for you to accustom yourself to play with either Black or White, for which purpose it is well to practise the attack, first with the White and then with the Black Pieces.

WHITE.	BLACK.
1. K's P. to K's 4th.	1. K's P. to K's 4th.

When the men are first arranged in battle order, it is seen that the only Pieces which have the power of moving are the Knights, and that to liberate the others it is indispensably necessary to move a Pawn. Now, as the

King's Pawn, on being moved, gives freedom both to the Queen and to the King's Bishop, it is more frequently played at the beginning of the game than any other. You will remember, in speaking of the Pawns it was shown that on certain conditions they have the privilege of going either one or two steps when they are first moved.

2. K's B. to Q's B's 4th.   2. K's B. to Q's B's 4th.

Thus far the game illustrative of the *King's Bishop's* opening is correctly begun. Each party plays his King's Bishop thus, because it attacks the most vulnerable point of the adverse position, viz., the *King's Bishop's Pawn*

3. Q. B's Pawn to B's 3d.   3. Q's Knight to B's 3d.

In playing this Pawn your object is afterwards to play Queen's Pawn to Queen's 4th square, and thus establish your Pawns in the centre; but Black foresees the intention, and thinks to prevent its execution by bringing another Piece to bear upon the square.

4. Q's Pawn to Q's 4th.   4. Pawn takes Q's Pawn.
5. Q's B's Pawn takes Pawn.   5. K's B. takes Pawn.

Here you have played without due consideration. Black's third move of Queen's Knight to Bishop's 3d square was a bad one, and afforded you an opportunity of gaining a striking advantage, but omitting this, you have enabled him to gain a valuable Pawn for nothing. Observe, now, your reply to his third move was good enough, (4. Queen's Pawn to Queen's 4th square), but when he took your Pawn with his, instead of taking again, you ought to have taken his *King's Bishop's Pawn* with your Bishop, giving check: the game would then most probably have gone on thus :—

5. *K's B. takes K. B. Pawn* (ch.)   5. *K. takes Bishop.*
6. *Queen to K. R's 5th (check).*   6. *K. to his B's square*
7. *Queen takes K's Bishop* (check).

In this variation, you see Black has lost his King's Bishop's Pawn, and what is worse, *has lost his privilege of castling*, by being forced to move his King; and although for a moment he had gained a Bishop for a Pawn, it was quite clear that he must lose a Bishop in return by the check of the adverse Queen at King's

Rook's 5th square. It is true that he need not have taken the Bishop, but still his King must have moved, and White could then have taken the King's Knight with his Bishop, having always the better position.

But now to proceed with the actual game:—

6. K's Knight to K's B's 3d.   6. Queen to K's B's 3d.

Bringing out the Knight is good play; you not only threaten to win his Bishop, but you afford yourself an opportunity of castling whenever it may be needful. Black would have played better in retiring the Bishop from the attack to Queen's Knight 3d square than in supporting it with the Queen.

7. Knight takes Bishop.   7. Queen takes Knight.

Both parties played well in their last moves. You rightly took off the Bishop, because supported by the Queen he menaced your Queen's Kt's Pawn, and Black properly retook with his Queen instead of the Knight, because having a Pawn ahead, it was his interest to exchange off the Queens.

8. Q's Knight to Q's 2d.   8. K's Knight to B's 3d.

You played correctly here in not exchanging Queens, and also in protecting your Bishop and your King's Pawn, both of which were attacked by the adverse Queen; but all this might have been done without impeding the movements of any of your Pieces, by simply playing Queen to King's 2d sq.; as it is, the Knight entirely shuts your Queen's Bishop from the field. Black properly brings another Piece to the attack of your King's Pawn:—

9. K. B's Pawn to B's 3d.   9. Q's Knight to King's 4th.

In protecting the King's Pawn with your K. Bishop's Pawn, you are guilty of a very common error among young players; as you improve, you will find that it is rarely good play to move the K. Bishop's Pawn to the third square—in the present instance, for example, you have deprived yourself of the power of castling, at least for some time, since the adverse Queen now commands the very square upon which your King, in castling on his own side, has to move. Black's last move is much more

INTRODUCTION. 47

sensible. He again attacks your Bishop, and by the same move brings his Q's Knight into co-operation with the King's, on the weak point of your position:—

10. Pawn to Q. Kt.'s 3d.   10. Q. takes Queen's Rook.

This is a serious blunder indeed. In your anxiety to save the threatened Bishop, which you feared to withdraw to Q. Kt.'s 3d sq., on account of the adverse Knight's giving check at your Queen's 3d square, you have actually left your Q's Rook *en prise!* Black takes it, of course, and having gained such an important advantage, ought to win easily.

11. Castles, (*i. e.*, plays K. to   11. Q's Kt. takes Bishop.
    his Kt.'s sq., and Rook to
    K. B.'s sq.)
12. Kt. takes Kt.   12. Castles.
13. Queen to her 2d.   13. Q. B's Pawn to B's 4th.

Your last move is very subtle; finding the mistake that Black had committed in not retreating his Queen directly after winning the Rook, you determine, if possible, to prevent her escape by gaining command of all the squares she can move to. Seeing the danger, Black throws forward this Pawn to enable him, if possible, to bring the Queen off, by playing her to her 5th sq., giving check.

14. Bishop to Q. Kt's 2d.   14. Q. takes Q. R's Pawn.

This move of the Bishop is well timed; it does not, to be sure, prevent the Queen from escaping for a move or two, but it gives you an attack, and very great command of the field.

15. Q. to K. Kt's 5th.   15. Knight to K.'s sq.

Very well played on both sides. By playing the Queen to K. Kt.'s 5th, you threatened to win his Knight by at once taking it with your Bishop, which he could not retake without opening check on his King. Instead of so moving, you might have played the Knight to Q. Rook's 5th sq., in which case, by afterwards moving the Rook to Q. Rook's square, it would have been impossible for his Queen to get away.

16. Q. to King's 3d.   16. K. R's Pawn to R's 3d.

You prudently retreated your Queen to guard her Knight's

Pawn; which it was important to save, on account of its protection to the Knight. Black played the King's R's Pawn to prevent your Queen returning to the same post of attack.

17. K. R's P. to R's 3d.   17. K. to his R's sq.

Here are two instances of what is called "lost time" at chess, neither move serving in the slightest degree to advance the game of the player. That you should have overlooked the opportunity of gaining the adverse Queen was to be expected. Similar advantages present themselves in every game between young players, and are unobserved.

18. K. B's Pawn to B's 4th.   18. Q. Kt's Pawn to Kt's 3d.

Again you have failed to see a most important move; you might have taken the K. Rook's Pawn with your Queen, giving check safely, because Black could not take your Queen without being in check with your Bishop. All this time, too, your opponent omits to see the jeopardy his Queen is in, and that as far as practical assistance to his other Pieces is concerned, she might as well be off the board.

19. K. Kt's Pawn to Kt's 4th.   19. Q. Kt's Pawn to Q. Kt's 4th.

Your last move is far from good. By thus attacking your Knight, Black threatens to win a Piece, because upon playing away the Knight you must leave the Bishop unprotected.

20. Pawn to K. Kt's 5th.   20. Pawn takes Knight.

Although your Knight was thus attacked, it might have been saved very easily. In the first place, by your taking the adversary's Q. B's Pawn, threatning to take his K's Rook, on his removing which, or interposing the Q's Pawn, you could have taken the Pawn which attacked your Knight; or, in the second place, by moving your Queen to her 2d square. In the latter case, if Black ventured to take the Knight, you would have won his Queen by taking the K. Kt.'s Pawn with your Bishop, giving check, and thus exposing his Queen to yours. Black would have been obliged to parry the check, either by taking the

Bishop or removing his King, and you would then have taken his Queen. This position is very instructive, and merits attentive examination.

21. B. to Q. B's 3d.	21. Pawn takes Q. Kt.'s Pawn.
22. Pawn to K. R's 4th.	22. Pawn to Q. Kt.'s 7th.

In such a position, the advance of your King's flank Pawns is a process too dilatory to be very effective.

23. Pawn to K. B's 5th.	23. Pawn to Q. Kt.'s 8th, becoming a Queen.

Now the fault of your tortoise-like movements with the Pawns becomes fatally evident. Black has been enabled to make a second Queen, and has an overwhelming force at command.

24. Rook takes Queen.	24. Queen takes Rook (check).

You had no better move than to take the newly-elected Queen, for two Queens must have proved irresistible.

25. King to his Kt.'s 2d.	25. Kt. to Queen's 3d.
26. K. Kt.'s Pawn to Kt.'s 6th.	26. P. takes Pawn.
27. P. takes Pawn.	27. Bishop to Q. Kt.'s 2d.

Here you have given another remarkable instance of lost opportunity. At your last move you might have redeemed all former disasters by checkmating your opponent in two moves. Endeavor to find out how this was to be accomplished.

28. K. R's Pawn to R's 5th.	28. Knight takes King's Pawn.
29. Bishop to King's 5th.	29. Kt. to K. Kt.'s 4th (discovering check).

Up to Black's last move you had still the opportunity of winning the game before mentioned.

30. King to Kt.'s 3d.	30. K's Rook to B's 6th (ch.)
31. King to R's 4th.	31. Q. to K. Bishop's 4th.

At this point you were utterly at the mercy of your antagonist, but fortunately he wanted the skill to avail himself properly of his vast superiority in force and position, or he might have won the game in half a dozen different ways.

32. Q. takes Rook.	32. Q. takes Queen.
33. B. takes K. Kt.'s Pawn (ch.)	33. King takes Bishop.

This was your last chance, and its success should serve

to convince you that in the most apparently hopeless situations of the game there is often a latent resource, if we will only have the patience to search it out. By taking the Bishop, Black has left your King, *who is not in check*, no move without going into check, and as you have neither Piece nor Pawn besides to play, you are *stalemated*, and the game is DRAWN.

If thoroughly acquainted with the information contained in the preceding sections, you may now proceed to the consideration of the openings; before you do this, however, it is necessary to apprise you that without a great abridgment of the notation adopted in the foregoing game, it would be impossible to compress within the limits of this work one-third of the variations which are required to be given. The following abbreviations will therefore be used throughout the remainder of our HANDBOOK :—

K.	for King.
Q.	Queen.
R.	Rook.
B.	Bishop.
Kt.	Knight.
P.	Pawn.
sq.	square.
adv.	adversary's.
ch.	check or checking.
dis ch.	discovering check.

The word "square" is only used to distinguish the first row of squares on which the superior Pieces stand at the commencement—thus, we say, Kt. to K's 2d, and omit the word square; but if the Kt. were played to K's *first* square or R's *first* square, the move would be described not as Kt. to K's or R's *first* square, but "Kt. to K's or R's square."

CHAPTER II.

THE KING'S KNIGHT'S OPENING

WHITE.	BLACK.
1. P. to K's 4th.	1. P. to K's 4th.
2. K's Kt. to B's 3d.	

Your second move gives the name to this opening, which is one of the most popular and instructive of all the various methods of commencing the game. The Kt., it will be observed, at once attacks the adverse Pawn, and the defence recommended by the best authors and the leading players of Europe, is for Black to reply 2. Q's Kt. to B's 3d. He has, however, many other ways of playing, and as the examination of these comparatively simple variations will serve to prepare you for the more complex and elaborate combinations of the best defences, it will be advisable to consider them previously. In the first place, then, Black may sustain his Pawn by playing—

1. P. to K. B's 3d.
2. K's B. to Q's 3d.
3. Q. to K. B's 3d.
4. P. to Q's 3d.

or, in the second place, he may leave it unprotected, and play—

5. K's Kt. to B's 3d.
6. K's B. to Q. B's 4th.
7. P. to K. B's 4th.
8. P. to Q's 4th.

He has thus eight different modes of play at his command, besides the move of Q's Kt. to B's 3d, in answer to your second move of K's Kt. to B's 3d. Each of these will form the subject of a separate game.

GAME THE FIRST.
The Damiano Gambit.

WHITE.	BLACK.
1. P. to K's 4th.	1. P. to K's 4th.
2. K's Kt. to B's 3d.	2. P. to K. B's 3d.
3. Kt. takes K's P.	3. P. takes Kt.
4. Q. to K. R's 5th (ch.)	4. P. to K. Kt's 3d.
5. Q. takes K's P. (ch.)	5. Q. to K's 2d.
6. Q. takes R.	6. K's Kt. to B's 3d.
7. P. to Q's 4th (best.)	7. Q. takes P. (ch.)
8. Q's B. to K's 3d.	8. Q. takes Q. B's P.
9. Q. takes Kt.	9. Q. takes Q. Kt's P.
10. K's B. to Q. B's 4th.	10. K. B. to Q. Kt's 5th (ch.)
11. Q's Kt. to Q's 2d.	11. Q. takes R. (ch.)
12. K. to his 2d.	12. Q. takes K's R.

and you give mate in two moves.

The foregoing moves are dependent on Black's taking the Kt., which is very bad play. His proper move, under the circumstances, is 3. Q. to K's 2d, as in the following example:—

WHITE.	BLACK.
1. P. to K's 4th.	1. P. to K's 4th.
2. K's Kt. to B's 3d.	2. P. to K. B's 3d.
3. K's Kt. takes P.	3. Q. to K's 2d.
4. K. Kt. to B's 3d (best)	4. P. to Q's 4th.
5. P. to Q's 3d.	5. P. takes K's P.
6. P. takes P.	6. Q. takes P. (ch.)
7. B. to K's 2d.	7. Q's B. to K. B's 4th
8. Kt. to Q's 4th.	8. Q's Kt. to B's 3d.
9. Kt. takes B.	9. Q. takes Kt.
10. Castles.	10. B. to Q's 3d.
11. B. to Q's 3d.	

You have an excellent position.

GAME THE SECOND.

WHITE.	BLACK.
1. P. to K's 4th.	1. P. to K's 4th.
2. K's Kt. to B's 3d.	2. K's B. to Q's 3d.

KING'S KNIGHT'S OPENING.

3. B. to Q. B's 4th.
4. P. to Q's 4th.
5. P. takes K. P.
6. K. Kt. to his 5th.
7. P. to K. B's 4th.
8. P. to K's 5th.
9. Q. to K's 2d.
10. B. to Q's 5th.
11. Q. Kt. to B's 3d.

3. K. Kt. to B's 3d.
4. Q. Kt. to B's 3d.
5. B. takes P.
6. Castles.
7. B. to Q's 5th.
8. Q. to K's 2d.
9. K. Kt. to K's sq.
10. K. B. to Q. Kt's 3d.
11. P. to K. R's 3d.

In reply, you may now play P. to K. R's 4th, having a capital game. If, instead of 11. P. to R's 3d, he play 11. Q. Kt. to Q's 5th, you move 12. Q. to her 3d, then B. to Q's 2d, and finally castle on the Q's side. If, however, in lieu of that move, he play 11. B. to Q. R's 4th, you can move 12. B. to Q's 2d, and presently castle on the Q's side; and lastly, if he play 11. K. to R's sq., then you take your Queen to K. R's 5th, and he cannot save the game.

GAME THE THIRD.

WHITE.	BLACK.
1. P. to K's 4th.	1. P. to K's 4th.
2. K. Kt. to B's 3d.	2. Q. to K. B's 3d.

It is seldom good to bring the Q. into play early in the game, unless for some decisive blow, because she is so easily assailable by the opponent's minor Pieces, and in attacking her he brings his forces into action.

3. K. B. to Q. B's 4th.   3. Q. to K. Kt's 3d. .

Black now attacks two undefended Pawns, but he can take neither without ruinous loss to him; for suppose on your playing P. to Q's 3d, to protect the K. P., he ventures to take the K. Kt. P., you immediately take the K. B. P. with your Bishop (ch.). If he then take the Bishop with his King, you attack his Quèen with your Rook, and on her retiring to R. 6th, you win her by K. Kt. to his 5th (ch.). On the other hand, you can leave the King's Pawn. and castle safely.

4. Castles.   4. Q. takes K. P.
5. K. B. takes B. P. (ch).   5. K. to Q's sq.

It is quite obvious that he would lose his Queen by the check of the Knight, if he took the Bishop.

6. Kt. takes K's P.   6. K. Kt. to B's 3d.

If he take the Kt., you will play R. to K's sq., compelling him either to take it with his Q. or be mated.

7. K. R. to K's sq.   7. Q. to K. B's 4th.
8. K. B. to K. Kt.'s 6th.   8. Q. to K's 3d.
9. Kt. to B's 7th (ch.), and gains the Queen.

GAME THE FOURTH.
PHILIDOR'S DEFENCE.

WHITE.	BLACK.
1. P. to K's 4th.	1. P. to K's 4th.
2. K. Kt. to B's 3d.	2. P. to Q's 3d.
3. P. to Q's 4th.	3. P. to K. B's 4th.
4. Q. P. takes P.	4. K. B. P. takes P.
5. Kt. to K. Kt's 5th.	5. P. to Q's 4th.
6. P. to K's 6th.	6. Kt. to K. R's 3d.
7. P. to K. B's 3d.	7. Q. Kt. to B's 3d.
8. B. to Q. Kt's 5th.	8. Q. to her 3d.
9. Q. Kt. to B's 3d.	9. Q. B. takes K. P.
10. K. Kt. takes B.	10. Q. takes Kt.
11. Q. takes Q's P.	11. Q. takes Q.
12. Kt. takes Q.	12. Castles.
13. P. takes K. P.	

You have a Pawn more than Black, and a better position

FIRST VARIATION OF THIS ATTACK,
Commencing at White's 7th move.

WHITE.	BLACK.
1. P. to K's 4th.	1. P. to K's 4th.
2. K. Kt. to B's 3d	2. P. to Q's 3d.
3. P. to Q's 4th.	3. P. to K. B's 4th.
4. Q P. takes P.	4. K. B. P. takes P.
5. Kt. to K. Kt's 5th	5. P. to Q's 4th.

KING'S KNIGHT'S OPENING.

WHITE	BLACK
6. P. to K's 6th.	6. Kt. to K. R's 3d.
7. Q. Kt. to B's 3d.	7. P. to Q. B's 3d.
8. K. Kt. takes K. R. P	8. Q. B. takes K. P. (best)
9. Kt. takes K. B.	9. K. takes Kt.
10. Q. Kt. takes K. P.	10. Kt. to K. Kt's 5th.
11. K. Kt. to K. Kt's 5th, with the better game.	

SECOND VARIATION OF THIS ATTACK,
Commencing at White's 8th move.

WHITE.	BLACK.
1. P. to K's 4th.	1. P. to K's 4th.
2. K. Kt. to B's 3d.	2. P. to Q's 3d.
3. P. to Q's 4th.	3. P. to K. B's 4th.
4. Q P. takes P.	4. K. B. P. takes P.
5. Kt. to K. Kt's 5th.	5. P. to Q's 4th.
6. P. to K's 6th.	6. Kt. to K. R's 3d.
7. Q. Kt. to B's 3d.	7. P. to Q. B's 3d.
8. K. Kt. takes K. P.	8. P. takes Kt.
9. Q. to K. R's 5th (ch.)	9. P. to K. Kt's 3d.
10. Q. to K's 5th.	10. K. R. to Kt's sq.
11 B. takes K. Kt.	11. B. takes B.
12. Q. R. to Q's sq.	12. Q. to K's 2d.
13. Kt. takes K. P.	13. Q. B. takes P.
14. R. to Q's 6th. (the winning move.)	14. Q. B. to K. B's 4th.
15. Kt. to B's 6th (ch.)	15. K. to B's sq. (best)
16. R. to Q's 8th (ch.)	16. K. to B's 2d.
17. B. to Q. B's 4th (ch.)	17. B. to K's 3d (best)
18. Kt. takes R., and wins.	

VARIATION OF THE DEFENCE IN THIS OPENING,
Beginning at Black's 3d move.

WHITE.	BLACK.
1. P. to K's 4th.	1. P. to K's 4th.
2. K. Kt. to B's 3d.	2. P. to Q's 3d.
3. P. to Q's 4th.	3. K. Kt. to B's 3d.
4. Q. B. to K. Kt's 5th	4. Q. B. to K. Kt's 5th

WHITE.	BLACK.
5. P. takes K P.	5. B. takes Kt.
6. Q. takes B.	6. P. takes P.
7. Q. to her Kt's 3d.	7. P. to Q. Kt's 3d.
8. K. B. to Q. B's 4th.	8. Q. to Q's 2d.
9. B. takes Kt.	9. P. takes B.
10. Q. Kt. to B's 3d.	10. K. B. to K. Kt's 2d
11. Q. R. to Q's sq.	11. Q. to K's 2d.
12. B. to Q. Kt's 5th (ch.)	12. P. to Q. B's 3d.
13. Kt. to Q's 5th,	

with an excellent game.

ANOTHER VARIATION OF THE DEFENCE,
Beginning also from Black's 3d move.

WHITE.	BLACK.
1. P. to K's 4th.	1. P. to K's 4th.
2. K. Kt. to B's 3d.	2. P. to Q's 3d.
3. P. to Q's 4th.	3. Q. B. to K. Kt's 5th.
4. P. takes P.	4. B. takes Kt.
5. Q. takes B.	5. P. takes P.
6. B. to Q. B's 4th.	6. Q. to K. B's 3d.
7. Q. to her Kt's 3d.	7. P. to Q. Kt's 3d.
8. Q. Kt. to B's 3d.	8. P. to Q. B's 3d.
9. Castles.	9. B. to Q's 3d.
10. P. to K. B's 4th.	10. P. takes P.
11. Q. B. takes P.	11. B. takes B. (best)
12. P. to K's 5th.	12. B. takes K. R. P. (ch.)

And White has the better game.

SUMMARY OF THE FOREGOING VARIATIONS IN PHILIDOR'S DEFENCE.

The result of the preceding analysis serves to prove that Q. P. one, as the second move of Black, is not a tenable defence; since, play as he can afterwards, if the best moves are adopted by the first player, he will always have a very insecure or a very constrained game.

KING'S KNIGHT'S OPENING.

GAMES

ILLUSTRATIVE OF PHILIDOR'S DEFENCE.

GAME I.—Mr. Morphy plays without seeing the Chess board or men, against M. Boucher, at Paris.

WHITE. (Mr. M.)	BLACK. (M. B.)
1. P. to K's 4th.	1. P. to K's 4th.
2. K. Kt. to K. B's 3d.	2. P. to Q's 3d.
3. P. to Q's 4th.	3. P. takes P.
4. Q. takes P.	4. Q. Kt. to Q. B's 3d.
5. K. B. to Q. Kt's 5th.	5. Q. B. to Q's 2d.
6. B. takes Kt.	6. B. takes B.
7. B. to K. Kt's 5th.	7. P. to K. B's 3d.
8. B. to K. R's 4th.	8. Kt. to K. R's 3d.
9. Q. Kt. to Q. B's 3d.	9. K. B. to K's 2d.
10. Castles on K's side.	10. Castles.
11. Q. to Q. B's 4th (ch.)	11. K. to R's sq.
12. K. Kt. to Q's 4th.	12. Q. to her 2d.
13. Q. R. to Q's sq.	13. K. R. to K. B's 2d.
14. P. to K. B's 4th.	14. P. to Q. R's 4th.
15. P. to K. B's 5th.	15. K. R. to K. B's sq.
16. K. Kt. to K's 6th.	16. K. R. to K. Kt's sq.
17. P. to Q. R's 4th.	17. Kt. to Kt's 5th.
18. Q. to K's 2d.	18. Kt. to K's 4th.
19. B. to K. Kt's 3d.	19. Q. to Q. B's sq.*
20. B. takes Kt.	20. Q. P. takes B.
21. K. R. to K. B's 3d.†	21. Q. B. to Q's 2d.‡
22. K. R. to K. R's 3d.‖	22. P. to K. R's 3d.
23. Q. to Q's 2d.	23. K. to R's 2d. §
24. Q. takes Q. B.	24. B. to Q's 3d.
25. K. R. takes K. R. P. (ch.)¶	25. K. takes R.
26. R. to Q's 3d.**	26. K. to R's 4th.
27. Q. to K. B's 7th (ch.)	

And wins; the battle having lasted about seven hours.

---

* To enable him to capture the Bishop, which is about to take the Kt., with the Q's Pawn.

† The attack looks already irresistible, but the actual finish is charmingly accomplished.

‡ By this move Black may be said to lose a Piece. His best course—but that a bad one—was possibly to retreat his Bishop to K's square.

‖ Threatening mate in two moves.

§ To avert the promised mate, by R. takes Pawn, &c.

¶ The termination is very pretty—quite an elegant little problem.

** And Black has no possible means of escape; for, if he play Q. to K's sq., White simply captures the Queen for nothing; if B. to Q. B's 4th (ch.), then follows K. to B's sq., &c.

CHESS HANDBOOK.

GAME II.—Between Mr. Morphy and Mr. Harrwitz.

WHITE. (Mr. M.)	BLACK. (Mr. H.)
1. P. to K's 4th.	1. P. to K's 4th.
2. K. Kt. to K. B's 3d.	2. P. to Q's 3d.
3. P. to Q's 4th.	3. P. takes P.
4. Q. takes P.	4. Q. Kt. to Q. B's 3d.
5. K. B. to Q. Kt's 5th.	5. Q. B. to Q's 2d.
6. B. takes Kt.	6. B. takes B.
7. B. to K. Kt's 5th.	7. P. to K. B's 3d.
8. B. to K. R's 4th.	8. Kt. to K. R's 3d.
9. Q. Kt. to B's 3d.	9. K. B. to K's 2d.
10. Castles on K's side.	10. Q. to Q's 2d.
11. Q. R. to Q's sq.	11. Castles on K's side.
12. Q. to B's 4th (ch.).	12. K. R. to K. B's 2d.
13. K. Kt. to Q's 4th.	13. Kt. to K. Kt's 5th.
14. P. to K. R's 3d.	14. Kt. to K's 4th.
15. Q. to K's 2d.	15. P. to K. Kt's 4th.*
16. B. to K. Kt's 3d.	16. K. R. to K. Kt's 2d.
17. K. Kt. to K. B's 5th.	17. K. R. to K. Kt's 3d.
18. P. to K. B's 4th.	18. P. takes P.
19. K. R. takes P.	19. K. to R's sq.
20. K. R. to K. R's 4th.	20. K. B. to his sq.
21. B. takes Kt.	21. K. B. P. takes B.
22. Q. R. to K. B's sq.	22. Q. to K's 3d.
23. Q. Kt. to Q. Kt's 5th.	23. Q. to K. Kt's sq.
24. Q. R. to K. B's 2d.	24. P. to Q. R's 3d.
25. Q. Kt. takes Q. B. P.†	25. Q. R. to Q. B's sq.
26. Q. Kt. to Q's 5th.	26. B. takes Kt.
27. K. P. takes B.	27. Q. R. to Q. B's 2d.‡
28. P. to Q. B's 4th.	28. B. to K's 2d.
29. K. R. to K. R's 5th.	29. Q. to K's sq.
30. P. to Q. B's 5th.§	30. Q. R. takes P.
31. K. R. takes P. (ch.)	31. K. takes R.
32. Q. to K. R's 5th (ch.)	32. K. to Kt. sq.
33. Kt. takes B. (ch.)	33. K. to Kt's 2d.‖
34. Kt. to K. B's 5th (ch.)	34. K. to Kt's sq.
35. Kt. takes Q. P.	

And Black cannot possibly save the game.

* Very imprudent in such a position and against such an opponent It must be admitted, however, that Black has no good move at this crisis.
† Perfectly sound, as the sequel shows.
‡ Taking the Pawn would have been injudicious; for example,

	27. Q. takes Pawn.
28. K. R. takes K. R. P. (ch.)	28. K. takes R. (best).
29. Q. to K. R's 5th. (ch.)	29. B. to K. R's 3d.
30. Kt. takes B.	30. K. R. takes Kt.
31. Q. to K. B's 5th (ch.)	31. Anything.
32. Q. takes Q. R., &c.	

§ The first step in a combination of admirable daring and ingenuity
‖ Had he taken the Knight it would have cost him his Queen.

KING'S KNIGHT'S OPENING.

GAME III.—Between **Mr. Morphy** and **Mr. Harrwitz**.

WHITE. (Mr. M.)	BLACK. (Mr. H.)
1. P. to K's 4th.	1. P. to K's 4th.
2. K. Kt. to K. B's 3d.	2. P. to Q's 3d.
3. P. to Q's 4th.	3. P. takes P.
4. Q. takes P.	4. Q. Kt. to Q. B's 3d.
5. K. B. to Q. Kt's 5th.	5. Q. B. to Q's 2d.
6. B. takes Kt.	6. B. takes B.
7. B. to K. Kt's 5th.	7. Kt. to K. B's 3d.
8. Q. Kt. to Q. B's 3d.	8. K. B. to K's 2d.
9. Castles on Q's side.	9. Castles.
10. K. R. to K's sq.	10. P. to K. R's 3d.
11. B. to K. R's 4th.	11. Kt. to K's sq.
12. B. takes B.	12. Q. takes B.
13. P. to K's 5th.	13. B. takes Kt.
14. P. takes B.	14. Q. to K. Kt's 4th (ch.)
15. K. to Q. Kt's sq.	15. P. takes P.
16. K. R. takes P.	16. Q. to K. Kt's 7th.
17. Kt. to Q's 5th.	17. Q. takes K. R. P.
18. K. R. to K's sq.	18. Q. to Q's 3d.
19. K. R. to K. Kt's sq.	19. K. to K. R's 2d.
20. Q. to K's 3d.	20. P. to K. B's 4th.
21. Kt. to K. B's 4th.	21. Q. to Q. Kt's 3d.
22. Q. to K's 2d.	22. K. R. to K. B's 2d.
23. Q. to Q. B's 4th.	23. Q. to K. B's 3d.
24. Kt. to K. R's 5th.*	24. Q. to K's 2d.
25. Q. R. to K's sq.	25. Q. to Q's 2d.
26. P. to Q. R's 3d.	26. Kt. to Q's 3d.
27. Q. to Q's 4th.	27. Q. R. to K. Kt's sq.
28. K. R. to K. Kt's 2d.	28. P. to Q. Kt's 3d.
29. Q. R. to K. Kt's sq.	29. Kt. to K's sq.
30. Q. to Q. B's 3d.	30. P. to K. B's 5th.†
31. Q. R. to K. R's sq.‡	31. Kt. to K. Kt's 3d.
32. Q. R. to K. Kt's sq.	32. Q. to Q's 4th.
33. Q. to K's sq.	33. P. takes Kt.
34. K. R. to K. Kt's 5th.§	34. Q. takes P.
35. Q. to K's 5th.	35. K. R. to K. B's 3d.
36. Q. to K's 7th (ch).	36. Q. R. to K. Kt's 2d.
37. Q. takes Kt.	37. P. takes R.
38. Q. to K's sq.	38. Q. to Q. B's 3d.
39. P. to K. B's 3d.	39. K. R. to K's 3d.
40. Q. to K. B's 2d.	40. Q. R. to K's 2d.

And White abandoned the game.

---

* This looks promising, but does not turn out well. He had better, perhaps, have played K. R. to K. Kt's 6th.
† Well played. White must now beware, for his Kt. is in sore peril.
‡ This will not save the Kt. The best move was K. R. to Kt's 4th
§ Merely desperate

GAME IV.—Between Mr. Morphy and Mr. Bird of London

WHITE. (Mr. B.)	BLACK. (Mr. M.)
1. P. to K's 4th.	1. P. to K's 4th.
2. Kt. to K. B's 3d.	2. P. to Q's 3d.
3. P. to Q's 4th.	3. P. to K. B's 4th.
4. Kt. to Q. B's 3d.	4. K. B. P. takes P.
5. Q. Kt. takes P.	5. P. to Q's 4th.
6. Kt. to K. Kt's 3d.	6. P. to K's 5th.
7. Kt. to K's 5th.	7. Kt. to K. B's 3d.
8. Q. B. to K. Kt's 5th.	8. B. to Q's 3d.
9. Kt. to K. R's 5th.	9. Castles.
10. Q. to Q's 2d.	10. Q. to K's sq.
11. P. to K. Kt's 4th.	11. Kt. takes K. Kt. P.
12. Kt. takes Kt.	12. Q. takes Kt.
13. Kt. to K's 5th.	13. Kt. to Q. B's 3d.
14. B. to K's 2d.	14. Q. to K. R's 6th.
15. Kt. takes Kt.	15. P. takes Kt.
16. B. to K's 3d.	16. R. to Q. Kt's sq.
17. Castles (Q. R.)	17. R. takes K. B. P.
18. B. takes R.	18. Q. to Q. R's 6th.
19. P. to Q. B's 3d.	19. Q. takes Q. R. P.
20. P. to Q. Kt's 4th.	20. Q. to Q. R's 8th. (ch.)
21. K. to B's 2d.	21. Q. to R's 5th. (ch.)
22. K. to Kt's 2d.	22. B. takes Q. Kt. P.
23. P. takes B.	23. R. takes P. (ch.)
24. Q. takes R.	24. Q. takes Q. (ch.)
25. K. to B's 2d.	25. P. to K's 6th.
26. B. takes P.	26. B. to K. B's 4th (ch.)
27. R. to Q's 3d.	27. Q. to Q. B's 5th (ch.)
28. K. to Q's 2d.	28. Q. to Q. R's 7th. (ch.)
29. K. to Q's square.	29. Q. to Kt's 8th (ch.)

And White resigns.

GAME V.—(By Philidor.)

WHITE.	BLACK.
1. P. to K's 4th.	1. P. to K's 4th.
2. K. Kt. to K. B's 3d.	2. P. to Q's 3d.
3. P. to Q's 4th.	3. P. to K. B's 4th.
4. P. takes K. P.	4. K. B. P. takes K. P.
5. Kt. to Kt's 5th.	5. P. to Q's 4th.
6. P. to K. B's 4th.*	6. K. B. to Q. B's 4th.
7. P. to Q. B's 4th.	7. P. to Q. B's 3d.
8. Q. Kt. to B's 3d.	8. K. Kt. to K's 2d.
9. P. to K. R's 4th.	9. P. to K. R's 3d.
10. K. Kt. to R's 3d.	10. Castles.
11. Q. Kt. to Q. R's 4th.	11. B. to Q. Kt's 5th (ch.)
12. B. to Q's 2d.	12. B. takes B. (ch.)
13. Q. takes B.	13. P. to Q's 5th.

* This is not the proper move; he should play 6. P. to K's 6th.

KING'S KNIGHT'S OPENING.

14. P. to Q. B's 5th.	14. P. to Q. Kt's 4th.
15. P. takes P. (in passing).	15. Q. R. P. takes P.
16. P. to Q. Kt's 3d.	16. Q. B. to K's 3d.
17. B. to K's 2d.	17. Kt. to K. B's 4th.
18. K. Kt. to his sq.	18. K. Kt. to Kt's 6th.
19. K. R. to his 2d.	19. P. to K's 6th.
20. Q. to her Kt's 2d.	20. P. to Q's 6th.
21. B. to K. B's 3d.	21. K. R. takes P.
22. Castles on Q's side.	22. K. R. takes Kt.
23. P. takes K. R.	23. Q. R. takes P.
24. P. to Q. R's 3d.	24. R. to Q. B's 5th (ch.)
25. K. to Q. Kt's sq.	25. R. to Q. B's 7th.
26. Q. to Kt's 4th.	26. Q. Kt. to R's 3d.
27. Q. to K. B's 4th.	27. Q. Kt. to B's 4th.
28. Q. takes K. Kt.	

And Black mates in two moves.

GAME THE FIFTH.
PETROFF'S DEFENCE.

WHITE.	BLACK.
1. P. to K's 4th.	1. P. to K's 4th.
2. K. Kt. to B's 3d	2. K. Kt. to B's 3d.
3. P. to Q's 4th.	3. P. takes P.
4. P. to K's 5th	4. Kt. to K's 5th (best)
5. Kt. takes P.	5. P. to Q's 3d (best).
6. P. takes P.	6. K. B. takes P.
7. K. B. to Q B's 4th.	7. K. B. to Q. B's 4th
8. Q. B. to K's 3d.	8. Castles.
9. Castles.	9. Q. Kt. to Q's 2d.

The game is equal.

VARIATION I.
Commencing at Black's 3d move.

WHITE.	BLACK.
1 P. to K's 4th.	1. P. to K's 4th.
2 K. Kt. to B's 3d	2. K. Kt. to B's 3d
3. P. to Q's 4th.	3. Kt. takes P.
4. K. B. to Q's 3d.	4. P. to Q's 4th.
5. Kt. takes K's P.	5. Kt. to Q's 3d.
6 P to Q. B's 4th	6. P. takes P.
7 K. Kt. takes P.	7 Q. B. to K's 3d.

8. Kt. to K's 3d. 8. B. to K's 2d.
9. Castles. 9. Castles.

You have the move, and somewhat the advantage of position.

VARIATION II.

Beginning at White's 5th move.

WHITE.	BLACK.
1. P. to K's 4th.	1. P. to K's 4th.
2. K. Kt. to B's 3d.	2. K. Kt. to B's 3d.
3. P. to Q's 4th.	3. P. takes P.
4. P. to K's 5th.	4. Kt. to K's 5th.
5. K. B. to Q's 3d.	5. K. Kt. to Q. B's 4th.
6. Kt. takes P.	6. P. to Q's 3d.
7. P. takes P.	7. K. B. takes P.
8. Castles.	8. Castles.

It would not be a good move for Black, instead of castling, to take your K. R. P. (ch.) and then to take the Kt., on account of your check with the B., which would leave his Q. exposed to capture.

VARIATION III.

Beginning at White's 3d move.

WHITE.	BLACK.
1. P. to K's 4th.	1. P. to K's 4th.
2. K. Kt. to B's 3d.	2. K. Kt. to B's 3d.
3. Kt. takes K's P.	3. Kt. takes P.
4. Q. to K's 2d.	4. Q. to K's 2d.
5. Q. takes Kt.	5. P. to Q's 3d.
6. P. to Q's 4th.	6. P. to K. B's 3d.
7. P. to K. B's 4th.	7. Q. Kt. to Q's 2d.
8. Q. Kt. to B's 3d.	8. Q. P. takes Kt.
9. Q. Kt. to Q's 5th.	9. Q. to her 3d.
10. Q. P. takes P.	10. P. takes P.
11. P. takes P.	11. Q. to her B's 3d
12. K. B. to Q. Kt.'s 5th.	12. Q. to her B's 4th.
13. P. to Q. Kt.'s 4th,	

Winning the Q. At his 12th move, Black might prolong the game by playing 12 Q. to K. Kt's 3d. but in that

KING'S KNIGHT'S OPENING.

case you would take 13. Q. B. P. with the Kt. (ch.), then take Q. with Q., and afterwards Q. R. with Kt.

VARIATION IV.
Beginning at Black's 3d move.

WHITE.	BLACK.
1. P. to K's 4th.	1. P. to K's 4th
2. K. Kt. to B's 3d.	2. K. Kt. to B's 3d.
3. Kt. takes K. P.	3. P. to Q's 3d.
4. Kt. to K. B's 3d.	4. Kt. takes K's P.
5. P. to Q's 4th.	5. P. to Q's 4th.
6. K. B. to Q's 3d.	6. K. B. to K's 2d.
7. Castles.	7. Q. Kt. to B's 3d.
8. P. to Q. B's 4th.	8. Q. B. to K's 3d.
9. P. to.Q. R's 3d.	9. Castles.

You are now enabled to play Q. to her B's 2d, and obtain a good attacking situation.

ANOTHER VARIATION,
Beginning at the 3d move of White.

WHITE.	BLACK.
1. P. to K's 4th.	1. P. to K's 4th.
2. K. Kt. to B's 3d.	2. K. Kt. to B's 3d.
3. K. B. to Q. B's 4th.	3. Kt. takes P.
4. Q. to K's 2d.	4. P. to Q's 4th.
5. Kt. takes K. P.	5. K. B. to Q. B. 4 (best)
6. P. to Q's 3d.	6. B. takes K. B. P. (ch.)
7. K. to Q's sq. (best)	7. B. to Q. Kt's 3d.
8. Kt. takes K. B. P.	8. Q. B. to K. Kt's 5th
9. Kt. takes Q.	9. B. takes Q. (ch.)
10. K. takes B.	10. Kt. to K. B's 7th.
11. R. to K. B's sq.	11. P. takes B.
12. Kt to K's 6th.	12. P. takes P. (ch.)
13 P. takes P.	13. K. to his 2d.
14. Kt. takes K. Kt. P.	14. R. to K. Kt's sq.
15. Kt. to K. B's 5th (ch.)	15. K. to his 3d.
16. Q. B. to K's 3d.	16. B. takes B.
17. Kt. takes B.	17. Kt to K. Kt.'s 5th.

The positions are equal, but you have a pawn more

Variation (A.)

Beginning at Black's 6th move.

WHITE.	BLACK.
1. P. to K's 4th.	1. P. to K's 4th.
2. K. Kt. to B's 3d.	2. K. Kt. to B's 3d.
3. K. B. to Q. B's 4th.	3. Kt. takes P.
4. Q. to K's 2d.	4. P. to Q's 4th.
5. Kt. takes K. P.	5. K. B. to Q. B's 4 (best)
6. P. to Q's 3d.	6. Q. P. takes B.
7. Q. takes Kt.	7. Castles.
8. Q. takes doubled P.	8. Q. to K's 2d.
9. P. to K. B's 4th.	9. Q. Kt. to B's 3d.
10. Q. to K's 4th.	10. K. R. to K's sq.
11. K. to Q's sq.	11. Q. to K. R's 5th.
12. P. to K. Kt.'s 3d.	12. Q. to K. R's 4th (ch.)
13. K. to Q's 2d.	13. Kt. takes Kt.
14. P. takes Kt.	14. R. takes P.

Winning easily.

Instead, however, of playing 12. P. to K. Kt's 3d, you might at that moment move Q. Kt. to Q's 2d.

12. Q. Kt. to Q's 2d.	12. Q. to K. R's 4th (ch.)
13. Q. Kt. to K. B's 3d (best)	13. Q. B. to K. Kt's 5th.

and now, play as you can, Black must gain a decided advantage by taking the K. Kt. with Kt., &c.

Variation,

Beginning at White's 11th move.

WHITE.	BLACK.
1. P. to K's 4th.	1. P. to K's 4th.
2. K. Kt. to B's 3d.	2. K. Kt. to B's 3d.
3. K. B. to Q. B's 4th.	3. Kt. takes P.
4. Q. to K's 2d.	4. P. to Q's 4th.
5. Kt. takes K. P.	5. K. B. to Q. B. 4th (best)
6. P. to Q's 3d.	6. Q P. takes B.
7. Q. takes Kt.	7. Castles.
8. Q. takes doubled P.	8. Q. to K's 2d.
9. P. to K. B's 4th.	9. Q. Kt. to B's 3d

KING'S KNIGHT'S OPENING.

10. Q. to K's 4th	10. K. R. to K's sq.
11. Q. Kt. to Q's 2d.	11. Q. to K. R's 5th (ch.)
12. P. to K. Kt.'s 3d.	12. Q. to K. R's 4th.
13. Q. Kt. to K. B's 3d.	13. Q. B. to K. B's 4th.
14. Q. to K's 2d. (best)	14. Q. B. to K. Kt's 5th
15. K. R. to B's sq.	15. Q. Kt. to Q's 5th.

And Black must win.

GAMES
ILLUSTRATIVE OF PETROFF'S DEFENCE.

GAME 1.—Mr. Morphy plays without seeing the Chess-board or men, against M. Potier, at Paris.

WHITE. (Mr. M.)	BLACK. (M. P.)
1. P. to K's 4th.	1. P. to K's 4th.
2. K. Kt. to K. B's 3d.	2. K. Kt. to K. B's 3d.
3. K. B. to Q. B's 4th.	3. Kt. takes K. P.
4. Q. Kt. to Q. B's 3d.	4. K. Kt. to K. B's 3d.*
5. Kt. takes K. P.	5. P. to Q's 4th.
6. K. B. to Q. Kt's 3d.	6. K. B. to K's 2d.
7. P. to Q's 4th.	7. P. to Q. B's 3d.
8. Castles.	8. Q. Kt. to Q's 2d.
9. P. to K. B's 4th.	9. Q. Kt. to Q. Kt's 3d.
10. Q. to K. B's 3d.	10. P. to K. R's 4th.
11. P. to K. B's 5th.	11. Q. to Q. B's 2d.
12. Q. B. to K. B's 4th.	12. K. B. to Q's 3d.
13. Q. R. to K's sq.	13. K. to B's sq.
14. Q. to K. Kt's 3d.	14. P. to K. R's 5th.
15. K. Kt. to Kt's 6th (ch.)†	15. K. to Kt's sq.
16. Q. B. takes B.	16. P. takes Q.
17. Q. B. takes Q.	17. P. takes Kt.
18. K. B. P. takes P.	18. P. takes K. R. P. (ch.)
19. K. to R's sq.	19. B. to K. Kt's 5th.
20. Q. R. to K's 7th.	20. Q. Kt. to Q's 2d.
21. Q. B. to K's 5th.	21. K. to B's sq.
22. Q. R. to K. B's 7th (ch.)‡	22. K. to Kt's sq.

* It is to be regretted that Mr. Potier did not take the Kt. rather than retreat, as many amateurs would have been pleased to see Mr. Morphy carrying out the attack of this interesting and comparatively novel début.
† Finely played.
‡ The termination of this *partie* is remarkably elegant and finished.

23. Kt. takes Q. P.	23. P. takes Kt.
24. K. B. takes P.	24. Q. Kt. to Q. Kt's 3d.
25. K. B. to Q. Kt's 3d.	

And Black abandons the game.

GAME II.—Played between Jose R. Capablanca, of Havana, the Pan-American champion, and Frank J. Marshall, of New York, the United States champion, at the New York Masters' Tournament, 1915.

WHITE. (Capablanca.)	BLACK. (Marshall.)
1. P. to K's 4th.	1. P. to K's 4th.
2. Kt. to K. B's 3d.	2. Kt. to K. B's 3d.
3. Kt. takes P.	3. P. to Q's 3d.
4. Kt. to K. B's 3d.	4. Kt. takes P.
5. Q. to K's 2d.	5. Q. to K's 2d.
6. P. to Q's 3d.	6. Kt. to K. B's 3d.
7. B. to Kt's 5th.	7. Q. takes Q. (ch.)
8. B. takes Q.	8. B. to K's 2d.
9. Kt. to B's 3d.	9. P. to K. R's 3d.
10. B. to R's 4th.	10. B. to K's 3d.
11. Castles. Q. R.	11. Kt. to B's 3d.
12. K. R. to K.	12. Castles. Q. R.
13. P. to Q's 4th.	13. P. to Q's 4th.
14. B. to Q. Kt's 5th.	14. Kt. to Q. Kt.
15. Kt. to K's 5th.	15. B. to Q. Kt's 5th.
16. Kt. to Kt's 6th.	16. K. R. to Kt.
17. P. to Q. R's 3d.	17. B. to Q's 3d.
18. B. to Kt's 3d.	18. P. takes Kt.
19. R. takes B.	19. B. takes B.
20. R. P. takes B.	20. Q. Kt. to Q's 2d.
21. Q. R. to K.	21. P. to Kt's 4th.
22. R. to K's 7th.*	22. P. to B's 3d.
23. B. to Q's 3d.	23. Q. R. to K.
24. B. to Kt's 6th.	24. R. takes R.
25. R. takes R.	25. K. to Q.
26. R. to K's 2d.	26. R. to B.
27. Kt. to Q.	27. Kt. to K. Kt.
28. K. to Q's 2d.	28. Kt. to K's 2d.
29. B. to Q's 3d.	29. Kt. to K. B's 4th.
30. B. takes Kt.	30. R. takes B.

Drawn.

* B. to Q's 3d at once would have held out better prospects for White.

KING'S KNIGHT'S OPENING.

GAME III.—Between M. Tchigorin and H. N. Pillsbury.

WHITE. (Mr. T.)	BLACK. (Mr. P.)
1. P. to K's 4th.	1. P. to K's 4th.
2. K. Kt. to B's 3d.	2. K. Kt. to B's 3d.
3. Kt. to B's 3d.	3. Kt. to B's 3d.
4. B. to Kt's 5th.	4. B. to Kt's 5th.
5. Castles.	5. Castles.
6. P. to Q's 3d.	6. P. to Q's 3d.
7. B. to Kt's 5th.*	7. B. takes Kt.
8. P. takes B.	8. Kt. to K's 2d.†
9. B. takes Kt.	9. P. takes B.
10. Q. to Q's 2d.	10. Kt. to Kt's 3d.
11. K. to R's sq.‡	11. K. to R's sq.
12. P. to Q's 4th.	12. R. to K. Kt's sq.
13. B. to Q's 3d.	13. Q. to K's 2d.
14. Q. R. to Kt's sq.§	14. P. to Kt's 3d.
15. Kt. to Kt's sq.	15. B. to K's 3d. !
16. P. to Q's 5th.?	16. B. to Q's 2d.
17. P. to Kt's 3d.	17. R. to Kt's 2d.
18. Q. R. to K's sq.	18. Q. R. to K. Kt's sq.‖
19. P. to B's 3d.¶	19. P. to K. R's 4th.!
20. R. to K's 2d.	20. Kt. to B's sq.
21. P. to K. B's 4th.	21. P. takes P.
22. Q. takes P.	22. Kt. to R's 2d.
23. Kt. to B's 3d.	23. B. to Kt's 5th.
24. Kt. to Q's 4th.**	24. P. to R's 5th.!
25. R. to K's 3d.	25. Q. to K's 4th.
26. P. takes P.?	26. B. to B's 6th (ch.)
27. Resigns.	

---

* NOTES by JAS. MASON.—In this familiar "double Lopez" predicament, 7. B. takes Kt. is highly recommended, if a dull but durable kind of game is desired.

† ... Something like a leap in the dark. If the doubled Pawn can be "dissolved" betimes, or the open file well used in attack, a safe landing may be confidently expected.

‡ More or less necessary, sooner or later. Black does not attempt to dissolve, just here; for then Q. to R's 6th, threatening Kt. to Kt's 5th, might be uncomfortable.

§ Routine—indirectly including the questionable 16. P. to Q's 5th? At once Kt. to Kt's sq., to be speedily followed by P. to Kt's 3d and P. to K. B's 4th, would have given the matter another and perhaps very different complexion.

‖ ... The difference is in favor of the young American representative, who presses it fully.

¶ Manifestly weakening. The Russian champion feels himself on the defensive, and at a loss how to continue. Thus the text move may be as good as any other.

** 24. Kt. to R's 4th would be much stronger, the importance of halting the advancing Rook Pawn duly considered. Going from bad to worse, the downright blunder two moves later caps the climax—and more need not be said.

GAME THE SIXTH.

WHITE.	BLACK.
1. P. to K's 4th.	1. P. to K's 4th.
2. K. Kt. to B's 3d.	2. K. B. to Q. B's 4th
3. Kt. takes K. P.	3. Q. to K's 2d.
4. P. to Q's 4th.	4. B. to Q. Kt.'s 3d.
5. K. B. to Q. B's 4th.	5. K. Kt. to B's 3d.
6. B takes B. P. (ch.)	6. K. to B's sq.
7. B. to Q. Kt.'s 3d.	7. Kt. takes K's P
8. Castles,	

And you have an excellent position.

GAME THE SEVENTH.

COUNTER GAMBIT IN THE KNIGHT'S OPENING.

WHITE.	BLACK.
1. P. to K's 4th.	1. P. to K's 4th.
2. K. Kt. to B's 3d.	2. P. to K. B's 4th.

This second move of Black gives the name of Counter Gambit to this game.

3. K. Kt. takes P. (best.)	3. Q. to K. B's 3d (best)
4. P. to Q's 4th.	4. P. to Q's 3d.
5. Kt. to Q. B's 4th.	5. P. takes K's P.
6. Q. Kt. to B's 3d.	6. P. to Q. B's 3d.
	or First Variation.
7. Q. Kt. takes K's P. (best)	7. Q. to K's 3d.
8. Q. to K's 2d.	8. P. to Q's 4th.
9. Q's Kt. to Q's 6th (ch.)	9. K. to Q's 2d.
10. Q. Kt. to K. B's 7th.	10. Q. P. takes K's Kt.
11. Q. takes Q. (ch.)	11. K. takes Q.
12. K. B. takes P. (ch.)	12. K. to his 2d.
13. Kt. takes R.	13. Q. B. to K's 3d.
14. K. B. to Q's 3d.	14. K. Kt. to B's 3d
15. Q. B. to K. Kt.'s 5th.	15. Q. B. to K. Kt's sq.
16. Castles, with a fine game.	

KING'S KNIGHT'S OPENING.

First Variation,
Beginning at Black's 6th move.

WHITE.	BLACK.
1. P. to K's 4th	1. P. to K's 4th.
2. K. Kt. to B's 3d.	2. P. to K. B's 4th.
3. K. Kt. takes P. (best)	3. Q. to K. B's 3d (best).
4. P. to Q.'s 4th.	4. P. to Q's 3d.
5. Kt. to Q. B's 4th.	5. P. takes K. P.
6. Q. Kt. to B's 3d.	6. Q. B. to K. B's 4th.
7. P. to K. Kt's 4th.	7. Q. B. to K. Kt's 3d.
8. K. B. to Kt's 2d	8. P. to Q. B's 3d.
9. B. takes K's P.	9 B. takes B.
10. Q. Kt. takes B.	10 Q. to K's 3d.
11. Q. to K's 2d.	11. P. to Q's 4th.
12. K. Kt. to Q's 6th (ch.)	

If now Black take the Knight with his Bishop, you retake with the Q. Kt. (ch.), then exchange Queens, and win the Q. Kt. P. He may, however, move 12. K. to his 2d, whereupon you check with K. Kt. at K. B's 5th, and afterwards liberate your other Kt.

Second Variation,
Beginning at Black's 6th move.

WHITE.	BLACK.
1. P. to K's 4th.	1. P. to K's 4th.
2. K. Kt. to B's 3d.	2. P. to K. B's 4th.
3. K. Kt. takes P. (best)	3. Q. to K. B's 3d. (best)
4. P. to Q's 4th.	4. P. to Q's 3d.
5. Kt. to Q. B's 4th.	5. P. takes K. P.
6. Q. Kt. to B's 3d.	6. K. Kt. to K's 2d.
7. P. to Q's 5th.	7. Q. to K. Kt's 3d.
8. Q. to her 4th.	8. Q B. to K. B's 4th
9. Q. Kt. to his 5th, gaining a Pawn.	

Third Variation,
From Black's 6th move.

WHITE.	BLACK.
1. P. to K's 4th.	1. P. to K's 4th.
2. K. Kt. to B's 3d.	2. P. to K. B's 4th.

3. K. Kt. takes P. (best)   3. Q. to K. B's 3d (best)
4. P. to Q's 4th.   4. P. to Q's 3d.
5. Kt. to Q. B's 4th.   5. P. takes K's P.
6. Q. Kt. to B's 3d.   6. Q. to K. Kt.'s 3d.
7. P. to K. B's 3d (best)   7. K. Kt. to B.'s 3d.
8. P. takes K's P.   8. Kt. takes P.
9. Q. to K's 2d.   9. Q. B. to K. B's 4th.
10. K. Kt. to Q's 2d.   10. Q. Kt. to B's 3d.
11. K. Kt. takes Kt.   11. Kt. takes Q. P.
12. Q. to her 3d, having won a Piece.

FOURTH VARIATION OF THIS GAME,
Beginning at Black's 4th move.

WHITE.   BLACK.
1. P. to K's 4th.   1. P. to K's 4th.
2. K. Kt. to B's 3d.   2. P. to K. B's 4th
3. Kt. takes K. P.   3. Q. to K. B's 3d.
4. P. to Q's 4th.   4. P. takes K. P.
5. K. B. to Q. B's 4th.   5. P. to Q. B's 3d.
6. B. to B's 7th (ch.)   6. K. to his 2d.
7. P. to K. R's 4th.   7. P. to K. R's 3d.
8. Q. to K. R's 5th.   8. K. to Q's 3d.
9. Q. B. to K. Kt's 5th.   9. P. takes B.
10. Q. takes R.,

and you have an easy game.

ANOTHER VARIATION,
Beginning at the 3d move of White

WHITE.   BLACK.
1 P. to K's 4th.   1. P. to K's 4th.
2. K. Kt. to B's 3d.   2. P. to K. B's 4th.
3. K. B. to Q. B's 4th.   3. P. takes K's P.
4. Kt. takes P.   4. Q. to K. Kt's 4th.
5. Kt. to K. B's 7th (best)   5. Q. takes K. Kt. P
6. R. to K. B's sq.   6. P. to Q's 4th.
7. Kt. takes R.   7. P. takes B.
8. Q. to K. R's 5th (ch.)   8. P. to K. Kt's 3d
9. Q. takes K. R. P.   9. Q. B. to K's 3d

KING'S KNIGHT'S OPENING.

10. Q. takes K. Kt. P. (ch.) 10. Q. takes Q.
11. Kt. takes Q.,

and you have "the exchange" and a Pawn advantage.

VARIATION OF THIS GAME,
Beginning at White's 3d move.

WHITE.	BLACK.
1. P. to K's 4th.	1. P. to K's 4th.
2. K. Kt. to B's 3d.	2. P. to K. B's 4th.
3. P. takes P.	3. P. to Q's 3d.
4. P. to Q's 4th.	4. P. to K's 5th.
5. Kt. to his 5th.	5. Q. B. takes P.
6. Q. to K's 2d.	6. P. to Q's 4th.
7. Q. to her Kt's 5th (ch.)	7. Q. Kt. to B's 3d
8 Q. takes Q. Kt. P.	8. Q. Kt. takes Q. P
9. B. to Q. Kt's 5th (ch.)	9. Kt. takes B.
10. Q. takes Kt. (ch.)	10. Q. to her 2d.
11. Q. to Q. Kt's 7th.	11. Q. R. to B's sq.
12. Q. takes Q. R. P.	12. P. to K. R's 3d.
13. Kt. to K. R's 3d.	13. B. takes Kt.
14. K. Kt. P. takes B.	14. Q. takes P.

And he has the superiority in position

GAME THE EIGHTH.

WHITE.	BLACK.
1. P. to K's 4th.	1. P. to K's 4th.
2. K. Kt. to B's 3d.	2. P. to Q's 4th
3. P takes P. (best)	3. Q. takes P.
4. Q. Kt. to B's 3d.	4. Q. to K's 3d.
5. B. to Q. Kt's 5th (ch.)	5. B. to Q's 2d.
6. Castles.	6. B. takes B.
7. Kt. takes B.	7. K. B. to Q's 3d.
8. R. to K's sq.	8. P. to K. B's 3d.
9. P. to Q's 4th.	9. P. to Q. B's 3d.
10. Q. P. takes P.	10. P. takes P.
11. K Kt takes P.	

Winning of course.

VARIATION.

WHITE.	BLACK.
1. P. to K's 4th.	1. P. to K's 4th.
2. K. Kt. to B's 3d.	2. P. to Q's 4th.
3. Kt. takes K's P.	3. Q. to K's 2d (best)
4. P. to Q's 4th.	4. P. to K. B's 3d.
5. Kt. to his 4th.	5. B. takes Kt.
6. Q. takes B.	6. Q. takes P. (ch.)
7. Q. takes Q. (ch.)	7. P. takes Q.

There is no advantage on either side.

GAMES

ILLUSTRATIVE OF THE PRECEDING VARIATIONS

GAME I.—Between Messrs. Cochrane and Staunton

WHITE. (Mr. C.)	BLACK. (Mr. S.)
1. P. to K's 4th.	1. P. to K's 4th.
2. K. Kt. to B's 3d.	2. P. to Q's 4th.
3. Kt. takes K. P.	3. Q. to K's 2d.
4. P. to Q's 4th.	4. P. to K. B's 3d.
5. Q. Kt. to B's 3d.	5. P. takes K. Kt.
6. Kt. takes Q. P.	6. Q. to K. B's 2d.
7. K. B. to Q. B's 4th.	7. Q. B. to K's 3d.
8. Castles.	8. P. to Q. B's 3d.
9. P. to K. B's 4th.	9. P. takes Kt.
10. B. P. takes P.	10. Q. to her 2d.
11. K. P. takes P.	11. B. takes P.
12. P. to K's 6th.	12. Q. to her B's 3d.
13. Q. to K. R's 5th (ch.)	13. P. to K. Kt's 3d.
14. Q. takes B.	14. K. Kt. to K's 2d.
15. Q. to K's 5th.	15. Q. takes B.
16. Q. takes R.	16. Kt. to K. B's 4th.
17. Q. B. to K. R's 6th.	17. Q. to her Kt's 5th.
18. Q. takes B. (ch.)	18. Q. takes Q.
19. B. takes Q.	19. K. takes B.
20. P. to K. Kt's 4th.	

Black surrenders.

KING'S KNIGHT'S OPENING.

GAME II.—Between MM. Jaenisch and Petroff.

WHITE. (M. J.)	BLACK. (M. P.)
1. P. to K's 4th.	1. P. to K's 4th.
2. K. Kt. to B's 3d.	2. P. to Q's 4th.
3. K. Kt. takes P.	3. Q. to K's 2d.
4. P. to Q's 4th.	4. P. to K. B's 3d.
5. Kt. to B's 3d.	5. P. takes P.
6. K. Kt. to Q's 2d.	6. P. to K. B's 4th.
7. K. B. to K's 2d.	7. Q. Kt. to B's 3d.
8. K. Kt. to Q. Kt's 3d.	8. K. Kt. to B's 3d.
9. Castles.	9. Q. to K. B's 2d.
10. P. to Q. B's 4th.	10. Q. B. to Q's 2d.
11. Q. B. to K. B's 4th.	11. Castles.
12. Q. Kt. to B's 3d.	12. P. to K. R's 3d.
13. P. to Q. R's 3d.	13. P. to K. Kt's 4th.
14. Q. B. to Q's 2d.	14. P. to K. B's 5th.
15. P. to Q's 5th.	15. Q. Kt. to K's 4th.
16. K. Kt. to Q's 4th.	16. K. B. to Q. B's 4th.
17. Q. B. to K's square.	17. K. R. to Kt's sq.
18. P. to Q. Kt's 4th.	18. K. B. to K's 2d.
19. P. to K. B's 3d.	19. P. to K's 6th.
20. Q. to her Kt's 3d.	20. P. to K. Kt's 5th.
21. P. to Q. B's 5th.	21. P. takes K. B. P.
22. Kt. takes P.	22. Kt. takes Kt. (ch.)
23. B. takes Kt.	23. Kt. to K. Kt's 5th.
24. Q. to her B's 4th.	24. K. to Kt's sq.
25. Q. to K's 4th.	25. Q. R. to K's sq.
26. P. to Q's 6th.	26. Q. B. to his 3d.
27. Q. to her 4th.	27. B. takes B.
28. R. takes B.	28. B. to K. Kt's 4th.
29. Q. Kt. to his 5th.	29. P. to Q. B's 3d.
30. P. to Q's 7th.	30. Q. R. to K's 3d.
31. B. to K. Kt's 3d.	31. P. takes Q. Kt.*
32. B. takes B. P. (ch.)	32. Kt. to K's 4th.
33. B. takes Kt. (ch.)	33. R. takes B.
34. Q. takes R. (ch.)	34. K. to R's sq.
35. R. takes Q.	35. P. to K's 7th.
36. Q. to K's 8th (ch.)	36. R. takes Q.
37. P. takes R., becomes a Queen (ch.), and wins.	

* If Black had taken the B. with K. B. P. at this point, the following moves show that he would have equally lost:—

	31. P. takes B.
32. Q. takes Kt.	32. P. takes P. (ch.)
33. K. to R's sq.	33. Q. takes Q. P.
34. Q. to K. Kt's 3d (ch.), and wins.	

GAME THE NINTH.

THE GIUOCO PIANO.

AN attentive examination of the eight separate methods of reply to your second move of K's Kt. to B's 3d in the antecedent games, will have enabled you to understand that four at least of these defences, viz.: P. to K. B's 3d, B. to Q's 3d, Q. to B's 3d, and B. to Q. B's 4th, are untenable and injurious for the game of the second player, and that the remaining four, if not absolutely bad for him, are unsatisfactory, because against the best attack, they leave the balance of advantage in favor of the party playing first.

It is now time to consider the consequences to both parties when Black, abandoning the objectionable or uncertain modes of play he has hitherto adopted, shall answer with the move which the best authorities at length concur in recommending as the proper one, *i. e.* 2. Q's Kt. to B's 3d. Upon his playing thus, you have the choice of three good moves: in the first place to play 3. K's B. to Q. B's 4th, as in the present game; secondly, 3. P. to Q's 4th; and thirdly, P. to Q. B's 3d. The two latter of which will form the subjects of games hereafter.

WHITE.	BLACK.
1. P. to K's 4th.	1. P. to K's 4th
2. K. Kt. to B's 3d.	2. Q. Kt. to B's 3d.
3. K. B. to Q. B's 4th.	3 K. B. to Q. B's 4th

It is generally admitted that Black's third move is the best he can adopt; and the opening now formed is that which the Italians have entitled the "Giuoco Piano;" an opening, less attacking than many others, but one perfectly safe for both players, and therefore always in request, and which usually generates games of the most solid and instructive kind.

4. P. to Q. B's 3d	4. K. Kt. to B's 3d (best)
5. P. to Q's 4th.	5. P. takes P.
6. P. to K's 5th.	6. P. to Q's 4th (best)

KING'S KNIGHT'S OPENING.   75

7. K. B. to Q. Kt's 5th.	7. K. Kt. to K's 5th.
8. B. takes Kt. (ch.)	8. P. takes B.
9. P. takes P.	9. B. to Q. Kt's 3d.
10. Castles.	10. Q. B. to K. Kt's 5th
11. Q. B. to K's 3d.	11. Castles.

The game is equal.

Variation I.

Beginning at Black's 6th move.

WHITE.	BLACK.
1. P. to K's 4th.	1. P. to K's 4th.
2. K. Kt. to B's 3d.	2. Q. Kt. to B's 3d.
3. K. B. to Q. B's 4th.	3. K. B. to Q. B's 4th.
4. P. to Q. B's 3d.	4. K. Kt. to B's 3d.
5. P. to Q's 4th.	5. P. takes P.
6. P. to K's 5th.	6. K. Kt. to K's 5th.
7. K. B. to Q's 5th	7. Kt. takes K. B's P.
8. K. takes Kt.	8. P. takes P. (dis. ch.)
9. K. to Kt's 3d.	9. P. takes Q. Kt's P.
10. Q. B. takes P.	10. Q. Kt. to K's 2d.
11. Q. to her B's 2d	11. P. to Q's 3d.
12. B. to K's 4th.	12. Kt. to K. Kt's 3d.
13. Q. Kt. to Q's 2d.	13. P. to Q. B's 3d.
14. Q. R. to Q's sq.	

And the game appears to me in your favor.

Remember that at your move 14. you must not, instead of playing Q. R. to Q's sq., take the Kt. with your B., and afterwards play 15. Q. Kt. to K's 4th, because after taking your B. with K. R's P., he might move Q. B. to K. B's 4th, and thus prevent you moving your Kt. advantageously.

Variation II.

Beginning at White's 6th move.

WHITE.	BLACK.
1. P. to K's 4th.	1. P. to K's 4th.
2. K. Kt. to B's 3d.	2 Q. Kt. to B's 3d.
3 K. B. to Q. B's 4th	3 K. B. to Q. B's 4th
4 P. to Q. B's 3d	4 K. Kt to B's 3d

5. P to Q's 4th.	5. P. takes P.
6. P. takes P.	6. B. to Q. Kt's 5th (ch.)
7. B. to Q's 2d.	7. B. takes B. (ch.)
8. Q. Kt. takes B.	8. P. to Q's 4th.
9. P. takes P.	9. Kt. takes P.
10. Q. to her Kt's 3d.	10. Q. Kt. to K's 2d.

The game is even.

VARIATION III.
Beginning at White's 5th move.

WHITE.	BLACK.
1. P. to K's 4th.	1. P. to K's 4th.
2. K. Kt. to B's 3d.	2. Q. Kt. to B's 3d.
3. K. B. to Q. B's 4th.	3. K. B. to Q. B's 4th
4. P. to Q. B's 3d.	4. K. Kt. to B's 3d.
5. Castles.	5. Kt. takes K's P.
6. Q. to K's 2d.	6. P. to Q's 4th.
7. B. to Q. Kt's 5th	7. Castles.
8. B. takes Q. Kt.	8. P. takes B.
9. Kt. takes K. P.	9. Q. B. to Kt's 2d.
10. P. to Q's 4th.	10. K. B. to Q. Kt's 3d.

There is no advantage on either side.

GAME THE TENTH.

WHITE.	BLACK.
1 P. to K's 4th.	1. P. to K's 4th.
2. K. Kt. to B's 3d.	2. Q's Kt. to B's 3d.
3. K. B. to Q. B's 4th.	3. K. B. to Q. B's 4th.
4. P. to Q. B's 3d.	4. K. Kt. to B's 3d.
5. P. to Q's 3d.	5. P. to Q's 3d.
6. P. to Q's 4th.	6. P. takes P.
7. P. takes P.	7. B. to Q. Kt's 3d.
8. Q. Kt. to B's 3d.	8. Q. B. to K. Kt's 5th
9. P. to Q's 5th.	9. Q. Kt. to K's 4th.

The game is equal.

GAME THE ELEVENTH.

WHITE.	BLACK.
1 P. to K's 4th.	1. P. to K's 4th.

KING'S KNIGHT'S OPENING.

2. K Kt. to B's 3d.
3. K B. to Q. B's 4th.
4. P. to Q. B's 3d.
5. P. to Q's 4th.
6. P. takes P.
7. B. to Q's 2d.
8. Q. Kt. takes B.
9. Q. to her Kt's 3d.
10. Castles.
11. Q. to her B's 2d.
12. Q. takes Kt.
13. Kt. takes Kt.
14. Q. to K's 2d.
15. Q. takes P.

2. Q. Kt. to B's 3d.
3. K. B. to Q. B's 4th.
4. P. to Q's 3d.
5. P. takes P.
6. B. to Q. Kt's 5th (ch.)
7. B. takes B. (ch.)
8. K. Kt. to B's 3d.
9. Castles.
10. Q. Kt. to R's 4th.
11. Kt. takes B.
12. Kt. takes K's P.
13. P. to Q's 4th.
14. P. takes Kt.

There is little difference in the positions, but your men are better disposed for immediate action, and you have the advantage of a Knight against a Bishop.

VARIATION I.

Beginning at White's 7th move.

WHITE.
1. P. to K's 4th.
2. K. Kt. to B's 3d.
3. K. B. to Q. B's 4th.
4. P. to Q. B's 3d.
5. P. to Q's 4th.
6. P. takes P.
7. K. to his B's sq.
8. Q. to her R's 4th.
9. P. takes B.
10. K. B. to Q. Kt's 5th.
11. K. to Kt's 2d.

BLACK.
1 P. to K's 4th.
2. Q. Kt. to B's 3d.
3. K. B. to Q. B's 4th.
4. P. to Q's 3d.
5. P. takes P.
6. B. to Q. Kt's 5th (ch.)
7. Q. B. to K. Kt's 5th.
8. B. takes Kt.
9. Q. to her 2d.
10. Castles.

And it appears to me that White has an unquestionable advantage.

GAME THE TWELFTH.

WHITE.
1. P. to K's 4th.

BLACK.
1. P. to K's 4th.

2. K. Kt. to B's 3d.   2. Q. Kt. to B's 3 l.
3. K. B. to Q. B's 4th.   3. K. B. to Q. B's 4th.
4. P. to Q. B's 3d.   4. P. to K. B's 4th.
5. P. to Q's 4th   5. K. B. P. takes K. P
6. K. Kt. takes K. P.   6. B. to Q. Kt's 3d.
7. Q. to K. R's 5th (ch.)   7. P. to K. Kt's 3d.
8. B. to K. B's 7th (ch.)   8. K. to B's sq.
9. Q. B. to K. R's 6th (ch)   9. Kt. takes B.
10. Q. takes Kt. (ch.)   10. K. to his 2d.
11. B. takes Kt's P.   11. Kt. takes Kt
12 Q. to K. Kt's 5th (ch.), and you must win.

GAME THE THIRTEENTH.

WHITE.   BLACK.
1. P. to K's 4th.   1. P. to K's 4th.
2. K. Kt. to B's 3d.   2. Q. Kt. to B's 3d.
3. K. B. to Q. B's 4th.   3. K. B. to Q. B's 4th.
4. P. to Q. B's 3d.   4. Q. to K's 2d.
5. P. to Q's 4th.   5. B. to Q. Kt's 3d.
6. P. takes K. P.   6. Kt. takes P.
7. Kt. takes Kt.   7. Q. takes Kt.
8. Castles.   8. P. to Q's 3d.
9. K. to R's sq.   9. Q's B. to K's 3d.

White has a little the better game.

VARIATION.

1. P. to K's 4th.   1. P. to K's 4th.
2. K. Kt. to B's 3d.   2. Q. Kt. to B's 3d.
3. K. B. to Q. B's 4th.   3. K. B. to Q. B's 4th.
4. P. to Q. B's 3d.   4. K. B. to Q. Kt.'s 3d
5. P. to Q's 4th.   5. P. to Q's 3d.
6. P. takes P.   6. P. takes P.
7. Q. takes Q. (ch.)   7. K. takes Q.
8. B. takes K. B's. P.,

and you have the better game.

GAME THE FOURTEENTH.

WHITE.   BLACK.
1 P. to K's 4th.   1. P. to K's 4th.

KING'S KNIGHT'S OPENING.

2. K's Kt. to B's 3d. 2. Q. Kt. to B's 3d.
3. K's B. to Q. B's 4th. 3. K's B. to Q. B's 4th.
4. Castles. 4. P. to Q's 3d.
5. P. to Q. B's 3d. 5. Q's B. to K. Kt's 5th
6. Q. to her Kt.'s 3d. 6. Q's B. takes Kt.
7. B. takes K. B. P. (ch.) 7. K. to K. B's sq.
8. K. Kt. P. takes Q. B. 8. Q. to K. B's 3d.
9. K. B. to K. R's 5th. 9. P. to K. Kt's 3d.
10. K. B. to Kt's 4th. 10. B. to Q. Kt's 3d.
11. Q. to her sq.

You have the better game.

GAME THE FIFTEENTH.

WHITE. BLACK.
1. P. to K's 4th. 1. P. to K's 4th.
2. K. Kt. to B's 3d. 2. Q. Kt. to B's 3d
3. K. B. to Q. B's 4th. 3. K. B. to Q. B's 4th.
4. P. to Q's 3d. 4. P. to Q's 3d.
5. P. to Q. B's 3d. 5. Q. to K. B's 3d.
6. Q. B. to K. Kt's 5th. 6. Q. to K. Kt's 3d.
7. Castles. 7. Q. B. to K. Kt's 5th.
8. Q. Kt. to Q's 2d. 8. K. Kt. to K. R's 3d.
9. P. to Q. Kt's 4th. 9. K. B. to Q. Kt's 3d.
10. P. to Q. R's 4th. 10. P. to Q. R's 4th (best)
11. P. to Q. Kt's 5th. 11. Kt. to Q's sq.
12. K. B. to Q's 5th.

The game is in your favor.

GAMES

ILLUSTRATIVE OF THE GIUOCO PIANO.

GAME I.—Between Mr. D. Harrwitz of Paris and Mr Capdebo, a strong Hungarian player.

WHITE. (Mr. C.) BLACK. (Mr. H.)
1. P. to K's 4th. 1. P. to K's 4th.
2. K. Kt. to B's 3d. 2. Q. Kt. to B's 3d.
3. K. B. to Q. B's 4th. 3. K. B. to Q. B's 4th.
4. P. to Q. B's 3d. 4. K. Kt. to Q. B's 3d.

5. P. to Q's 4th.	5. P. takes P.
6. P. takes P.	6. K. B. to Q. Kt's 5th (ch.
7. Q. B. to Q's 2d.	7. K. B. takes Q. B. (ch.)
8. Q. Kt. takes B.	8. P. to Q's 4th.
9. P. takes P.	9. K. Kt. takes P.
10. Q. to K's 2d (ch.)	10. B. to K's 3d.
11. B. to Kt's 5th.	11. Castles.
12. B. takes Kt.	12. P. takes B.
13. Castles (with K. R.)	13. Q. R. to Kt's sq.
14. P. to Q. Kt's 3d.	14. Kt. to K. B's 5th.
15. Q. to Q. R's 6th.	15. K. R. to K's sq.
16. K. R. to K's sq.	16. Q. to Q's 2d.
17. Kt. to K's 5th.	17. Q. takes P.
18. Q. Kt. to B's 3d.	18. Q. to Q. Kt's 3d.
19. Q. takes Q.	19. R. takes Q.
20. Q. R. to B's sq.	20. P. to K. B's 3d.
21. K. Kt. to Q. B's 4th.	21. Q. R. to R's 3d.

And Black ultimately won.

GAME II.—Played at the Philadelphia Athenæum, between Mr. McCabe and Mr. H. P. Montgomery.

WHITE. (Mr. McC.)	BLACK. (Mr. M.)
1. P. to K's 4th.	1. P. to K's 4th.
2. Kt. to K. B's 3d.	2. Q. Kt. to B's 3d.
3. K. B. to Q. B's 4th.	3. K. B. to Q. B's 4th.
4. P. to Q. B's 3d.	4. P. to K. B's 4th.
5. P. to Q's 3d.	5. K. Kt. to B's 3d.
6. P. takes P.	6. P. to Q's 4th.
7. B. to Q. Kt's 5th.	7. Q. to her 3d.
8. Castles.	8. Castles.
9. P. to Q. Kt's 4th.	9. B. to Kt's 3d.
10. P. to K. R's 3d.	10. Q. B. takes P.
11. B. takes Kt.	11. P. takes B.
12. P. to Q's 4th.	12. P. to K's 5th.
13. Kt. to K's 5th.	13. P. to Q. R's 4th.
14. Q. B. to R's 3d.	14. P. takes P.
15. B. takes P.	15. P. to Q. B's 4th.
16. P. takes P.	16. B. takes P.
17. B. takes B.	17. Q. takes B.
18. Q. to Q's 4th.	18. Q. to Q's 3d.
19. Kt. to K. Kt's 4th.	19. B. takes Kt.
20. P. takes B.	20. Kt. takes P.
21. P. to K. Kt's 3d.	21. Q. to K. R's 3d.
22. R. to Q's sq.	22. Q. checks.
23. K. moves.	23. R. takes P. (ch.), and wins

GAME III.—Between Mr. Horwitz and Mr. Staunton.

WHITE. (Mr. S)	BLACK. (Mr. H.)
1. P. to K's 4th.	1. P. to K's 4th.
2. K. Kt. to B's 3d.	2. Q. Kt. to B's 3d.

KING'S KNIGHT'S OPENING.   81

3. K. B. to Q. B's 4th.	3. K. B. to Q. B's 4th.
4. P. to Q. B's 3d.	4. P. to Q's 3d.
5. P. to Q's 4th.	5. P. takes P.
6. P. takes P.	6. B. to Q. Kt's 3d.
7. Q. Kt. to B's 3d.	7. Q. B. to K. Kt's 5th.
8. Q. B. to K's 3d.	8. K. Kt. to B's 3d.
9. P. to Q. R's 3d.	9. Castles.
10. K. B. to K's 2d.	10. K. R. to K's sq.
11. P. to Q's 5th.	11. Q. Kt. to K's 4th.
12. Kt. takes Kt.	12. Q. B. takes K. B.
13. Q. takes B.	13. R. takes Kt.
14. B. takes K. B.	14. Q. R. P. takes B.
15. Castles on K's side.	15. Kt. takes K. P.
16. Kt. takes Kt.	16. P. to K. B's 4th.
17. P. to K. B's 3d.	17. P. takes Kt.
18. P. takes P.	18. Q. to K's 2d.
19. Q. R. to K's sq.	19. Q. R. to K's sq.
20. K. R. to K. B's 4th.	20. P. to K. R's 3d.*
21. Q. to K. B's 3d.†	21. R. takes Q. P.
22. Q. R. to K. B's sq.‡	22. R. to K's 4th.
23. K. R. to K. B's 7th.	23. Q. to K's 3d. §
24. K. R. takes Q. B. P.	24. R. takes K. P.
25. R. takes Q. Kt. P	25. P. to Q's 4th.
26. P. to K. R's 3d.‖	26. R. to K's 8th.
27. R. takes R.	27. Q. takes R. (ch.)
28. Q. to K. B's sq.¶	28. Q. to K's 6th (ch.)

---

* Black would have gained no advantage by taking the Q. P. at this juncture, or by advancing his P. to K. Kt's 4th, to attack the Rook. The move in the text was not made without due deliberation, and we believe it the best on the board.

† White designedly gives up the Queen's Pawn, to get a counter attack with his combined forces.

‡ Queen to her Knight's 3d would have been worse than useless.

§ Had he gone to Queen's square, to protect his threatened Pawn, White would have won the King's Knight's Pawn. (*e. g.*)

WHITE.	BLACK.
	23. Q to Q's sq.
24. R. takes K. Kt. P. (ch.)	24. K. takes R.
25. Q. to K. B's 7th (ch.)	25. K. to R's sq.
26. K. R. to K. B's 6th.	26. R. to K. R's 4th.
27. Q. takes K. R.	27. Q. takes R.
28. Q. takes R. (ch.), &c.	

‖ A most important move. Black dare not now advance his Q. P. on account of Q. to B's 7th (ch.), which would enable White to double his Rooks on the adversary's K. Kt. P., and thus win easily.

¶ K. to R's 2d would have been very bad play, because Black would have checked with his Q. at K's 4th; and if then the Queen were interposed, he would have taken the Q. and played R. to K's 8th ch.), and afterwards R. to Q. Kt's 6th.

29. Q. to K. B's 2d.	29. Q. to her B's 8th (ch.)
30. K. to R's 2d.	30. R. to K. B's sq.
31. Q. to her 4th.	31. R. to K. B's 3d.*
32. Q. takes P. (ch.)	32. K. to R's 2d.
33. Q. to K's 5th.	33. R. to K. Kt's 3d.†
34. R. to K's 7th.	34. Q. to her 7th.
35. Q. to K's 4th.	35. Q. to her 3d (ch.)
36. R. to K's 5th.	36. K. to Kt's sq.
37. Q. to her 5th (ch.)	37. Q. takes Q.
38. R. takes Q.	38. K. to B's 2d.
39. R. to Q. Kt's 5th.	39. K. to his 2d.
40. P. to K. Kt's 4th.	40. K. to Q's 2d.
41. K. to Kt's 3d.	41. K. to Q. B's 3d.
42. R. to K's 5th.	42. R. to Q's 3d.
43. R. to K's 3d.	43. K. to Q. B's 4th.
44. P. to K. R's 4th.	44. P. to K. Kt's 3d.
45. K. to B's 4th.	45. K. to Q's 5th.
46. R. to K's 4th (ch.)	46. K. to Q's 4th.
47. R. to K's 8th.	47. R. to K. B's 3d (ch.)
48. K. to his 3d.	48. K. to Q. B's 5th.
49. R. to K's 4th (ch.)	49. K. to Q's 4th.
50. R. to K. B's 4th.	50. R. to Q. B's 3d.
51. R. to Q. Kt's 4th.	51. R. to K's 3d (ch.)
52. K. to Q's 3d.	52. R. to K. B's 3d.
53. R. to Q. Kt's 5th (ch.)‡	53. K. to Q. B's 3d.
54. R. to K's 5th.	54. K. to Q's 3d.
55. R. to Q. Kt's 5th.	55. K. to Q. B's 3d.
56. R. to Q. Kt's 4th.	56. R. to B's 6th (ch.)
57. K. to his 2d.	57. R. to K. R's 6th.
58. R. to K. B's 4th.	58. R. takes K. R. P.
59. R. to B's 6th (ch.)	59. K. to Kt's 4th.
60. R. takes K. Kt. P.	60. R. to R's 7th (ch.)
61. K. to B's 3d.	61. R. takes Q. Kt. P.
62. R. takes K. R. P.	62. R. to Q. Kt's 6th (ch.)
63. K. to B's 4th.	63. R. takes Q. R. P.
64. P. to Kt's 5th.	64. R. to Q. R's 8th.
65. R. to K. R's 4th.	65. K. to Q. B's 4th.
66. P. to Kt's 6th.	66. R. to Q. R's 2d.
67. K. to his B's 5th.	67. P. to Kt's 4th.
68. R. to K. Kt's 4th.	68. P. to Kt's 5th.§
69. P. to Kt's 7th.	69. R. takes P.
70. R. takes R.	70. P. to Kt's 6th.
71. K. to his 4th.	71. K. to Kt's 5th.
72. K. to Q's 3d.	

And Black surrenders.

---

* He could not save all the Pawns attacked.

† Threatening to take the K. Kt. P. with his Rook, and then check with the Queen at her Bishop's 3d.

‡ K. to his 3d would have been better.

§ This was ill-judged. He should have played R. to K. Kt' 2d, or Q. R's square.

KING'S KNIGHT'S OPENING.

GAME IV.—Between A. A. Alechine, of St. Petersburg, and Dr. S. Tarrasch, of Nuremburg.

WHITE. (Alechine.)	BLACK. (Tarrasch.)
1. P. to K's 4th.	1. P. to K's 4th.
2. Kt. to K. B's 3d.	2. Kt. to Q. B's 3d.
3. B. to B's 4th.	3. B. to B's 4th.
4. P. to B's 3d.	4. Q. to K's 2d.*
5. P. to Q's 4th.	5. B. to Kt's 3d.
6. Castles.	6. P. to Q's 3d.
7. P. to Q. R's 4th.	7. P. to Q. R's 3d.
8. B. to K's 3d.	8. B. to Kt's 5th.
9. P. to Q's 5th.	9. Kt. to Kt.
10. P. to R's 5th.†	10. B. takes B.
11. P. takes B.	11. Kt. to K. B's 3d.
12. Q. Kt. to Q's 2d.	12. Q. Kt. to Q's 2d.
13. Q. to K.	13. Kt. to B's 4th.
14. Q. to Kt.	14. B. to B.
15. P. to Q. Kt's 4th.	15. Q. Kt. to Q's 2d.
16. Kt. to R's 4th.	16. P. to K. Kt's 3d.
17. Q. to K.	17. P. to B's 3d.
18. Kt. (R's 4th) to B's 3d.‡	18. P. takes P.
19. P. takes P.	19. P. to K's 5th.
20. Kt. to Kt's 5th.	20. P. to R's 3d.
21. Kt. to R's 3d.	21. Q. to K's 4th.
22. R. to B.	22. Kt. to Kt's 5th.§
23. Kt. to B's 4th.	23. P. to K. Kt's 4th.
24. P. to R's 3d.	24. Kt. (Kt's 5th) to B's 3d.
25. Kt. to K's 2d.	25. Kt. takes P.
26. B. takes Kt.	26. Q. takes B.
27. Kt. to Q's 4th.‖	27. Q. to K's 4th.¶
28. Kt. to B's 4th.	28. Q. to Q's 4th.
29. Kt. to B's 5th.	29. K. to B.
30. Kt. (B's 5th) takes Q. P.	30. R. to K. R's 2d.
31. R. to Q.	31. Q. to B's 3d.
32. R. to Q's 4th.	32. P. to Kt's 4th.
33. P. takes P. e. p.	33. B. to Kt's 2d.
34. Kt. to R's 5th.	34. Resigns.

* This variation of the Giuoco Piano leads to an interesting game, but is seldom played. Black's object is to maintain his centre by avoiding the exchange of Pawns when White plays P. to Q's 4th.

† B. takes B., followed by Q. Kt. to Q's 2d, would have given White a slight advantage in Pawn positions, but Alechine shines more in combination than in position play, and preferred forcing his opponent to make the exchange in order that he might retake with the King's Bishop's Pawn, and thus open the file for his Rook.

‡ Black having played P. to K. Kt's 3d, the Knight had no longer any future at R's 4th.

§ A faulty maneuver, which has the effect of forcing White's Knight into a better position than it held before. Black, however, had the worst of the game in any case. If, instead of the text move, he had played 22. . . . Kt. takes P., then 23. Kt. to B's 4th, and he would have had nothing better than 23. . . . Kt. (Q's 4th) to B's 3d, remaining with a very cramped position, for if 23 . . . Kt. takes B. P., then 24. B. takes P. (ch.), and if 23. . . . Kt. (Q's 2d) to B's 3d, then 24. B. takes Kt., Kt. takes B.; 25. Kt. to B's 4th, and wins.

‖ Threatening to win a piece by R. to B's 5th, for the Knight could not interpose at K's 4th, because of P. to Q. B's 4th winning the Queen.

¶ A weak move, which leads to immediate disaster. His best defense would have been Kt. to B.

CHESS HANDBOOK.

GAME V.—Between M. St. Amant and Mr. Staunton.

WHITE. (Mr. S.)	BLACK. (M. St. A.)
1. P. to K's 4th.	1. P. to K's 4th.
2. K. B. to Q. B's 4th.	2. K. B. to Q. B's 4th
3. K. Kt. to B's 3d.	3. Q. Kt. to B's 3d.
4. P. to Q. B's 3d.	4. Q. to K's 2d.
5. P. to Q's 4th.	5. P. takes P.*
6. Castles.	6. Q. Kt. to K's 4th.
7. Kt. takes Kt.	7. Q. takes Kt.
8. P. to K. B's 4th.	8. P. takes Q. B. P. (dis. ch.)
9. K. to R's sq.	9. Q. to her 5th.
10. Q. to her Kt's 3d.	10. Kt. to K. R's 3d.
11. Q. Kt. takes P.	11. Castles.
12. P. to K. R's 3d.†	12. P. to Q. B's 3d.
13. P. to K. B's 5th.	13. Q. to K. B's 3d.
14. P. to K's 5th.‡	14. Q. to K. R's 5th.
15. Q. B. takes Kt.	15. Q. takes Q. B.
16. Kt. to K's 4th.	16. B. to Q's 5th.
17. Kt. to Q's 6th.	17. Q. to K. R's 4th.
18. B. takes K. B. P. (ch.)	18. R. takes B.
19. P. to K. Kt's 4th.	19. B. takes K. P.§
20. Q. R. to K's sq.	20. Q. takes K. R. P. (ch.)
21. Q. takes Q.	21. B. takes Kt.
22. R. to K's 8th (ch.)	22. B. to his sq.
23. K. R. to K's sq.	23. P. to Q's 4th.
24. Q. R. to Q's 8th.	24. R. to Q's 2d.
25. K. R. to K's 8th.	25. R. takes Q. R.
26. R. takes R.	26. P. to Q. Kt's 3d.
27. Q. to K's 3d.	27. Q. B. to Kt's 2d.
28. R. takes R.	28. B. takes R.
29. Q. to K's 6th (ch.)	29. K. to R's sq.
30. Q. to K. B's 7th.	

Black resigns.

---

* The proper move is B. to Q. Kt's 3d. Taking the Pawn gives an immediate advantage to White.

† If White play P. to K. B's 5th at this point, his opponent may move Kt. to K. Kt's 5th, threatening to play afterwards Q. to K. Kt's 8th (ch.), and then mate with his Kt. at B's 7th.

‡ From this move the attack is very lively and interesting.

§ There appears to be nothing better, bad as this is.

KING'S KNIGHT'S OPENING.

GAME VI.—Played by correspondence between Mr. Cheney, of Syracuse, N. Y., and two Amateurs of Utica, N. Y.

WHITE. (Utica.)	BLACK. (Syracuse.)
1. P. to K's 4th.	1. P. to K's 4th.
2. K. Kt. to B's 3d.	2. Q. Kt. to B's 3d.
3. K. B. to Q. B's 4th.	3. K. B. to Q. B's 4th.
4. P. to Q. B's 3d.	4. K. Kt. to B's 3d.
5. P. to Q's 4th.	5. P. takes P.
6. P. to K's 5th.	6. P. to Q's 4th.
7. B. to Q. Kt's 5th.	7. Kt. to K's 5th.
8. B. takes Kt. (ch.)	8. P. takes B.
9. P. takes P.	9. B. to Q. Kt's 3d.
10. Castles.	10. Q. B. to K. Kt's 5th
11. B. to K's 3d.	11. Castles.
12. P. to K. R's 3d.	12. B. to K. R's 4th.
13. P. to K. Kt's 4th.	13. B. to K. Kt's 3d.
14. K. Kt. to R's 2d.	14. P. to K. B's 4th.
15. P. to K. B's 3d.	15. Kt. to Kt's 6th.
16. R. to K's square.	16. P. to K. B's 5th.
17. B. to K. B's 2d.	17. Q. to K's 2d.
18. Kt. to Q. B's 3d.	18. P. to K. R's 4th.
19. Q. to Q. R's 4th.	19. B. to K's sq.
20. P. to Q. Kt's 4th.	20. Q. to K's 3d.
21. Q. to Q. Kt's 3d.	21. B. to Q's 2d.
22. Q. Kt. to K's 2d.	22. P. to K. R's 5th.
23. K. Kt. to K. B's sq.	23. P. to Q. R's 4th.
24. K. Kt. takes Kt.	24. R. P. takes Kt.
25. B. takes P.	25. P. takes B.
26. P. to Q. R's 3d.	26. Q. to K. R's 3d.
27. K. to Kt's 2d.	27. B. takes K. Kt. P.
28. B. P. takes B.	28. B. takes Q. P.
29. Q. R. to Q.	

Black announced mate in four moves.

GAME VII.—Between Mr. Popert and another fine player of London.

WHITE. (Mr. P.)	BLACK. (Mr. —.)
1. P. to K's 4th.	1. P. to K's 4th.
2. K. Kt. to B's 3d.	2. Q. Kt. to B's 3d.
3. K. B. to Q. B's 4th.	3. K. B. to Q. B's 4th.
4. P. to Q. B's 3d.	4. K. Kt. to B's 3d.
5. Castles.*	5. K. Kt. takes P.
6. P. to Q's 4th.	6. P. to Q's 4th.
7. K. B. to Q. Kt's 5th.	7. P. takes Q. P.
8. P. takes P.	8. K. B. to Q's 3d.

---

* Castling before moving the Q. B. P., and before the adverse K. Kt. is in the field, appears safer play.

CHESS HANDBOOK.

9. K. Kt. to K's 5th.	9. B. takes Kt.
10. P. takes B.	10. Castles.
11. P. to K. B's 4th.	11. P. to K. B's 4th.
12. Q Kt. to B's 3d.	12. Q. B. to K's 3d.
13. Q. B. to K's 3d.	13. P. to Q. R's 3d.
14. B. takes Kt.	14. P. takes B.
15. Q. R. to Q. B's sq.*	15. Q. to K's sq.
16. Q. to her B's 2d.†	16. Q. R. to Kt's sq.
17. Kt. takes Kt.	17. K. B. P. takes Kt.
18. Q. takes Q. B. P.	18. Q. R. takes Q. Kt. P.
19. Q. takes Q.	19. R. takes Q.
20. P. to K. B's 5th.‡	20. B. to his sq.
21. Q. R. takes P.	21. Q. R. to K's 7th.
22. B. to Q's 4th.	22. Q. R. to Q's 6th.
23. B. to Q. B's 3d.	23. R. to Q's 8th.
24. P. to K. B's 6th.	24. P. takes P.
25. P. takes P.	25. Q. B. to K's 3d.
26. R. to K. Kt's 7th (ch.)	26. K. to R's sq.
27. B. to K's 5th.	27. B. to K. Kt's sq.
28. R. to K's 7th.	28. B. to K. B's 2d.

White now checkmates in two more moves.

GAME VIII.—Between Mr. Buckle and Mr. Harrwits

WHITE. (Mr. B.)	BLACK. (Mr. H.)
1. P. to K's 4th.	1. P. to K's 4th.
2. K. Kt. to B's 3d.	2. Q. Kt. to B's 3d.
3. K. B. to Q. B's 4th.	3. K. B. to Q. B's 4th.
4. Castles.	4. K. Kt. to B's 3d.
5. Q. Kt. to B's 3d.	5. P. to Q's 3d.
6. P. to K. R's 3d.	6. Castles.
7. P. to Q's 3d.	7. Q. B. to K's 3d.
8. K. B. to Kt's 3d.	8. Q. Kt. to K's 2d.
9. Q. Kt. to K's 2d.	9. Q. Kt. to K. Kt's 3d.
10. Q. Kt. to K. Kt's 3d.	10. P. to Q. B's 3d.
11. P. to Q. B's 3d.	11. P. to Q's 4th.
12. P. to Q's 4th.	12. Q. P. takes K. P.
13. Q. P. takes B.	13. P. takes Kt.
14. Q. takes P.	14. Q. B. takes K. B.
15. P. takes B.	15. K. Kt. to Q's 4th.
16. Kt. to K. B's 5th.§	16. P. to Q. Kt's 3d.
17. P. takes Kt. P.	17. Q. takes P.

* Threatening to exchange the Kt., and then take Q. B. P. with the Rook.

† Intending again to take the Kt., and thus win a Pawn.

‡ Well played, the advance of this Pawn secures to him an irresistible attack.

§ This is a very attacking position for the Kt., and generally occasions great embarrassment to an adversary.

KING'S KNIGHT'S OPENING.

18. P. to Q. B's 4th.	18. K. Kt. to K. B's 5th
19. B. takes K. Kt.	19. Q. Kt. takes B.
20. K. R. to Q's sq.*	20. Q. to Q. B's 2d.
21. Q. takes Q. B. P.	21. K. R. to Q. B's sq.
22. Q. takes Q.	22. R. takes Q.
23. Kt. to Q's 6th.	23. Kt. to K's 7th (ch.)
24. K. to B's sq.	24. Kt. to Q's 5th.
25. P. to Q. Kt's 4th.	25. P. to K. B's 4th.
26. P. to Q. B's 5th.	26. K. R. to Q. Kt's sq.
27. Q. R. to R's 4th.	27. P. to K. Kt's 3d.
28. K. R. to Q. R's sq.	28. Kt. to Q. B's 7th.
29. R. takes P.	29. R. takes R.
30. R. takes R.	30. Kt. takes Q. Kt. P.
31. R. to Q. Kt's 7th.†	31. R. takes R.
32. Kt. takes R.	32. K. to B's 2d.
33. K. to K's 2d.	33. K. to K's 2d.
34. K. to Q's 2d.	34. K. to Q's 2d.
35. Kt. to R's 5th.	35. Kt. to R's 3d.
36. Kt. to Q. Kt's 3d.	36. K. to Q. B's 3d.
37. K. to Q. B's 3d.	37. Kt. takes P.
38. Kt. takes Kt.	38. K. takes Kt.
39. P. to K. R's 4th.	39. P. to K. R's 3d.
40. P. to K. B's 3d.	40. P. to K. Kt's 4th.
41. P. to K. R's 5th.	41. P. to K's 5th.
42. P. takes P.	42. K. B. P. takes P.
43. P. to K. Kt's 4th.	43. K. to Q's 4th.
44. P. to Q. Kt's 4th.	44. K. to K's 4th.
45. P. to Q. Kt's 5th.	45. K. to K. B's 5th.
46. P. to Q. Kt's 6th.	46. P. to K's 6th.
47. P. to Q. Kt's 7th.	47. K. to B's 6th.
48. P. becomes a Queen.	

And wins.‡

---

* Prudently taking possession of an "open file."
† White plays with remarkable care and judgment here.
‡ The termination of this game is an improving lesson in Pawn play.

Captain Evans's Gambit
GAME THE FIRST.

WHITE.	BLACK.
1. P. to K's 4th.	1. P. to K's 4th.
2. K. Kt. to B's 3d.	2. Q. Kt. to B's 3d.
3. K. B. to Q. B's 4th.	3. K. B. to Q. B's 4th.
4. P. to Q. Kt's 4th.	4. B. takes Q. Kt. P. (best)
5. P. to Q. B's 3d.	5. B. to Q. R's 4th.
6. Castles.	6. P. to Q's 3d (best)
7. P. to Q's 4th.	7. P. takes P.
8. P. takes P.	8. B. to Q. Kt's 3d.
9. B. to Q. Kt's 2d.	9. K. Kt. to B's 3d.
10. P. to Q's 5th.	10. Q. Kt. to K's 2d.
11. B. takes K. Kt.	11. P. takes B.
12. K. Kt. to Q's 4th.	12. B. takes Kt.

Equal game.

First Variation,
Commencing at Black's 4th move.

WHITE.	BLACK.
1. P. to K's 4th.	1. P. to K's 4th.
2. K. Kt. to B's 3d.	2. Q. Kt. to B's 3d.
3. K. B. to Q. B's 4th	3. K. B. to Q. B's 4th.
4. P. to Q. Kt's 4th.	4. Q. Kt. takes Kt. P.
5. P. to Q. B's 3d.	5. Kt. to Q. B's 3d.

(See Second Variation.)

Second Variation,
Commencing at Black's 5th move.

WHITE.	BLACK.
1. P. to K's 4th.	1. P. to K's 4th.
2. K. Kt. to B's 3d.	2. Q. Kt. to B's 3d.
3. K. B. to Q. B's 4th	3. K. B. to Q. B's 4th.
4. P. to Q. Kt's 4th.	4. B. takes Q. Kt. P.
5. P. to Q. B's 3d.	5. K. B. to Q. B's 4th
6. P. to Q's 4th.	6. P. takes P.
7. P. takes P	7. B. to Q. Kt's 3d.
8. Castles.	8. P. to Q's 3d.

9. P. to Q's 5th. 9. Q. Kt. to K's 2d.
10. Q. B. to Q. Kt's 2d. 10. K. Kt. to B.'s 3d.

Same position as in the game given first

VARIATION III.
Beginning at White's 6th move.

WHITE.	BLACK.
1. P. to K's 4th.	1. P. to K's 4th.
2. K. Kt. to B's 3d.	2. Q. Kt. to B's 3d.
3. K. B. to Q. B's 4th.	3. K. B. to Q. B's 4th
4. P. to Q. Kt's 4th.	4. B. takes Kt. P.
5. P. to Q. B's 3d.	5. B. to Q. B's 4th.
6. Castles.	6. P. to Q's 3d.
7. P. to Q's 4th.	7. P. takes P.
8. P. takes P.	8. B. to Q. Kt's 3d.
9. Q. B. to Q. R's 3d.	9. K. Kt. to B's 3d.
10. P. to K's 5th.	10. P. takes P.
11. Q. to her Kt's 3d.	

And your game is preferable to Black's.

GAME THE SECOND.

WHITE.	BLACK.
1. P. to K's 4th.	1. P. to K's 4th.
2. K. Kt. to B's 3d.	2. Q. Kt. to B's 3d.
3. K. B. to Q. B's 4th.	3. K. B. to Q. B's 4th
4. P. to Q. Kt's 4th.	4. B. takes Kt. P.
5. P. to Q. B's 3d.	5. B. to Q. R's 4th.
6. Castles.	6. K. Kt. to B's 3d.
7. K. Kt. to his 5th.	7. Castles.
8. P to K. B's 4th.	8. P. to Q's 4th.
9. P. takes Q. P.	9. K. Kt. takes P.
10. P. to Q's 4th.	10. P. to K. R's 3d.
11. Q. to her Kt's 3d.	11. P. takes Kt.
12. B. takes Kt.	12. K. P. takes B. P.
13. P to K. Kt's 3d.	13. Kt. to K's 2d.

Black has the advantage.

Variation I.

Beginning at White's 7th move.

WHITE.	BLACK.
1. P. to K's 4th.	1. P. to K's 4th.
2. K. Kt. to B's 3d.	2. Q. Kt. to B's 3d.
3. K. B. to Q. B's 4th.	3. K. B. to Q. B's 4th.
4. P. to Q. Kt's 4th.	4. B. takes Kt. P.
5. P. to Q. B's 3d.	5. B. to Q. R's 4th.
6. Castles.	6. K. Kt. to B's 3d.
7. P. to Q's 4th.	7. P. takes P.
8. P. to K's 5th.	8. K. Kt. to K's 5th.
9. Q. to her Kt's 3d.	9. Castles.
10. Q. B. to Q. R's 3d	10. P. to Q's 3d.
11. Q. B. P. takes P.	11. K. B. to Q. Kt's 3a.
12. Q. to K's 3d.	12. Q. B. to K. B's 4th
13. B. to Q's 5th.	

And you win a piece.

GAME THE THIRD

Varying from the preceding at Black's 7th move.

WHITE.	BLACK.
1 P. to K's 4th.	1. P. to K's 4th.
2. K. Kt. to B's 3d.	2. Q. Kt. to B's 3d.
3. K. B. to Q. B's 4th.	3. K. B. to Q. B's 4th
4. P. to Q. Kt's 4th.	4. B. takes Kt. P.
5. P. to Q. B's 3d.	5. B. to Q. R's 4th.
6. Castles.	6. K. Kt. to B's 3d.
7. P. to Q's 4th.	7. Castles.
8. P. takes K. P.	8. Kt. takes K. P.
9. Q. to Q's 3d.	9. Kt. to Q. B's 4th
10. Q. to her 5th.	10. Kt. to K's 3d.
11. Q. B. to Q. R's 3d.	11. K. R. to K's sq.

You may then move 12. K. to R's sq., or 12. P. to K Kt's 3d., and have a good game.

KING'S KNIGHT'S OPENING.

GAMES
ILLUSTRATIVE OF THE EVANS GAMBIT.

GAME I.—Between Mr. Morphy and Mr. Anderssen.

WHITE. (Mr. M.)	BLACK. (Mr. A.)
1. P. to K's 4th.	1. P. to K's 4th.
2. K. Kt. to B's 3d.	2. Q. Kt. to B's 3d.
3. K. B. to Q. B's 4th.	3. K. B. to Q. B's 4th.
4. P. to Q. Kt's 4th.	4. B. takes P.
5. P. to Q. B's 3d.	5. B. to Q. R's 4th.
6. P. to Q's 4th.	6. K. P. takes Q. P.
7. Castles.	7. K. Kt. to B's 3d.
8. P. to K's 5th.	8. P. to Q's 4th.
9. K. B. to Q. Kt's 5th.	9. K. Kt. to K's 5th.
10. P. takes P.	10. Castles.
11. B. takes Kt.	11. P. takes B.
12. Q. to Q. R's 4th.	12. B. to Q. Kt's 3d.
13. Q. takes Q. B. P.	13. Q. B. to K. Kt's 5th.
14. Q. B. to Q. Kt's 2d.	14. B. takes Kt.
15. P. takes B.	15. K. Kt. to his 4th.
16. Q. Kt. to Q's 2d.	16. K. R. to K's sq.
17. K. to R's sq.	17. K. Kt. to K. R's 6th.
18. P. to K. B's 4th.	18. Q. to K. R's 5th.
19. Q. takes Q. P.	19. Kt. takes P. (ch.)
20. K. to Kt's sq.	20. Kt. to Q's 6th.
21. Q. B. to B's 3d.	21. Kt. takes K. B. P.
22. Q. to K. B's 3d.	22. Kt. to R's 6th (ch.)
23. K. to R's sq.	23. Kt. to K. Kt's 4th.
24. Q. to K. Kt's 2d.	24. Q. R. to Q's sq.
25. R. to K. Kt's sq.	25. P. to K. R's 3d.
26. Q. R. to K. B's sq.	26. Q. to K. R's 6th.
27. Q. to Q. B's 6th.	27. Q. to her 2d.
28. Q. to K. Kt's 2d.	28. B. takes Q. P.
29. B. takes B.	29. Q. takes B.
30. Kt. to K. B's 3d.	30. Q. to her 4th.
31. P. to K. R's 4th.	31. Kt. to K's 3d.
32. Q. to K. Kt's 4th	32. Q. to Q. B's 3d.
33. R. to K. Kt's 2d.	33. R. to Q's 6th.
34. Q. to K. B's 5th.	34. K. R. to Q's sq.
35. Q. to K. B's 6th.	35. Q. to Q's 4th.
36. Q. to K. B's 5th.	36. R. to Q's 8th.
37. R. takes R.	37. Q. takes R. (ch.)
38. K. to R's 2d.	38. R. to Q's 6th.
39. R. to K. B's 2d.	39. R. to K's 6th.
40. Kt. to Q's 2d.	40. R. to K's 7th.
41. Q. takes P. (ch.)	41. K. to R's sq.
42. Kt. to K's 4th.	42. R. takes R. (ch.)
43. Kt. takes R.	43. Q. to Q's 4th.
44. Kt. to K. Kt's 4th.	44. Q. takes R. P. (ch.)

45. K. to Kt's 3d.	45. Q. to Q. Kt's 6th (ch.)
46. K. to R's 2d.	46. Q. to Q. B's 7th (ch.)
47. K. to Kt's 3d.	47. Q. to Q. B's 6th (ch.)
48. K. to R's 2d.	48. Q. to Q. B's 3d.
49. P. to K. R's 5th.	49. P. to Q. R's 4th.
50. Kt. to K. B's 6th.	50. P. takes Kt.
51. Q. takes P. (ch.)	51. K. to Kt. sq.
52. Q. to Kt's 6th (ch.)	52. K. to B's sq.
53. Q. takes R. P. (ch.)	53. K. to his sq.
54. Q. to Kt's 6th (ch.)	54. K. to Q's 2d.
55. P. to K. R's 6th.	55. Q. to her 4th.
56. P. to K. R's 7th.	56. Q. takes P. (ch.)
57. K. to Kt's sq.	57. Kt. to K. Kt's 4th.
58. P. to R's 8th (2d Q.)	58. Q. takes Q.
59. Q. takes Kt.	59. Q. to her 5th (ch.)
60. K. to B's sq.	60. P. to Q. R's 5th.
61. Q. to K. B's 5th (ch.)	61. K. to Q. B's 3d.
62. Q. to Q. B's 8th.	62. K. to Q. Kt's 4th.
63. K. to his sq.	63. P. to Q. B's 4th.
64. Q. to Q. Kt's 7th (ch.)	64. K. to Q. B's 5th.
65. Q. to K. B's 7th (ch.)	65. K. to Q. B's 6th.
66. Q. to K. B's 3d (ch.)	66. Q. to her 6th.
67. Q. to K. B's 6th (ch.)	67. K. to Q. Kt's 6th.
68. Q. to Q. Kt's 6th (ch.)	68. K. to B's 7th.
69. Q. to Q. R's 7th.	69. Q. to Q. B's 6th (ch.
70. K. to K's 2d.	70. P. to R's 6th.
71. Q. to Q. R's 4th (ch.)	71. K. to Kt's 7th.
72. Q. to Kt's 5th (ch.)	72. Q. to Kt's 6th.

And White resigns.

GAME II.—Between Mr. Mead, of N. Y., and another strong player.

WHITE. (Mr. —.)	BLACK. (Mr. M.)
1. P. to K's 4th.	1. P. to K's 4th.
2. K. Kt. to B's 3d.	2. Q. Kt. to B's 3d.
3. K. B. to Q. B's 4th.	3. K. B. to Q. B's 4th.
4. P. to Q. Kt's 4th.	4. B. takes P.
5. P. to Q. B's 3d.	5. B. to Q. R's 4th.
6. Castles.	6. K. Kt. to K's 2d.
7. P. to Q's 4th.	7. P. takes P.
8. K. Kt. to Kt's 5th.	8. Q. Kt. to K's 4th.
9. K. B. to Q. Kt's 3d.	9. P. to Q's 4th.
10. P. takes P.	10. P. to K. R's 3d.
11. P. to K. B's 4th.	11. B. to K. Kt's 5th.
12. Q. to K's sq.	12. P. takes Kt.
13. P. takes Kt.	13. Kt. takes P.
14. Q. to K. Kt's 3d.	14. B. to K's 7th.
15. K. B. to Q. R's 4th (ch.)	15. P. to Q. B's 3d.
16. Q. B. takes P.	16. Q. to Q. Kt's 3d.
17. P. to Q. B's 4th.	17. P. to Q's 6th (dis. ch.)

KING'S KNIGHT'S OPENING.

18. R. to K. B's 2d.	18. Q. to Q. Kt's 7th.
19. P. takes Kt.	19. Q. takes Q. R.
20. P. to K. R's 3d.	20. B. to Q. Kt's 3d.
21. P. takes P.	21. B. takes R. (ch.)
22. K. takes B.	22. Q. to Q's 5th (ch.)
23. Q. B. interposes.	23. Q. takes K. B.
24. P. takes P.	24. Q. R. to Q. Kt's sq.
25. Q. takes K. Kt. P.	25. Q. to K. R's 5th (ch.)
26. K. to Kt's sq.	26. Q. R. takes P.
27. Kt. to Q's 2d.	27. Q. to K. R's 2d.
28. Q. to K. B's 6th.	28. Castles.
29. Q. to Q. B's 6th.	29. Q. R. to K's 2d.
30. Kt. to K's 4th.	30. Q. to K. Kt's 3d.
31. Kt. to K. B's 6th (ch.)	31. K. to R's sq.
32. Q. to Q's 6th.	32. R. to K. Kt's sq.
33. Kt. takes R.	33. Q. takes Q.
34. P. takes Q.	34. R. takes B.
35. P. to Q's 7th.	35. P. to Q's 7th.
36. P. queens.	36. P. queens (ch.)
37. Q. takes Q.	37. B. takes Q.

And White resigns.

GAME III.—Between Mr. Anderssen and Mr. Hillel.

WHITE. (Mr. A.)	BLACK. (Mr. H.)
1. P. to K's 4th.	1. P. to K's 4th.
2. K. Kt. to B's 3d.	2. Q. Kt. to B's 3d.
3. K. B. to Q. B's 4th.	3. K. B. to Q. B's 4th.
4. P. to Q. Kt's 4th.	4. B. takes P.
5. P. to Q. B's 3d.	5. B. to Q. R's 4th.
6. P. to Q's 4th.	6. P. takes P.
7. Castles.	7. B. to Q. Kt's 3d.
8. P. takes P.	8. P. to Q's 3d.
9. P. to K. R's 3d.	9. Q. to K. B's 3d.
10. B. to Q. Kt's 2d.	10. K. Kt. to R's 3d.
11. Q. Kt. to Q's 2d.	11. Castles.
12. P. to K's 5th.	12. P. takes P.
13. P. takes P.	13. Q. to K's 2d.
14. Q. Kt. to K's 4th.	14. B. to K's 3d.
15. B. to Q's 3d.	15. B. to K. B's 4th.
16. Kt. to K. B's 6th (ch.	16. P. takes Kt.
17. P. takes P.	17. Q. to K's sq.
18. Q. to Q's 2d.	18. B. to K's 6th.
19. P. takes B.	19. B. takes B.
20. Q. takes B.	20. Q. R. to Q's sq.
21. Q. to Q. R's 3d.	21. K. Kt. to B's 4th.
22. Q. R. to K's sq.	22. Q. to K's 5th.
23. Kt. to Kt's 5th.	23. Q. to K. R's 5th.
24. P. to K's 4th.	24. K. Kt. to Q's 5th.
25. Kt. to K. B's 3d.	25. Kt. takes Kt. (ch.)

26. Q. takes Kt.	26. Q. R. to Q's 7th.
27. B. to Q. B's 3d	27. R. takes Q. R. P.
28. P. to K's 5th.	28. Kt. to Q's 5th.
29. B. takes Kt.	29. Q. takes B. (ch.)
30. K. to R's sq.	30. K. to R's sq.
31. Q. R. to K's 4th.	31. Q. to Q. Kt's 7th.
32. Q. R. to K. R's 4th.	32. Q. takes K. P.
33. Q. to Q's 3d.	33. P. to K. R's 4th.
34. Q. to K. B's 5th.	34. Q. takes Q.
35. K. R. takes Q.	35. K. to R's 2d.
36. R. to K. Kt's 5th.	36. K. to R's 3d.
37. Q. R. takes P.	

Mate.

GAME IV.—Between Mr. Morphy and Mr. Marache

WHITE. (Mr. Marache.)	BLACK. (Mr. Morphy.)
1. P. to K's 4th.	1. P. to K's 4th.
2. Kt. to K. B's 3d.	2. Kt. to Q. B's 3d.
3. B. to Q. B's 4th.	3. B. to Q. B's 4th.
4. P. to Q. Kt's 4th.	4. B. takes P.
5. P. to Q. B's 3d.	5. B. to R's 4th.
6. P. to Q's 4th.	6. P. takes P.
7. P. to K's 5th.	7. P. to Q's 4th.
8. P. takes P. *en passant*.	8. Q. takes P.
9. Castles.	9. K. Kt. to K's 2d.
10. Kt. to K. Kt's 5th.	10. Castles.
11. B. to Q's 3d.	11. B. to K. B's 4th.
12. B. takes B.	12. Kt. takes B.
13. B. to Q. R's 3d.	13. Q. to K. Kt's 3d.
14. B. takes R.	14. Q. takes Kt.
15. B. to R's 3d.	15. P. takes P.
16. B. to Q. B's sq.	16. Q. to Kt's 3d.
17. B. to K. B's 4th.	17. R. to Q's sq.
18. Q. to Q. B's 2d.	18. Q. Kt. to Q's 5th.
19. Q. to K's 4th.	19. K. Kt. to Kt's 6th
20. Q. takes Q.	20. Q. Kt. Mates.

KING'S KNIGHT'S OPENING.

THE TWO KNIGHTS' DEFENCE.

THIS, like the Evans Gambit, and the Queen's Pawn Game or Scotch Gambit, is a variation merely of the Giuoco Piano; the second player, instead of moving at his 3d move, K. B. to Q. B's 4th, bringing out his K. Kt. to B's 3d.

GAME THE FIRST.

WHITE.	BLACK.
1. P. to K's 4th.	1. P. to K's 4th.
2. K. Kt. to B's 3d.	2. Q. Kt. to B's 3d.
3. K. B. to Q. B's 4th.	3. K. Kt. to B's 3d.
4. K. Kt. to his 5th.	4. P. to Q's 4th.
5. P. takes P.	5. K. Kt. takes P.
6. K. Kt. takes K. B. P.	6. K. takes Kt.
7. Q. to K. B's 3d (ch.)	7. K. to his 3d.
8. Q. Kt. to Q. B's 3d.	8. Q. Kt. to K's 2d.
9. P. to Q's 4th.	9. P. to Q. B's 3d.
10. Q. B. to K. Kt's 5th.	10. P. to K. R's 3d.
11. Q. B. takes Kt.	11. B. takes B.
12. Castles on Q's side.	12. K. R. to B's sq
13. Q. to K's 4th.	13. Q. to her 3d.
14. K. R. to K's sq.	14. R. to K. B's 4th.
15. P. to K. Kt's 4th.	15. B. to Kt's 4th (ch)
16. K. to Kt's sq.	16. R. to B's 5th.
17. Q. to K. R's 7th.	17. B. to K. B's 3d.
18. P. takes P.	18. B. takes P.
19. B. takes Kt. (ch.)	19. P. takes B.
20. Kt. takes P.	

And you must win easily.

GAME THE SECOND.

WHITE.	BLACK.
1. P. to K's 4th.	1. P. to K's 4th.
2. K. Kt. to B's 3d.	2. Q. Kt. to B's 3d
3. K. B. to Q. B's 4th.	3. K. Kt. to B's 3d.
4. K. Kt. to his 5th.	4. K. Kt. takes K P.
5. B. takes K. B. P. (ch.)	5. K to his 2d

6. P. to Q's 3d.   6. Kt. to K. B's 3d
7. B. to Q. Kt's 3d.   7. P. to Q's 4th.
8. P. to K. B's 4th.   8. Q. B. to K. Kt's 5th
9. Q. to her 2d.   9. P. to K. R's 3d.
10. P. takes K. P   10. Q. Kt. takes P.
11. Q. to K's 3d.   11. P. takes Kt.
12. Q. takes Kt. (ch.)   12. K. to B's 2d.
13. Castles.   13. B. to Q's 3d
14. Q. takes Q. P. (ch.)
And you must win.

GAME

ILLUSTRATIVE OF THE TWO KNIGHTS' GAME

Game I.—Between Von H. der Laza and Mr. M.

WHITE. (V. H. d. L.)   BLACK. (Mr. M.)
1. P. to K's 4th.   1. P. to K's 4th.
2. K. Kt. to B's 3d.   2. Q. Kt. to B's 3d.
3. K. B. to Q. B's 4th.   3. K. Kt. to B's 3d.
4. K. Kt. to his 5th.   4. P. to Q's 4th.
5. P. takes P.   5. Kt. takes P.
6. Kt. takes K. B. P.   6. K. takes Kt.
7. Q. to K. B's 3d (ch.)   7. K. to his 3d.
8. Q. Kt. to B's 3d.   8. Q. Kt. to K's 2d.
9. P. to Q's 4th.   9. P. to Q. Kt's 4th.
10. Kt. takes P.   10. P. to Q. B's 3d.
11. Kt. to Q. B's 3d.   11. Q. to her Kt's 3d.
12. P. takes K. P.   12. Q. B. to Kt's 2d.
13. Kt. to K's 4th.   13. Q. to Kt's 5th (ch.)
14. Q. B. to Q's 2d.   14. Q. takes K. B.
15. Q. to K. Kt's 4th (ch.)   15. K. takes P.
16. P. to K. B's 4th (ch.)   16. K. to Q's 5th.
17. P. to Q. B's 3d (ch.)   17. Kt. takes B. P.
18. B. takes Kt. (ch.)   18. K. takes Kt.
19. P. to B's 5th (dis. ch.)   19. K. to Q's 4th.
20. Castles on Q's side (ch).   20. K. to B's 4th.
21. P. to Q. Kt's 4th (ch.)   21. K. to Kt's 4th.
22. P. to Q. R's 4th (ch.)   22. K. takes P.
23. Q. takes Q.   23. Kt. to Q's 4th.
24. K. to Q. Kt's 2d, and wins.

KING'S KNIGHT'S OPENING.

THE KNIGHT'S GAME OF RUY LOPEZ.

GAME THE FIRST.

WHITE.	BLACK.
1. P. to K's 4th.	1. P. to K's 4th.
2. K. Kt. to B's 3d.	2. Q. Kt. to B's 3d.
3. K. B. to Q. Kt's 5th.	3. K. Kt. to B's 3d.

By his 3d move, White threatens to take the Q. Kt. with his B., and then to take the K. P. with his K. Kt., winning the P.

4. Q. to K's 2d.	4. K. B. to K's 2d.
5. P. to Q. B's 3d.	5. P. to Q's 3d.
6. P. to Q's 4th.	6. P. takes P.
7. Kt. takes P.	7. B. to Q's 2d.
8. Kt. takes Q. Kt.	8. B. takes Kt.
9. B. takes B. (ch.)	9. P. takes B.

And his Bishop is locked, and the position altogether in your favor.

GAME THE SECOND.

WHITE.	BLACK.
1. P. to K's 4th.	1. P. to K's 4th.
2. K. Kt. to B's 3d.	2. Q. Kt. to B's 3d.
3. K. B. to Q. Kt's 5th.	3. K. B. to Q. B's 4th.
4. P. to Q. B's 3d.	4. Q. to K. B's 3d.
5. Castles.	5. K. Kt. to K's 2d.
6. P. to Q's 4th.	6. P. takes P.
7. Q. B. to K. Kt's 5th.	7. Q. to K. Kt's 3d.
8. B. takes K. Kt.	8. Q. Kt. takes B.
9. P. takes P.	9. B. to Q. Kt's 3d.
10. Q. Kt. to B's 3d.	10. Castles.

Your game is a little better developed.

VARIATION I.
Beginning at Black's 4th move.

WHITE.	BLACK.
1. P. to K's 4th.	1. P. to K's 4th.
2. K. Kt. to B's 3d.	2. Q. Kt. to B's 3d.
3. K. B. to Q. Kt's 5th.	3. K. B. to Q. B's 4th.
4. P. to Q. B's 3d.	4. P. to Q's 3d.
5. P. to Q's 4th.	5. P. takes P.
6. P. takes P.	6. B. to Q. Kt's 5th (ch.)
7. K. to his 2d.	7. P. to Q's 4th.
8. Q. to her R's 4th.	8. P. takes K. P.
9. B. takes Kt. (ch.)	9. P. takes B.
10. Q. takes P. (ch.)	10. Q. B. to Q's 2d.
11. Q. takes K. P. (ch.)	

And the game is much in your favor.

GAMES

ILLUSTRATIVE OF RUY LOPEZ'S KNIGHT'S GAME

GAME I.—A memorable partie from the St. Petersburg Masters' Tournament of 1914, between Dr. Emanuel Lasker, of Berlin, the world's champion, and Jose R. Capablanca. With this game Dr. Lasker won first place in the tournament, Mr. Capablanca finishing second.

WHITE. (Lasker.)	BLACK. (Capablanca.)
1. P. to K's 4th.	1. P. to K's 4th.
2. Kt. to K. B's 3d.	2. Kt. to Q. B's 3d.

98   CHESS HANDBOOK.

3. B. to Kt's 5th.   3. P. to Q. R's 3d.
4. B. takes Kt.   4. Q. P. takes B.
5. P. to Q's 4th.   5. P. takes P.
6. Q. takes P.   6. Q. takes Q.
7. Kt. takes Q.   7. B. to Q's 3d.
8. Kt. to Q. B's 3d.   8. Kt. to K's 2d.
9. Castles.   9. Castles.
10. P. to B's 4th.*   10. R. to K.†
11. Kt. to Kt's 3d.‡   11. P. to B's 3d.§
12. P. to B's 5th.‖   12. P. to Q. Kt's 3d.
13. B. to B's 4th.   13. B. to Kt's 2d.¶
14. B. takes B.   14. P. takes B.
15. Kt. to Q's 4th.   15. Q. R. to Q.**
16. Kt. to K's 6th.   16. R. to Q's 2d.
17. Q. R. to Q.   17. Kt. to B.
18. R. to B's 2d.   18. P. to Q. Kt's 4th.
19. K. R. to Q's 2d.††   19. Q. R. to K's 2d.
20. P. to Q. Kt's 4th.‡‡   20. K. to B's 2d.
21. P. to Q. R's 3d.   21. B. to R.§§
22. K. to B's 2d.‖‖   22. R. to R's 2d.¶¶
23. P. to Kt's 4th.   23. P. to R's 3d.
24. R. to Q's 3d.   24. P. to Q. R's 4th.
25. P. to K. R's 4th.   25. P. takes P.*
26. P. takes P.   26. Q. R. to K's 2d.†
27. K. to B's 3d.   27. R. to Kt.
28. K. to B's 4th.‡   28. P. to Kt's 3d.§
29. R. to Kt's 3d.   29. P. to Kt's 4th (ch.)‖
30. K. to B's 3d.   30. Kt. to Kt's 3d.¶
31. P. takes P.   31. R. P. takes P.
32. R. to R's 3d.   32. R. to Q's 2d.
33. K. to Kt's 3d.**   33. K. to K.††
34. Q. R. to K. R.   34. B. to Kt's 2d.
35. P. to K's 5th.   35. Q. P. takes P.‡‡
36. Kt. to K's 4th.   36. Kt. to Q's 4th.
37. K. Kt. to B's 5th.§§   37. B. to B.
38. Kt. takes R.   38. B. takes Kt.
39. R. to R's 7th.   39. R. to B.
40. R. to R.   40. K. to Q.
41. R. to R's 8th (ch.)   41. R. to B.
42. Kt. to B's 5th.   42. Resigns.

NOTES BY DR. E. LASKER.

* Capablanca here detected several weaknesses; it was difficult to protect the K. P., although it threatened to advance in due course, even if with indifferent effect; and, further, the White Knight on Q's 4th could be pinned by means of B. to Q. B's 4th. He saw this quickly and played with hardly any hesitation.

† This threatened 11....B. to B's 4th; 12 B. to K's 3d, Kt. to Q's 4th or Kt. to B's 4th.

‡ Parrying the threat. Now P. to K's 5th might be a strong move, inasmuch as the K. B. has only one flight square. After brief consideration, Capablanca made his move.

§ At this point Black felt perfectly secure and hopeful. The fact that White's K. P. is weak was only too apparent.

‖ A piece of finesse which Capablanca did not expect. This advance seemingly makes the K. P. a candidate for death. Upon closer inspection, however, one sees that the Pawn can nevertheless stand, and the move, notwithstanding all these surface weaknesses, has much

KING'S KNIGHT'S OPENING.

GAME II.—Between Dr. E. Lasker and Wm. Steinitz.

WHITE. (Dr. L.)	BLACK. (Mr. S.)
1. P. to K's 4th.	1. P. to K's 4th.
2. Kt. to K. B's 3d.	2. Kt. to Q. B's 3d.
3. B. to Kt's 5th.	3. P. to Q's 3d.
4. P. to Q's 4th.	4. B. to Q's 2d.
5. Kt. to B's 3d.	5. K. Kt. to K's 2d.

in compensation. It hinders the K. B. P., the Q. B., as well as the K. Kt., and, in addition, forces the exchange of the strong K. B.

¶ It was only after long deliberation that Black determined upon this course. The alternative is 13....B. takes B.; 14 R. takes B., P. to B's 4th; 15 Q. R. to Q., B. to Kt's 2d; 16 R. to B's 2d, Q. R. to Q.; 17 R. takes R., R. takes R.; 18 R. to Q's 2d, R. takes R.; 19 Kt. takes R. And now White practically has a Pawn plus, for it is difficult to make the doubled Q. B. Pawn yield adequate results.

** Black here played very thoughtfully. He did not wish to delay his development with B. to Q. B. and planned, with regard to the Knight which forces its way to K's 6th, to drive it off later. For the time being, however, he attacked nothing.

†† The Rooks are doubled at exactly the right time. It was important to nail the Knight down to Q. B. square by means of pressure upon the Queen's Pawn.

‡‡ And now the Q. B. Pawn is crippled. Strategically, Black is beaten, for he plays without the co-operation of the Q. B. This Bishop can be brought into action only through loss of some sort.

§§ Neither would 21....Kt. to Kt's 3d; 22 R. takes P., Kt. to B's 5th have yielded any fruit. To be sure, Pawns are menaced by the Knight at B's 5th, but the likely continuation in that case is 23 Kt. to Q's 8th (ch.), followed by Kt. takes B. and R. takes B. P.

‖‖ And now to beleaguer the Black King. The necessary preparations are tedious, but the attack will assuredly eventuate.

¶¶ A sortie, which, however, has no strength.

* Here Capablanca moved with nervous haste. He was in fear of White's attack, but saw no possibility of escaping it.

† Dispirited, the Rook turns back. Black resigns himself to undergo a long siege.

‡ The break with P. to Kt's 5th requires the most careful preparation. First of all, the Rooks must be doubled on the K. Kt. file.

§ Not to permit White time for these preparations.

‖ If Black exchanges Rooks on the Kt. file, the White King, after duly paving the way, will finally push through by way of Kt's 4th and R's 5th. And yet P. takes P. was the only chance. Now follows a fearful attack, to which eventually all of the Black forces must fall victims.

¶ Offering the Q. P., but the open file is more important.

** P. to K's 5th is threatened. The same move would hold good in case of Kt. to B's 5th.

†† Parries the threat, but merely for the time being.

‡‡ If, B. P. takes P., then also Kt. to K's 4th, in which case the K. Kt. Pawn would fall. The White Pawns, unrestrained, would then go on.

§§ Threatens Kt. takes B., followed by Kt. to Q's 6th (ch.)—
(Translated from "Mittag.")

6. B. to K's 3d.*	6. Kt. to Kt's 3d.†
7. Q. to Q's 2d.	7. B. to K's 2d.
8. Castles Q. R.	8. P. to Q. R's 3d.
9. B. to K's 2d.	9. P. takes P.
10. Kt. takes P.	10. Kt. takes Kt.
11. Q. takes Kt.‡	11. B. to K. B's 3d.
12. Q. to Q's 2d.	12. B. to B's 3d.§
13. Kt. to Q's 5th.	13. Castles.
14. P. to K. Kt's 4th.‖	14. R. to K's sq.¶
15. P. to Kt's 5th.?	15. B. takes Kt.
16. Q. takes B.**	16. R. to K's 4th.!
17. Q. to Q's 2d.	17. B. takes P.
18. P. to K. B's 4th.	18. R. takes P.
19. P. takes B.	19. Q. to K's 2d.
20. Q. R. to B's sq.††	20. R. takes B.
21. B. to B's 4th.	21. Kt. to R's sq.
22. P. to K. R's 4th.	22. P. to Q. B's 3d.
23. P. to Kt's 6th!‡‡	23. P. to Q's 4th.
24. P. takes R. P. (ch)	24. K. takes P.
25. B. to Q's 3d (ch.)	25. K. to Kt's sq.
26. P. to R's 5th.	26. R. to K's sq.
27. P. to R's 6th.	27. P. to K. Kt's 3d.
28. P. to R's 7th (ch.)	28. K. to Kt's 2d.
29. K. to Kt's sq.	29. Q. to K's 4th.
30. P. to R's 3d.§§	30. P. to Q. B's 4th.
31. Q. to B's 2d.	31. P. to B's 5th.!
32. Q. to R's 4th.	32. P. to B's 3d.
33. B. to B's 5th.!‖‖	33. K. to B's 2d.

*White in this instance had probably made up his mind to adopt the plan frequently employed by Gunsberg in the Giuoco Piano, namely, playing Q. to Q's 2d and Castling rapidly on the Queen's side.—Gunsberg.

† ... Black's difficulty is how to dispose of the Kt. Now Kt's 3d in this instance, although perhaps preferable, is not a good place either, subject as it must be to an early attack from the K. R. P.—Hoffer.

‡ If 11. B. takes Kt., Kt. to B's 5th; and the Kt. cannot be captured on account of B. to Kt's 4th winning the Queen.—*Leeds Mercury.*

§ ... There seems little use in this move. Either he can Castle now; if not, then it is proof positive that his defence is bad.—Gunsberg.

‖ This premature advance is admirably taken advantage of by Steinitz.—*Leeds Mercury.*

¶ ... Although this looks like a defensive move (to make room for the Kt.) it is a subtle design which was entirely overlooked by Lasker.—Hoffer.

** But here is a great mistake, which ought to lose the game. 16. P. takes Q., B. would have averted the loss of a Pawn, but at the expense of position and attack; he was outplayed by Steinitz up to this point.

†† From this move to the end Lasker exhibits most marvellous power of resource. With 20. Q. R. to B's sq. he commenced one of the most ingenious attacks.

‡‡ One of the moves which will make this game memorable. The object is, if P. takes P. to open up the Rook's file by P. to R's 5th. Allowance must of course be made for the fact that, being two Pawns behind, White has nothing to lose and everything to gain by desperate tactics.—Gunsberg.

§§ Exhibiting consummate coolness in a "do or die" predicament.—Pollock.

‖‖ 33. B. to B's 5th is evidence with what perfect lucidity Lasker detects the weak spots, and how immediately he takes advantage of his opponent's slightest omission or commission.—Hoffer.

KING'S KNIGHT'S OPENING.

WHITE	BLACK
34. K. R. to Kt's sq.	34. P. takes B.
35. Q. to R's 5th (ch.)	35. K. to K's 2d.
36. R. to Kt's 8th.	36. K. to Q's 3d. ?
37. R. takes P.	37. Q. to K's 3d.
38. R. takes R.	38. Q. takes R.
39. R. takes B. P. (ch.)	39. K. to B's 4th.*
40. Q. to R's 6th. †	40. R. to K's 2d.
41. Q. to B's 2d. !	41. Q. to Q's 2d.‡
42. Q. to Kt's sq. (ch.)	42. P. to Q's 5th.
43. Q. to Kt's 5th (ch.)	43. Q. to Q's 4th.
44. R. to K. B's 5th.	44. Q. takes R.
45. Q. takes Q. (ch.)	45. K. to Q's 3d.
46. Q. to B's 6th (ch.)	46. Resigns.

THE QUEEN'S PAWN GAME, OR SCOTCH GAMBIT.

GAME THE FIRST.

WHITE.	BLACK.
1. P. to K's 4th.	1. P. to K's 4th.
2. K. Kt. to B's 3d.	2. Q. Kt. to B's 3d
3. P. to Q's 4th.	3. Kt takes P.

It is from your third move the opening derives its name of "The Queen's Pawn Game."

WHITE	BLACK
4. Kt. takes Kt.	4. P. takes Kt.
5. Q. takes P.	5. Kt. to K's 2d.
6. K. B. to Q. B's 4th.	6. Kt. to Q. B's 3d.
7. Q. to her 5th.	7. Q. to K. B's 3d (best)
8. Castles.	8. B. to K's 2d.

You have a better opened game, but the superiority is not important.

VARIATION I.
Beginning at White's 4th move.

WHITE.	BLACK.
1. P. to K's 4th.	1. P. to K's 4th.
2. K. Kt. to B's 3d.	2. Q. Kt. to B's 3d.
3. P. to Q's 4th.	3. Kt. takes P.

* . . . Imprudent. The King should make for safety in the corner, *via* B's 2d.—Mason.

† Threatening R. to B's 8th.—Gunsberg.

‡ . . . 41. Q to Q's 2d is a final blunder. 41. R to Q's 2d should have been played, or R. to K's 3d. The game is now over. It will be readily admitted that it is a well-earned victory which none will grudge the plucky young player.—Hoffer.

. . . We really cannot see a satisfactory move, for if R. to K's 3d, then follows Q. to B's 2d (ch.), and R. to B's 8th. Or if Q. to Q's sq. then likewise Q. to B's 2d (ch.) should gain some advantage, as, on King playing to Kt's 4th, White could continue with P. to R's 4th (ch) and Q. to Q. B's 5th, &c.—Gunsberg.

4. Kt. takes P.
5. K. B. to Q. B's 4th.
6. Castles.
7. Kt. to K. Kt's 4th.

4. Kt. to K's 3d.
5. K. Kt. to B's 3d.
6. P. to Q's 3d.
7. B. to K's 2d.

Your game is less confined than his, but you have very little advantage.

GAME THE SECOND.

WHITE.	BLACK.
1. P. to K's 4th.	1. P. to K's 4th.
2. K. Kt. to B's 3d.	2. Q. Kt. to B's 3d
3. P. to Q's 4th.	3. P. takes P.
4. K. B. to Q. B's 4th.	4. K. B. to Q. B's 4th
5. P. to Q. B's 3d.	5. P. to Q's 6th.
6. P. to Q. Kt.'s 4th.	6. B. to Q. Kt.'s 3d.
7. P. to Q. Kt.'s 5th.	7. Q. to K's 2d.
8. Castles.	8. Kt. to K's 4th.
9. Kt. takes Kt.	9. Q. takes Kt.
10. Q. to her Kt's 3d.	10. Q. to K. B's 3d,
11 P. to K's 5th.	K's 2d.

You have a fine game.

VARIATION I.

Beginning at White's 5th move.

WHITE.	BLACK.
1. P. to K's 4th.	1. P. to K's 4th.
2. K. Kt. to B's 3d	2. Q. Kt. to B's 3d.
3. P. to Q's 4th.	3. P. takes P.
4. K's B. to Q. B's 4th.	4. K. B. to Q. B's 4th
5. K. Kt. to his 5th.	5. K. Kt. to R's 3d. (best)
6 Kt. takes K. B's P.	6. Kt. takes Kt.
7. B. takes Kt. (ch.)	7. K. takes B.
8. Q. to K. R's 5th (ch.)	8. P. to K. Kt's 3d
9. Q. takes B.	9. P. to Q's 3d.
10. Q. to her Kt's 5th.	10. P. to Q. R's 3d.
11. Q. to her 3d.	11. K. to Kt's 2d.
12. Castles.	12. Q. B. to K's 3d.

13. P. to Q. B's 3d.   13. Q. to K. B's 3d.
14. B. to Q's 2d.
   You appear to me to have the better game

Variation II.
Beginning at White's 5th move.

WHITE.	BLACK.
1. P. to K's 4th.	1. P. to K's 4th.
2. K. Kt. to B's 3d.	2. Q. Kt. to B's 3d.
3. P. to Q's 4th.	3. P. takes P.
4. K. B. to Q. B's 4th.	4. K. B. to Q. B's 4th
5. Castles.	5. P. to Q's 3d.
6. P. to Q. B's 3d.	6. P. takes P.
7. Q. Kt. takes P.	7. K. Kt. to K's 2d.
8. K. Kt. to his 5th.	8. Kt. to K's 4th.

And he has at least as good a game as you have. This variation serves to prove that your castling on the 5th move is less advisable than the move of 5. P. to Q B's 3d.

Variation III.,
Beginning at Black's 4th move.

WHITE.	BLACK.
1. P. to K's 4th.	1. P. to K's 4th.
2. K. Kt. to B's 3d.	2. Q. Kt. to B's 3d.
3. P. to Q's 4th.	3. P. takes P.
4. K. B. to Q. B's 4th.	4. P. to Q's 3d.

Black now relinquishes the defence of the P. he has gained, but he also in some degree neutralizes your attack

| 5. P. to Q. B's 3d. | 5. P. takes P. |
| 6. Q. Kt. takes P. | |

You have certainly the advantage in position.

Variation IV.,
Beginning also at Black's 4th move.

WHITE.	BLACK.
1. P. to K's 4th.	1. P. to K's 4th.
2. K. Kt. to B's 3d.	2. Q. Kt. to B's 3d

3. P. to Q's 4th.   3. P. takes P.
4. K. B. to Q. B's 4th.   4. Q. to K. B's 3d.
5. Castles.   5. P. to Q's 3d.
6. P. to Q. B's 3d.   6. P. to Q's 6th.
7. Q. takes P.   7. Q. to K. Kt's 3d.
8. Q. B. to K. B's 4th.   8. B. to K's 2d.
9. Q. Kt. to Q. R's 3d.   9. P. to Q. R's 3d.
10. Q. Kt. to Q. B's 2d.   10. K. Kt. to R's 3d.

Your game is better opened, but there is no very striking disparity in the positions.

GAME THE THIRD.

WHITE.   BLACK.
1. P. to K's 4th.   1. P. to K's 4th.
2. K. Kt. to B's 3d.   2. Q. Kt. to B's 3d.
3. P. to Q's 4th.   3. P. takes P.
4. K. B. to Q. B's 4th.   4. B. to Q. Kt's 5th (ch.)
5. P. to Q. B's 3d.   5. P. takes P.
6. Castles.   6. P. to Q. B's 7th.
7. Q. takes P.   7. P. to Q's 3d.
8. P. to Q. R's 3d.   8. B. to Q. B's 4th.
9. P. to Q. Kt's 4th.   9. B. to Q. Kt's 3d.
10. Q. B. to Kt's 2d.   10. K. Kt. to B's 3d.

The game is about even.

GAME THE FOURTH.

MR. COCHRANE'S ATTACK.

WHITE.   BLACK.
1 P. to K's 4th.   1. P. to K's 4th.
2. K. Kt. to B's 3d.   2. Q. Kt. to B's 3d.
3. P. to Q's 4th.   3. P. takes P.
4. K. B. to Q. B's 4th.   4. K. B. checks.
5. P. to Q. B's 3d.   5. P. takes P.
6. P. takes P.   6. B. to Q. R's 4th.
7. P. to K's 5th.   7. P. to Q's 4th (best)

P. to K's 5th is the move adopted by Mr Cochrane.

KING'S KNIGHT'S OPENING.

8. Q. takes P.
9. B. takes Q.
10. K. B. takes Q. Kt.(ch.)
11. Q. B. to K. B's 4th.
12. Castles.
13. P. to K. R's 3d.

8. Q. takes Q.
9. K. Kt. to K's 2d
10. Kt. takes B.
11. Castles.
12. K. R. to K's sq.

The game is equal.

VARIATION.

WHITE.	BLACK.
1. P. to K's 4th.	1. P. to K's 4th.
2. K. Kt. to B's 3d.	2. Q. Kt. to B's 3d.
3. P. to Q's 4th.	3. P. takes P.
4. K. B. to Q. B's 4th.	4. K. B. checks.
5. P. to Q. B's 3d.	5. P. takes P.
6. P. takes P.	6. B. to Q. R's 4th.
7. Castles.	7. P. to Q's 3d.
8. P. to K's 5th.	8. Q's B. to K's 3d.
9. B. takes B.	9. P. takes B.
10. Q. to her Kt's 3d.	10. Q. to B's sq.
11. P. takes Q's P.	11. P. takes P.
12. K's Kt. to his 5th.	

Followed by R. to K's sq., and you appear to me to have a better game than Black.

GAME THE FIFTH.

WHITE.	BLACK.
1 P. to K's 4th.	1. P. to K's 4th.
2. K. Kt. to B's 3d.	2. Q. Kt. to B's 3d.
3. P. to Q's 4th.	3. P. takes P.
4. K. B. to Q. B's 4th.	4. K. B. checks.
5. P. to Q. B's 3d.	5. P. takes P.
6. Castles.	6. P. takes Q. Kt. P
7. Q. B. takes P.	7. K. B. to his sq.
8. Q. Kt. to B's 3d	8. K. Kt. to R's 3d.
9. P. to K's 5th.	9. K. B. to K's 2d.
10. Q. Kt. to K's 4th.	10. Castles.

11. Q. to her 2d.   11. P. to Q's 3d.
12. Kt. to K. B's 6th (ch.)
    You have an excellent attack.

VARIATION,
Beginning at Black's 7th move.

WHITE.	BLACK.
1. P. to K's 4th.	1. P. to K's 4th.
2. K. Kt. to B's 3d.	2. Q. Kt. to B's 3d.
3. P. to Q's 4th.	3. P. takes P.
4. K. B. to Q. B's 4th.	4. K. B. checks.
5. P. to Q. B's 3d.	5. P. takes P.
6. Castles.	6. P. takes Q. Kt. P
7. Q. B. takes P.	7. K. to B's sq.
8. P. to K's 5th.	8. Q. to K's 2d.
9. P. to Q. R's 3d.	9. B. to Q. B's 4th.
10. Q. Kt. to B's 3d.	10. P. to Q's 3d.
11. Q. Kt. to Q's 5th.	11. Q. to her 2d.
12. R. to K's sq.	12. P. takes K. P.
13. Q. B. takes P.	13. Kt. takes B.
14. Kt. takes Kt.	14. Q. to her sq.
15. Kt. takes K. B. P.	

And you must win.

GAME THE SIXTH.

WHITE.	BLACK.
1. P. to K's 4th.	1. P. to K's 4th.
2. K. Kt. to B's 3d.	2 Q. Kt. to B's 3d.
3. P. to Q's 4th.	3. P. takes P.
4. Kt. takes P.	4. Q. to K. R's th.
5. K. Kt. to Q. Kt's 5th.	5. K. B. to Q. B's 4th
6. Q. to K. B's 3d.	6. Q. Kt. to Q's 5th.
7. Kt. takes Q. B. P. (ch.)	7. K. to Q's sq. (best)
8. Q. to K. B's 4th	8. Kt. takes Q. B. P. (ch.)
9. K. to Q's sq.	9. Q. takes Q.
10. B. takes Q.	10. Kt. takes Q. R.
11. Kt. takes Q R	

I believe the best answering moves have been made by Black, and now, upon surveying the aspect of the board, there can be no question, I apprehend, that your game is much superior. The Kt. which has captured your Rook, he can never extricate, while, to secure yours in the same position, he must lose many moves, and thus afford you ample time for the development of your remaining forces.

VARIATION,
Beginning at Black's 5th move.

WHITE.	BLACK.
1. P. to K's 4th.	1. P. to K's 4th.
2. K. Kt. to B's 3d.	2. Q's Kt. to B's 3d.
3. P. to Q's 4th.	3. P. takes P.
4. Kt. takes P.	4. Q. to K. R's 5th.
5. Kt. to Q. Kt's 5th.	5. Q. takes K's P. (ch.)
6. B. to K's 2d.	6. K. to Q's sq.
7. Castles.	7. P. to Q. R's 3d.
8. Q. Kt. to B's 3d.	8. Q. to K's sq.
9. K. Kt. to Q's 4th.	

And again, I believe, with the strangely changed positions of his King and Queen, and the facility afforded you for bringing the Pieces into immediate action, that the game is very much in your favor.

GAME THE SEVENTH.
Varying from the preceding at Black's 4th move.

WHITE.	BLACK.
1. P. to K's 4th.	1. P. to K's 4th.
2 K. Kt. to B's 3d.	2. Q. Kt. to B's 3d.
3. P. to Q's 4th.	3. P. takes P.
4. Kt. takes P.	4. K. B. to Q. B's 4th
5. Kt. takes Q. Kt.	5. Q. to K. B's 3d.
6. Q. to K. B's 3d.	6. Q. takes Q.
7. P. takes Q.	7. Q. Kt. P. takes Kt.
8. Q. B. to K. B's 4th.	8. P. to Q's 3d.
9. K. B to Q. B's 4th	9. Q. B. to K's 3d.
10. Q. Kt. to Q's 2d.	

And the game is in every respect equal.

GAMES

ILLUSTRATIVE OF THE QUEEN'S PAWN GAME OR SCOTCH GAMBIT.

GAME I.—Played by Telegraph, in the Match between Philadelphia and New York, in 1858.

WHITE. (Phila.)	BLACK. (N. Y.)
1. P. to K's 4th.	1. P. to K's 4th.
2. Kt. to K. B's 3d.	2. Q. Kt. to B's 3d.
3. P. to Q's 4th.	3. P. takes P.
4. B. to Q. B's 4th.	4. B. to Q. B's 4th.
5. P. to Q. B's 3d.	5. Kt. to K. B's 3d.*
6. P. to K's 5th.	6. P. to Q's 4th.
7. B. to Q. Kt's 5th.	7. K. Kt. to K's 5th.
8. P. takes P.	8. B. to Q. Kt's 3d.
9. Q. Kt. to Q's 2d.†	9. Castles.
10. B. takes Kt.	10. P. takes B.
11. Q. to Q. B's 2d.‡	11. Kt. takes Kt.
12. B. takes Kt.	12. B. to K. Kt's 5th.§
13. Kt. to K. Kt's 5th.‖	13. P. to K. Kt's 3d.
14. Q. to Q. B's 3d.	14. P. to K. B's 3d.¶
15. P. to K. R's 3d.	15. B. to K. B's 4th.**
16. Kt. to K. B's 3d.	16. B. to K's 5th.††
17. B. to K. B's 4th.‡‡	17. P. takes P.
18. B. takes P.	18. Q. to K's 2d.§§
19. Castles. Q. side.‖‖	19. P. to Q. B's 4th.
20. K. R. to K's sq.¶¶	20. P. takes P.***
21. B. takes P.	21. P. to Q. B's 4th.
22. B. to K's 5th.	22. Q. R. to K's sq.†††
23. B. to K. Kt's 3d.	23. Q. to Q. Kt's 2d.‡‡‡

* The best move.
† Preparatory to the move of Q. to Q. B's 2d.
‡ Threatening to win Q. B. P. or take Kt. with Kt., winning Q. P.
§ If Black had played B. to Q. R's 3d, to prevent White Castling on King's side, White would have won a piece by P. to Q. R's 4th.
‖ A premature move.
¶ The best move.
** Better than taking Kt., as White would then have opened the Rock's file.
†† Better than P. takes P.
‡‡ The best move.
§§ Intending to advance Q. B. P. A strong move.
‖‖ An impudent move, in the face of such an attack.
¶¶ A strong move.
*** P. to K. B's 5th perhaps stronger.
††† Weak. We cannot see its object. Why not Q. R. to Q's sq?
‡‡‡ The best move.

KING'S KNIGHT'S OPENING.

24. Kt. to K's 5th.*	24. P. to Q's 5th.
25. Q. to Q. B's 4th.	25. B. to Q's 4th.
26. Q. to Q. R's 4th.†	26. R. to K's 3d.‡
27. Kt. to K. Kt's 4th.	27. P. to K. R's 4th.
28. R. takes R.	28. B. takes R.
29. Q. to Q. B's 2d.	29. K. to R's 2d.
30. R. to K's sq.§	30. B. to K. B's 4th.¶
31. Q. to Q's 2d.¶	31. P. takes Kt.
32. P. takes P.	32. Q. to Q's 4th.**
33. R. to K. R's sq. (ch.)††	33. K. to K. Kt's sq.
34. P. takes B.	34. Q. takes K. B. P.
35. Q. to K. R's 6th.	35. P. to K. Kt's 4th.
36. B. to Q's 6th.‡‡	36. R. to K. B's 3d.
37. Q. to K. R's 5th.§§	37. Q. to K. Kt's 3d.‖‖
38. Q. to K. R's 8th. (ch.)	38. K. to B's 2d.
39. R. to K's sq.¶¶	And Black resigns.

GAME II.—Played by Correspondence between New York and Philadelphia.

WHITE. (Phila.)	BLACK. (N. Y.)
1. P. to K's 4th.	1. P. to K's 4th.
2. K. Kt. to B's 3d.	2. Q. Kt. to B's 3d.
3. P. to Q's 4th.	3. Q. Kt. takes P.
4. Kt. takes Kt.	4. P. takes Kt.
5. K. B. to Q. B's 4th.	5. Q. to K. B's 3d.
6. Castles.	6. B. to Q. B's 4th.
7. P. to K's 5th.	7. Q. to K. B's 4th.
8. P. to Q. B's 3d.	8. P. takes P.
9. Kt. takes P.	9. Kt. to K's 2d.
10. K. B. to Q's 3d.	10. Q. to K's 3d.

---

* Preparatory to Kt. to Kt's 4th, and then B. to K's 5th.
† Preventing Black's contemplated move with the Q.
‡ With a view of withdrawing the B. and playing the R. to R's 3d.
§ The first move of a combination, which gave the victory to Philadelphia.
‖ Insures the winning of the Kt.
¶ A powerful move, as it compels Black to take the Kt., and thereby opens White's R's file.
** If B. takes P., White would have played Q. to K. Kt's 5th, threatening to check K. and Q. with R., or win the R.
†† An all important check before taking B., as it prevented an interposition of R. to R's 4th.
‡‡ A very attacking move. Much better than B. to K's 5th.
§§ A better move than checking, as it prevented Black's K. escaping to B's 2d, and then to K's 3d. White also threatened P. to K. Kt's 4th.
‖‖ Black would have lost the R. had they taken the B. by a check at K's 8th, and afterwards at his 7th.
¶¶ The *coup de grace*.

11. Kt. to K's 4th.	11. B. to Q's 5th.
12. Kt. to Kt's 5th.	12. Q. to Q. Kt's 3d.
13. Q. to K. R's 5th.	13. P. to K. Kt's 3d.
14. Q. to K. R's 6th.	14. B. takes K. P.
15. K. R. to K's sq.	15. Q. to K. B's 3d.
16. Kt. to K. B's 3d.	16. P. to Q's 3d.
17. B. to K. Kt's 5th.	17. Q. to K's 3d.
18. Kt. takes B.	18. P. takes Kt.
19. Q. R. to Q. B's sq.	19. K. R. to K. B's sq.
20. B. to Q. B's 4th.	20. Q. to K. B's 4th.
21. B. takes Kt.	21. K. takes B.
22. P. to K. B's 4th.	22. P. to K's 5th.
23. B. to Q's 3d.	23. B. to K's 3d.
24. B. takes P.	24. Q. to Q. R's 4th.
25. Q. to K. R's 4th (ch.)	25. K. to Q's 2d.
26. K. R. to Q's sq. (ch.)	26. K. to K's sq.
27. K. to K. R's sq.	27. P. to Q. B's 3d.
28. R. takes Q. B. P.	28. Q. R. to Q's sq.
29. Q. R. to Q. B's sq.	29. R. takes R.
30. R. takes R.	30. P. to K. R's 4th.
31. Q. to K. B's 6th.	31. B. to Q. B's sq.
32. B. takes Q. Kt. P.	

And New York resigns, as they must lose their Q., or be mated in a few moves.

GAME III.—Between Dr. Emanuel Lasker and A. A. Alechine.

WHITE. (Alechine.)	BLACK. (Dr. Lasker.)
1. P. to K's 4th.	1. P. to K's 4th.
2. Kt. to K. B's 3d.	2. Kt. to Q. B's 3d.
3. P. to Q's 4th.	3. P. takes P.
4. Kt. takes P.	4. Kt. to B's 3d.
5. Kt. to Q. B's 3d.	5. B. to Kt's 5th.
6. Kt. takes Kt.	6. Kt. P. takes Kt.
7. B. to Q's 3d.	7. P. to Q's 4th.
8. P. takes P.	8. P. takes P.
9. Castles.	9. Castles.
10. B. to K. Kt's 5th.	10. B. to K's 3d.*
11. Q. to B's 3d.	11. B. to K's 2d.
12. K. R. to K.	12. P. to K. R's 3d.
13. B. takes P.†	13. P. takes B.
14. R. takes B.	14. P. takes R.
15. Q. to Kt's 3d (ch.)	15. K. to R.
16. Q. to Kt's 6th.	16. Drawn.‡

* Here Dr. Lasker varies from Capablanca, who, in his game against two allies at Moscow, played B. takes Kt., followed it up by driving the B. and then with R. to K. and Q. to Q's 3d.

† This and the following sacrifice, though it leads only to a draw, forms a highly interesting variation of the opening.

‡ Black cannot prevent the perpetual check by Q. to K., on account of Q. takes P. (ch.), followed by Q. to Kt's 5th (ch.).

KING'S KNIGHT'S OPENING.   111

GAME IV.—Between Messrs. Cochrane and Deschapelles

WHITE. (Mr. C.)	BLACK. (M. D.)
1. P. to K's 4th.	1. P. to K's 4th.
2. K. Kt. to B's 3d.	2. Q. Kt. to B's 3d.
3. P. to Q's 4th.	3. P. takes P.
4. K. B. to Q. B's 4th.	4. K. B. to Q. B's 4th.
5. K. Kt. to Kt's 5th.	5. Q. Kt. to K's 4th.*
6. K. B. takes B. P. (ch.)	6. Q. Kt. takes B.
7. Kt. takes Kt.	7. B. to Q. Kt's 5th (ch.)
8. P. to Q. B's 3d.	8. P. takes P.
9. P. takes P.	9. K. B. takes P. (ch.)
10. Q. Kt. takes B.	10. K. takes Kt.
11. Q. to her 5th (ch.)	11. K. to B's sq.
12. Q. B. to R's 3d (ch.)	12. P. to Q's 3d.
13. P. to K's 5th.	13. Q. to K. Kt's 4th.
14. P. takes P.	14. Q. takes Q.
15. P. takes P. (dis. ch.)	15. K. to B's 2d.
16. Kt. takes Q.	16. Q. B. to Q's 2d.
17. Castles on K's side.	17. Q. R. to Q. B's sq.
18. B. to Q's 6th.	18. K. to his 3d.
19. Q. B. to K. Kt's 3d.	19. Q. B. to his 3d.
20. Q. R. to Q's sq.	20. B. takes Kt.
21. K. R. to K's sq. (ch.)	21. K. to B's 3d.
22. Q. R. takes B.	22. K. Kt. to R's 3d.
23. Q. R. to his 5th.	23. Kt. to K. B's 4th.
24. Q. R. to Q. B's 5th.	24. Kt. takes B.
25. K. B. P. takes Kt.	25. K. to B's 2d.
26. K. R. to Q's sq.	26. K. R. to K's sq.
27. K. R. to Q's 3d.	27. K. R. to K's 2d.
28. Q. R. to K. B's 5th (ch.)	28. K. to his square.†
29. Q. R. to Q's 8th (ch.)	29. R. takes R.
30. R. to K. B's 8th (ch.)	30. K. takes R.
31. P. takes R., becoming a Q. (ch.)	

And White wins.

THE QUEEN'S BISHOP'S PAWN GAME IN THE KING'S KNIGHT'S OPENING

GAME THE FIRST.

WHITE.	BLACK.
1. P. to K's 4th.	1. P. to K's 4th.
2. K. Kt. to B's 3d.	2. Q. Kt. to B's 3d.

---

* This is not the correct move, he should have played K. Kt. to K's 3d.
† K. to his 3d would have saved the game.

3. P. to Q. B's 3d
4. P. to Q's 4th.
5. Kt. takes K. P.
6. K. B. to Q. Kt.'s 5th.
7. B. takes Q. Kt.
8. Q. B. to K. Kt.'s 5th.
9. P. to Q. Kt's 4th.
10. Castles.
11. P. to K. B's 3d.
12. P. takes K. P.
13. Q. Kt. to Q's 2d.

3. P. to K. B's 4th.
4. P. takes K. P.
5. K. Kt. to B's 3d.
6. P. to Q. R's 3d.
7. Q. Kt. P. takes B.
8. Q. R. to Kt's sq.
9. Q. B. to Kt's 2d.
10. P. to Q's 4th.
11. B. to K's 2d.
12. Castles (best)

And you have a clear **Pawn** more and a much **better** game than he has.

VARIATION I.

Beginning at Black's 3d move.

WHITE.
1. P. to K's 4th.
2. K. Kt. to B's 3d.
3. P. to Q. B's 3d.
4. K. B. to Q. Kt's 5th.
5. Kt. takes K. P.
6. Q. to her R's 4th.
7. B. takes Kt. (ch.)
8. Q. takes K. P.

BLACK.
1. P. to K's 4th.
2. Q. Kt. to B's 3d.
3. P. to Q's 4th.
4. P. takes K. P.
5. Q. to K. Kt's 4th
6. Q. takes Kt.
7. K. to Q's sq.

Gaining a Pawn and a superior position.

GAME THE SECOND.

WHITE.
1. P. to K's 4th.
2. K. Kt. to B's 3d.
3. P. to Q. B's 3d.
4. P. to Q's 4th.
5. P. takes K. P.
6. K. B. to Q. Kt's 5th.
7. K. Kt. to Q's 4th.
8. P. takes B

BLACK.
1. P. to K's 4th.
2. Q. Kt. to B's 3d.
3. K. Kt. to B's 3d.
4. K. Kt takes K. P.
5. P. to Q's 4th.
6. K. B. to Q. B's 4th
7. B. takes Kt.
8. Castles.

KING'S KNIGHT'S OPENING.

VARIATION I.

Beginning at Black's 3d move.

WHITE.	BLACK.
1. P. to K's 4th.	1. P. to K's 4th.
2. K. Kt. to B's 3d.	2. Q. Kt. to B's 3d.
3. P. to Q. B's 3d.	3. K. B. to B's 4th.
4. P. to Q. Kt's 4th.	4. B. to Q. Kt's 3d.
5. P. to Q. Kt's 5th.	5. Q. Kt. to R's 4th.
6. Kt. takes K. P.	6. Q. to K's 2d.
7. P. to Q's 4th.	7. P. to Q's 3d.
8. B. to. Q. R's 3d.	8. P. to K. B's 3d.
9. Kt. to K. B's 3d.	9. Q. takes K. P. (ch.)
10. B. to K's 2d.	10. K. Kt. to R's 3d.
11. Castles.	11. Castles.
12. K. B. to Q's 3d.	

And you have an undoubted advantage of situation.

GAMES

ILLUSTRATIVE OF THE QUEEN'S BISHOP'S PAWN GAME IN THE KING'S KNIGHT'S OPENING.

GAME I.—Between Messrs. Harrwitz and Staunton.

WHITE. (Mr. S.)	BLACK. (Mr. H.)
1. P. to K's 4th.	1. P. to K's 4th.
2. K. Kt. to B's 3d.	2. Q. Kt. to B's 3d.
3. P. to Q. B's 3d.	3. P. to K. B's 4th.
4. P. to Q's 4th.	4. K. B. P. takes P.
5. Kt. takes P.	5. K. Kt. to B's 3d.
6. K. B. to Q. Kt's 5th.	6. P. to Q. R's 3d.
7. B. takes Kt.	7. Q. Kt. P. takes B.
8. Q. B. to K. Kt's 5th.	8. Q. R. to Q. Kt's sq.
9. P. to Q. Kt's 4th.	9. Q. B. to Kt's 2d.
10. Q. to Q. R's 4th.	10. P. to Q's 4th.
11. Castles.*	11. P. to K. R's 3d.
12. Q. B. to K. R's 4th.	12. Q. to her 3d.

* The following moves will show the probable result of taking the P. with Kt.:—

11. Kt. takes Q. B. P.	11. Q. to her 2d.
12. P. to Q. Kt's 5th.	12. R. to Q. R's sq.

(His best move; if P. takes P., then White plays Q. to her R's 7th.)

| 13. Q. to her sq. | 13. P. takes P., or B. takes Kt |

And White has little if any advantage.

13. B. to K. Kt's 3d.
14. Q. Kt. to Q's 2d.
15. Q. Kt. to his 3d.
16. Q. Kt. to R's 5th.
17. Q. to B's 2d.
18. P. to K. B's 3d.
19. R. takes P.
20. Q. R. to K's sq.
21. K. Kt. takes Q. B. P.
22. B. takes Q.
23. Q. to K. Kt's 6th (ch.)
24. Kt. takes B. (ch.)

13. K. R. to K. Kt's sq.
14. Q. R. to Q. B's sq.
15. Kt. to Q's 2d.
16. Kt. to Kt's 3d.
17. Q. B. to Q. R's sq.
18. P. takes P.
19. Q. to K's 3d.
20. K. B. to K's 2d.
21. Q. takes R. (ch.)
22. B. takes Kt.
23. K. to Q's sq.

And wins.

GAME II.—Between Mr. Horwitz and Captain Evans

WHITE. (Capt. E.)
1. P. to K's 4th.
2. K. Kt. to B's 3d.
3. P. to Q. B's 3d.
4. P. to Q's 4th.
5. P. to K's 5th.
6. Q. Kt. takes P.
7. Q. B. to K. Kt's 5th.
8. K. B. to Q. B's 4th.
9. P. takes P. in passing.
10. Q. to K's 2d.
11. Kt. takes Kt.
12. Castles.
13. Q. Kt. to Q's 5th.
14. Q. B. takes Kt.
15. Kt. takes B. (ch.)
16. K. R. to Q's sq.
17. B. to Q. Kt's 3d.
18. R. to Q's 2d.
19. Q. R. to Q's sq.
20. Q. takes P.
21. R. takes B.
22. R. takes R.
23. Q. to her sq.
24. R. to Q's 8th (ch.)
25. Q. takes R. (ch.)
26. Kt. to Q. B's 6th (ch.)

BLACK. (Mr. H.)
1. P. to K's 4th.
2. Q. Kt. to B's 3d.
3. P. to K. B's 4th.
4. P. takes Q. P.
5. P. takes Q. B. P.
6. K. B. to Q. Kt's 5th.
7. K. Kt. to K's 2d.
8. P. to Q's 4th.
9. Q. takes P.
10. Q. Kt. to Q's 5th.
11. Q. takes Kt.
12. Q. B. to Q's 2d.
13. Castles on Q's side.
14. B. takes B.
15. K. to Kt's sq.
16. Q. to K. R's 5th.
17. Q. to K. R's 3d.
18. P. to K. B's 5th.
19. P. to K. B's 6th.
20. P. to Q. R's 3d.
21. R. takes R.
22. Q. to her B's 8th (ch.)
23. Q. takes Kt. P.
24. R. takes R.
25. K. to R's 2d.

And White mates in four moves.

GAME III.—Between Captain Evans and Mr. Henderson

WHITE. (Capt. E.)
1. P. to K's 4th.
2. K. Kt. to B's 3d.
3. P. to Q. B's 3d.
4. K. B. to Q. Kt's 5th.
5. Q. to her R's 4th.

BLACK. (Mr. H.)
1. P. to K's 4th.
2. Q. Kt. to B's 3d.
3. P. to Q's 4th.
4. Q. B. to K. Kt's 5th.
5. Q. to her 3d.

KING'S KNIGHT'S OPENING.

6. Kt. takes K. P.	6. Q. takes Kt.
7. B. takes Q. Kt. (ch.)	7. P. takes B.
8. Q. takes P. (ch)	8. K. to his 2d.
9. P. to K. B's 3d.	9. R. to Q's sq.
10. P. to Q's 4th.	10. Q. to K's 3d.
11. Q. takes Q. B. P. (ch.	11. R. to Q's 2d.
12. Q. to Q. B's 5th (ch.)	12. K. to his sq.
13. Q. to Q. B's 8th (ch.)	13. R. to Q's sq.
14. Q. takes Q. (ch.)	14. B. takes Q.
15. P. to K's 5th.	15. P. to K. B's 4th.
16. Kt. to Q's 2d.	16. Kt. to K. R's 3d.
17. Kt. to Q. Kt's 3d.	17. Kt. to K. B's 2d.
18. P. to K. B's 4th.	18. B. to K's 2d.
19. P. to K. R's 4th.	19. Kt. to K. R's 3d.
20. K. to his 2d.	20. B. to Q's 2d.
21. K. to his B's 3d.	21. B. to Q. Kt's 4th.
22. P. to K. Kt's 3d.	22. B. to Q's 6th.
23. Kt. to Q's 2d.	23. Kt. to K. Kt's 5th.
24. K. R. to K's sq.	24. P. to K. R's 3d.
25. P. to Q. Kt's 3d.	25. R. to Q. B's sq.
26. B. to Q. Kt's 2d.	26. P. to K. Kt's 4th.
27. P. to K. R's 5th.	27. P. takes B. P.
28. P. takes P.	28. R. to K. Kt's sq.
29. R. to K. R's sq.	29. K. to B's 2d.
30. R. to K. R's 3d.	30. K. to his 3d.
31. R. to Q. B's sq.	31. R. to K. Kt's 2d.
32. P. to Q. B's 4th.	32. P. takes P.
33. Kt. takes P.	33. B. to K's 5th (ch.)
34. K. to his 2d.	34. B. to K. Kt's 7th.
35. R. to K. Kt's 3d.	35. B. to K's 5th.
36. P. to Q. R's 3d.	36. Q. R. to K. Kt's sq.
37. Q. R. to K. Kt's sq	37. B. to K. R's 5th.
38. R. to K. R's 3d.	38. B. to K. B's 7th.
39. R. to Q. B's sq.	39. Q. B. to K. Kt's 7th.
40. R. to Q's 3d.	40. B. to K. R's 5th.
41. Kt. to Q's 6th.	41. Kt. to K. B's 7th.
42. K. R. to Q. B's 3d.	42. Kt. to K's 5th.
43. P. to Q's 5th (ch.)	43. K. takes P.
44. R. to Q's 3d (ch.)	44. K. to K's 3d.
45. Kt. takes Kt.	45. P. takes Kt.
46. R. to Q's 6th (ch.)	46. K. to B's 4th.
47. P. to K's 6th.	47. B. to K. B's 6th (ch.)
48. K. to his 3d.	48. R. to K. Kt's 7th.
49. R. to Q. B's 5th (ch.)	49. K. to K. Kt's 5th.
50. R. to Q's 2d.	50. R. takes R.
51. K. takes R.	51. K. takes K. B. P.
52. B. to K's 5th (ch.)	52. K. to K. Kt's 5th.
53. K. to his 3d.	53. B. to K. Kt's 4th (ch.)
54. K. to Q's 4th.	54. P. to K's 6th.
55. R. to Q. B's sq.	55. R. to Q's sq. (ch.)
56. K. to Q. B's 3d.	56. R. to Q. B's sq. (ch.)

And Black wins.

CHAPTER III.

THE KING'S BISHOP'S OPENING.

The Two Kings' Bishops' Game
GAME THE FIRST.

WHITE.	BLACK.
1. P. to K's 4th.	1. P. to K's 4th.
2. K. B. to Q. B's 4th.	2. K. B. to Q. B's 4th.
3. P. to Q. B's 3d.	3. K. Kt. to B's 3d.
4. P. to Q's 4th.	4. P. takes P.
5. P. to K's 5th.	5. P. to Q's 4th.
6. P. takes Kt.	6. P. takes B.
7. P. takes K. Kt. P	7. R. to K. Kt's sq.
8. Q. to K. R's 5th.	8. Q. to K's 2d (ch.)
9. K. to Q's sq.	9. R. takes P.
10. K. Kt. to B's 3d	10. Q. Kt. to B's 3d.
11. K. R. to K's sq.	11. Q. B. to K's 3d.
12. R. takes B.	12. Q. takes R.
13. Q. takes B.	13. P. to Q. Kt's 3d.
14. Q. to her Kt.'s 5th	14. R. takes K. Kt. P.

I prefer your game.

GAME THE SECOND.

WHITE.	BLACK.
1 P. to K's 4th.	1. P. to K's 4th.
2. K. B. to Q. B's 4th.	2. K. B. to Q. B's 4th.
3. P. to Q. B's 3d.	3. Q. to K's 2d.
4. K. Kt. to B's 3d.	4. P. to Q's 3d (best)
5. P. to Q's 4th.	5. P. takes P.
6. Castles	6. P. takes Q. B. P.

KING'S BISHOP'S OPENING.

7. P. to Q. Kt's 4th.   7. B. to Q. Kt's 3d.
8. Q. Kt. takes P.   8. K. Kt. to B's 3d.
9. Q. Kt. to Q's 5th.   9. Kt. takes Kt.
10. P. takes Kt.   10. Castles.
11. Q. B. to Q. Kt's 2d. 11. Q. B. to K. Kt's 5th
12. K. R. to K's sq.   12. Q. to her sq.

Your attack is hardly an equivalent for his extra Pawn

GAME THE THIRD.
THE ITALIANS' DEFENCE.

WHITE.	BLACK.
1. P. to K's 4th.	1. P. to K's 4th.
2. K. B. to Q. B's 4th.	2. K. B. to Q. B's 4th.
3. P. to Q. B's 3d.	3. Q. to K. Kt's 4th.
4. Q. to K. B's 3d.	4. Q. to K. Kt's 3d (best)
5. K. Kt. to K's 2d.	5. P. to Q's 3d.
6. P. to Q's 4th.	6. B. to Q. Kt's 3d.
7. P. takes P.	7. P. takes P.
8. K. Kt. to his 3d.	8. K. Kt. to B's 3d.
9 P. to K. R's 3d.	

The game is equal.

GAME THE FOURTH.
LEWIS'S COUNTER GAMBIT.

WHITE.	BLACK.
1. P. to K's 4th.	1. P. to K's 4th.
2. K. B. to Q. B's 4th.	2. K. B. to Q. B's 4th.
3. P. to Q. B's 3d.	3. P. to Q's 4th.
4. B. takes P.	4. K. Kt. to B's 3d.
5. Q. to K. B's 3d.	5. Castles.
6. P. to Q's 4th.	6. P. takes P.
7 Q. B. to K. Kt's 5th.	7. P. takes P.
8. Q. Kt. takes P.	8. Q. Kt. to Q's 2d
9. Castles.	9. P. to Q. B's 3d.
10. B. to Q. Kt's 3d.	10. Q. to K's 2d.

The game is even.

GAME THE FIFTH.

WHITE.	BLACK.
1 P. to K's 4th.	1. P. to K's 4th.
2. K. B. to Q. B's 4th.	2. K. B. to Q. B's 4th.
3. P. to Q. B's 3d.	3. Q. Kt. to B's 3d.
4. P. to Q's 4th.	4. B. to Q. Kt's 3d (bes
5. K. Kt. to K's 2d.	5. K. Kt. to B's 3d.
6. Q. to her 3d.	6. Castles.
7. P. to K. B's 4th.	7. P. takes Q. P.
8. P. to K's 5th.	8. P. to Q's 4th.
9. B. to Q. Kt's 3d.	9. K. Kt. to K's 5th.
10. Q. B. P. takes P.	10 P. to K. B's 4th.
11. Q. Kt. to B's 3d.	11 Q. B. to K's 3d.

And the game is even.

GAME THE SIXTH.

WHITE.	BLACK.
1. P. to K's 4th.	1. P. to K's 4th.
2. K. B. to Q. B's 4th.	2. K. B. to Q. B's 4th.
3. K. Kt. to B's 3d.	3. P. to Q's 3d.
4. P. to Q. B's 3d.	4. K. Kt. to B's 2d.
5. P. to Q's 4th.	5. P. takes P.
6. P. takes P.	6. B. to Q. Kt's 5th (ch.)
7. B. to Q's 2d.	7. B. takes B. (ch.)
8. Q. Kt. takes B.	8. P. to Q's 4th.
9. P. takes P.	9. Kt. takes P.
10. Q. to her Kt's 3d.	10. P. to Q. B's 3d.
11. Castles.	11. Castles.

You have the move, and your Pieces are in better play.

GAME THE SEVENTH.

WHITE.	BLACK.
1. P. to K's 4th.	1. P. to K's 4th.
2. K. B. to Q. B's 4th.	2. K. B. to Q. B's 4th.
3. Q. to K. B's 3d.	3. K. Kt. to B's 3d.
4. P. to K. Kt's 4th.	4. P to Q's 4th.

KING'S BISHOP'S OPENING.

5. K. B. takes Q. P.   5. Q. B. takes P.
6. Q. to Q. Kt's 3d.   6. K. Kt. takes K. B.
7. P. takes Kt.   7. K. B. to Q. Kt's 3d
8. Q to K. Kt's 3d.   8. Q. to K. B's 3d.

Black has the better game.

GAME THE EIGHTH.

WHITE.	BLACK.
1. P. to K's 4th.	1. P. to K's 4th.
2. K. B. to Q. B's 4th.	2. K. B. to Q. B's 4th.
3. Q. to K. Kt's 4th.	3. Q. to K. B's 3d.
4. P. to Q's 4th.	4. B. takes P.
5. K. Kt. to B's 3d.	5. Q. Kt. to B's 3d.
6. Q. to K. Kt's 3d.	6. P. to Q's 3d.
7. Q. B. to K. Kt's 5th.	7. Q. to K. Kt's 3d.
8. Q. Kt. to Q's 2d.	8. P. to K. R's 3d.

Black has the advantage.

GAME THE NINTH.

WHITE.	BLACK.
1. P. to K's 4th.	1. P. to K's 4th.
2. K. B. to Q. B's 4th.	2. K. B. to Q. B's 4th
3. Q. to K. R's 5th.	3. Q. to K's 2d.
4. K. Kt. to B's 3d.	4. P. to Q's 3d.
5. K. Kt. to his 5th.	5. K. Kt. to B's 3d.
6. Q. takes K. B. P. (ch.) (best)	6. Q. takes Q.
7. B. takes Q. (ch.)	7. K. to his 2d.
8. B. to Q. B's 4th.	8. P. to K. R's 3d.
9. Kt. to K. B's 3d.	9. Kt. takes K. P.

You have no advantage.

GAME THE TENTH.

WHITE.	BLACK.
1. P. to K's 4th.	1. P. to K's 4th.
2. K. B. to Q: B's 4th.	2. K. B. to Q. B's 4th

3. P. to Q's 4th.   3. B. takes P.
4. K. Kt. to B's 3d.   4. Q. Kt. to B's 3d.
5. P. to Q. B's 3d.   5. B. to Q. Kt's 3d.
6. K. Kt. to his 5th.   6. K. Kt. to R's 3d.
7. Q. to K. R's 5th.   7. Castles.
   Black maintains his Pawn.

GAME THE ELEVENTH.
McDonnell's Double Gambit.

WHITE.	BLACK.
1. P. to K's 4th.	1. P. to K's 4th.
2. K. B. to Q. B's 4th	2. K. B. to Q. B's 4th
3. P. to Q. Kt's 4th.	3. B. takes Kt. P.
4. P. to K. B's 4th.	4. P. to Q's 4th.
5. P. takes Q. P.	5. P. to K's 5th.
6. K. Kt. to K's 2d.	6. K. Kt. to B's 3d.
7 Castles.	7. Castles.
8 Q. Kt. to B's 3d.	8. P. to Q. B's 3d.
9. P. takes P.	9. Q. Kt. takes P.
10. K. to R's sq.	10. Q. B. to K. Kt's 5th

Your game is inferior to his.

GAME THE TWELFTH.

WHITE.	BLACK.
1. P. to K's 4th.	1. P. to K's 4th.
2. K. B. to Q. B's 4th.	2. K. B. to Q. B's 4th
3. P. to K. B's 4th.	3. B. takes K. Kt.
4. Q. to K. R's 5th.	4. Q. to K's 2d.
5. R. takes B.	5. P. to Q's 3d.
6. P to K. B's 5th.	6. K. Kt. to B's 3d.
7. Q. to K. Kt's 5th.	7. K. Kt. takes K. P
8. Q. takes K. Kt. P.	8. Q. to K. B's 3d.
9. K B. takes K. B. P. (ch.)	9. K. to his 2d.
10. Q. takes Q. (ch.)	10. Kt. takes Q.
11. K. B. to Q. Kt's 3d.	11. Q. B. takes P.

The game is in Black's favor.

GAME THE THIRTEENTH.
THE LOPEZ GAMBIT

WHITE.	BLACK.
1. P. to K's 4th.	1. P. to K's 4th.
2. K. B. to Q. B's 4th.	2. K. B. to Q. B's 4th.
3. Q. to K's 2d.	3. P. to Q's 3d.
4. P. to K. B's 4th.	4. Kt. to K. B's 3d.
5. K. Kt. to B's 3d.	5. Q. to K's 2d.
6. P. to Q's 3d.	6. Q. B. to K. Kt's 5th.
7. P. takes P.	7. P. takes P.
8. Q. B. to K. Kt's 5th.	8. Q. Kt. to Q's 2d.
9. Q. Kt. to Q's 2d.	9. Castles on Q's side.
10. Castles on Q's side.	

The positions are equal.

GAME THE FOURTEENTH.

WHITE.	BLACK.
1. P. to K's 4th.	1. P. to K's 4th.
2. K. B. to Q. B's 4th.	2. K. B. to Q. B's 4th.
3. Q. to K's 2d.	3. Q. to K's 2d.
4. P. to K. B's 4th.	4. K. Kt. to B's 3d.
5. K. Kt. to B's 3d.	5. P. to Q's 3d.
6. Q. Kt. to B's 3d.	6. P. to Q. B's 3d.
7. P. to Q's 3d.	7. Q. B. to K. Kt's 5th.
8. P. to K. B's 5th.	8. Q. Kt. to Q's 2d.
9. Q. B. to K. Kt's 5th.	9. P. to K. R's 3d.
10. Q. B. to K. R's 4th.	10. P. to K. Kt's 4th.

The game is quite even.

GAME THE FIFTEENTH.

WHITE.	BLACK.
1. P. to K's 4th.	1. P. to K's 4th.
2. B. to Q. B's 4th	2. B. to Q. B's 4th.
3. Q. to K's 2d.	3. Q. Kt. to B's 3d.
4. P. to Q. B's 3d.	4. K. Kt. to B's 3d
5 P to K. B's 4th.	5 B. takes K. Kt.

6. R. takes B. 6. Castles
7. P. to Q's 3d. 7. P. to Q's 4th.
8. K. B. takes Q. P. 8. K. Kt. takes B.
9. P. takes Kt. 9. P. takes K. B. P.
10. Q. B. takes P 10. R. to K's sq.
11. B. to K's 3d. 11. Kt. to K's 4th.
12. P. to K. R's 3d. 12. B. to K. B's 4th.
13. P. to Q's 4th. 13. B. to Q's 6th.

And by afterwards moving the Kt. to Q. B's 5th, Black must win at least a Piece.

VARIATION,

Beginning at White's 4th move.

WHITE. BLACK.
1. P. to K's 4th. 1. P. to K's 4th.
2. K. B. to Q. B's 4th. 2. K. B. to Q. B's 4th.
3. Q. to K's 2d. 3. Q. Kt. to B's 3d.
4. K. B. takes K. B. P. (ch.) 4. K. takes B.
5. Q. to her B's 4th (ch.) 5. P. to Q's 4th.
6. Q. takes B. 6. P. takes K. P.
7. Q. to her B's 4th (ch.) 7. Q. B. to K's 3d.
8. Q. takes P. 8. K. Kt. to B's 3d

And you have an inferior game.

GAMES

ILLUSTRATIVE OF THE PRECEDING ANALYSES.

GAME I.—Played some years since between Messrs. Popert and Staunton.

WHITE. (Mr. S.) BLACK. (Mr. P.)
1. P. to K's 4th. 1. P. to K's 4th.
2. K. B. to Q. B's 4th. 2. K. B. to Q. B's 4th.
3. P. to Q. B's 3d. 3. P. to Q's 3d.*
4. K. Kt. to B's 3d.† 4. K. Kt. to B's 3d.
5. P. to Q's 4th. 5. P. takes P.
6. P takes P. 6. B. checks.

---

* Not so good a move as K. Kt. to B's 3d, or Q. to K. Kt's 4th.
† P. to Q's 4th would perhaps have been stronger play.

KING'S BISHOP'S OPENING.

7. B. to Q's 2d.
8. Q. Kt. takes B.
9. B. to Q's 3d.
10. P. to Q. R's 3d.
11. Q. to Q. B's 2d.
12. Q. R. to Q. B's sq.
13. P. to K's 5th.
14. Kt. takes B.
15. P. to K. Kt's 3d.
16. P. to Q. Kt's 4th
17. Q. to Q's 2d.
18. Castles.
19. Q. R. to B's 3d.
20. Kt. to K. R's 4th.
21. P. to K. B's 4th.
22. P. to K. Kt's 4th.
23. P. takes B. P
24. Kt. takes Kt.
25. K. to R's sq.
26. Q. R. to Q. B's sq.
27. Q. to Q. B's 2d.
28. K. R. to K. Kt's sq.
29. R. takes R.
30. R. to K. Kt's sq. (ch.)
31. Q. to K. B's 2d.
32. B. to K's 2d.
33. Q. to K. R's 4th.
34. B. to K. R's 5th.
35. R. to K. Kt's 3d.
36. B. to K. Kt's 6th.§
37. B. to K. B's 7th.
38. R. takes Q.
39. K. to Kt's 2d, and wins.

7. B. takes B. (ch.)
8. Castles.*
9. Kt. to Q. B's 3d.
10. Q. B. to K. Kt's 5th
11. P. to K. R's 3d.
12. P. to Q's 4th.
13. B. takes Kt.
14. Kt. to K. R's 4th.
15. P. to K. Kt's 3d.
16. Q. to Q's 2d.†
17. K. to R's 2d.
18. Q. R. to K's sq.
19. Kt. to Q's sq.
20. P. to Q. B's 3d.
21. P. to K. B's 4th.
22. Kt. to K. Kt's 2d.
23. K. Kt. takes P.
24. P. takes Kt.
25. K. R. to K. Kt's sq.
26. Q. to K. B's 2d.
27. Q. R. to K. B's sq.
28. Kt. to K's 3d.
29. K. takes R.
30. K. to R's sq.
31. Q. to K. R's 4th.‡
32. Q. to K. B's 2d.
33. Q. to K. R's 2d.
34. Kt. takes Q. P.
35. P. to Q. Kt's 3d.
36. Q. to K. Kt's 2d.
37. R. takes B.‖
38. K. takes R.

GAME II.—Between two Amateurs.

WHITE.	BLACK.
1. P. to K's 4th.	1. P. to K's 4th.
2. K. B. to Q. B's 4th.	2. K. B. to Q. B's 4th.
3. P. to Q. B's 3d.	3. Q. to K. Kt's 4th.
4. Q. to K. B's 3d.	4. Q. to K. Kt's 3d.
5. K. Kt. to K's 2d.	5. P. to Q's 3d.
6. P. to Q's 4th.	6. P. takes P.
7. P. takes P.	7. B. to Q. Kt's 3d.

* P. to Q's 4th is a better move at this point.
† Intending, if the Q. Kt. P. should be played on his Kt., to move Q. to K. Kt's 5th.
‡ A lost move.
§ It would have been more decisive if played to K. B's 7th at once.
‖ If the Q. takes B., mate follows in three moves.

8. P. to K's 5th.   8. K. Kt. t K's 2d
9. P. to K's 6th.   9. P. to K. B's 3d.
10. Q. Kt. to B's 3d.   10. Castles.
11. K. Kt. to K. B's 4th.   11. Q. to K's sq.
12. Q. B. to K's 3d.   12. Q. Kt. to Q. B's 3d.
13. Q. R. to Q's sq.   13. K. to R's sq.
14. P. to K. R's 4th.   14. Q. Kt. to Q's sq.
15. P. to K. R's 5th.   15. P. to K. B's 4th.
16. Q. Kt. to Q's 5th.   16. Q. B. takes P.
17. Kt. takes Kt.   17. Q. takes Kt.
18. Kt. to K. Kt's 6th (ch.)   18. P. takes Kt.
19. P. takes P. (dis. ch.)

And White gives checkmate in three moves.

GAME III.—THE LOPEZ GAMBIT.—Between Messrs. De la Bourdonnais and McDonnell.

WHITE. (M. De la B.)   BLACK. (Mr. McD.)
1. P. to K's 4th.   1. P. to K's 4th.
2. K. B. to Q. B's 4th.   2. K. B. to Q. B's 4th.
3. Q. to K's 2d.   3. K. Kt. to B's 3d.
4. P. to Q's 3d.   4. Q. Kt. to B's 3d.
5. P. to Q. B's 3d.   5. Q. Kt. to K's 2d.
6. P. to K. B's 4th.   6. P. takes P.*
7. P. to Q's 4th.   7. K. B. to Kt's 3d.
8. Q. B. takes P.   8. P. to Q's 3d.
9. K. B. to Q's 3d.   9. Q. Kt. to K. Kt's 3d
10. Q. B. to K's 3d.   10. Castles.
11. P. to K. R's 3d.   11. K. R. to K's sq.
12. Q. Kt. to Q's 2d.   12. Q. to K's 2d.
13. Castles on Q's side.   13. P. to Q. B's 4th.
14. K. to Kt's sq.   14. P. takes P.
15. P. takes P.   15. P. to Q. R's 4th
16. K. Kt. to B's 3d.   16. Q. B. to Q's 2d.
17. P. to K. Kt's 4th.   17. P. to K. R's 3d.
18. Q. R. to K. Kt's sq.   18. P. to Q. R's 5th
19. P. to K. Kt's 5th.   19. P. takes P.
20. B. takes P.   20. P. to Q. R's 6th.
21. P. to Q. Kt's 3d.   21. Q. B. to his 3d.
22. Q. R. to K. Kt's 4th.   22. K. B. to Q. R's 4th.
23. P. to K. R's 4th.   23. B. takes Q. Kt.
24. Kt. takes B.   24. Q. R. to his 4th.
25. P. to K. R's 5th.   25. R. takes B.
26. R. takes R.   26. Kt. to K. B's 5th
27. Q. to K. B's 3d.   27. Kt. takes B.
28. P. to Q's 5th.   28. Kt. takes Q. P.
29. K. R. to K. Kt's sq.†   29. Kt. to B's 6th (ch.)

* In this opening it is not advisable for the second player to take the gambit P. with his K. P.

† This portion of the game is full of interest and instruction, and 's remarkably well played.

KING'S BISHOP'S OPENING.

30. K. to R's sq.	30. B. takes K. P.
31. R. takes K. Kt. P. (ch.)	31. K. to R's sq.
32. Q. to K. Kt's 3d.	32. B. to K. Kt's 3d.
33. K. R. P. takes B.	33. Q. to K's 8th (ch.)
34. R. takes Q.*	34. R. takes R. (ch.)
35. Q. takes R.	35. Kt. takes Q.
36. R. to R's 7th (ch.)	36. K. to Kt's sq.
37. P. takes K. B. P. (ch.)	37. K. takes R.
38. P. one, becoming a Queen.	38. Kt. mates.

GAME IV.—THE LOPEZ GAMBIT.

WHITE.	BLACK.
1. P. to K's 4th.	1. P. to K's 4th.
2. K. B. to Q. B's 4th.	2. K. B. to Q. B's 4th.
3. Q. to K's 2d.	3. Q. Kt. to B's 3d.
4. B. takes K. B. P. (ch.)	4. K. takes B.
5. Q. to her B's 4th (ch.)	5. P. to Q's 4th.
6. Q. takes B.	6. P. takes P.
7. Q. to her B's 4th (ch.)	7. Q. B. to K's 3d.
8. Q. takes P.	8. K. Kt. to B's 3d.
9. Q. to K. R's 4th.	9. Q. Kt. to Q's 5th.
10. Q. Kt. to R's 3d.	10. P. to K's 5th.
11. P. to Q. B's 3d.	11. P. to K. Kt's 4th.†
12. Q. takes K. Kt. P.	12. K. R. to K. Kt's sq.
13. Q. to K's 3d.	13. Q. Kt. to K. B's 4th.
14. Q. to K's 2d.	14. R. takes K. Kt. P.
15. Q. Kt. to B's 2d.	15. Q. to her 3d.
16. Q. Kt. to K's 3d.	16. Kt. takes Kt.
17. Q. P. takes Kt.	17. Q. R. to K. Kt's sq.
18. Q. to K. B's sq.	18. Q. R. to Q's sq.
19. Q. to K's 2d.	19. Kt. to his 5th.
20. Kt. to R's 3d.	20. Kt. to K's 4th.
21. Kt. to K. B's 4th.	21. Kt. to K. B's 6th (ch.)
22. K. to his B's sq.	

And Black can checkmate in six moves.

GAME V.—Between Messrs. Cochrane and Staunton.

WHITE. (Mr. S.)	BLACK. (Mr. C.)
1. P. to K's 4th.	1. P. to K's 4th.
2. B. to Q. B's 4th.	2. B. to Q. B's 4th.
3. K. Kt. to B's 3d.	3. Q. Kt. to B's 3d.
4. P. to Q. Kt's 4th.‡	4. B. takes Q. Kt. P.
5. P. to Q. B's 3d.	5. B. to Q. R's 4th.
6. Castles.	6. B. to Q. Kt's 3d.
7. P. to Q's 4th.	7. P. takes Q. P.

---

* White loses the game by this move.
† The game from this point forward is admirably conducted by Black.
‡ We have now the same position brought about which occurs in the Evans Gambit.

8. K. Kt. takes P.	8. Kt. takes Kt.
9. P. takes Kt.	9. P. to Q's 3d.
10. P. to Q. R's 4th.	10. P. to Q. B's 3d.
11. P. to Q. R's 5th.	11. K. B. to Q. B's 2d.*
12. Q. to her Kt's 3d.	12. Q. to K's 2d.
13. Q. B. to Q. R's 3d.	13. Q. to K. B's 3d.
14. Q. Kt. to Q. B's 3d.	14. Q. to K. Kt's 3d.
15. Q. Kt. to K's 2d.	15. K. Kt. to K. R's 3d.
16. P. to K's 5th.	16. P. to Q's 4th.
17. K. B. to Q's 3d.	17. Kt. to K. B's 4th
18. Q. to her Kt's 4th.	18. K. B. to Q's sq.
19. Q. to her Kt's sq.	19. Q. to K. R's 4th.
20. Kt. to K. Kt's 3d.	20. Kt. takes Kt.
21. K. B. P. takes Kt.	21. K. B. takes Q. R. P.
22. K. B. to K. B's 5th.	22. K. B. to Q. Kt's 3d.
23. Q. to her Kt's 4th.	23. Q. to K. Kt's 4th.
24. K. B. takes Q. B.	24. Q. R. takes B.
25. P. to K's 6th.	25. P. takes P.

White announced mate in eight moves.

GAME VI.—Between Messrs. Walker and Daniels.

WHITE. (Mr. W.)	BLACK. (Mr. D.)
1. P. to K's 4th.	1. P. to K's 4th.
2. B. to Q. B's 4th.	2. B. to Q. B's 4th.
3. P. to Q. B's 3d.	3. P. to Q's 4th.
4. B. takes Q. P.	4. K. Kt. to B's 3d.
5. Q. to her Kt's 3d.	5. Castles.
6. K. Kt. to B's 3d.	6. P. to Q. B's 3d.†
7. B. takes K. B. P. (ch.)‡	7. R. takes B.
8. Kt. takes K. P.	8. Q. to K's 2d.
9. Q. takes R. (ch.)	9. Q. takes Q.
10. Kt. takes Q.	10. K. takes Kt.
11. P. to Q's 4th.	11. B. to Q. Kt's 3d.
12. P. to K. B's 3d.	12. Q. B. to K's 3d.
13. Q. B. to K's 3d.	13. Q. Kt. to R's 3d.
14. K. to B's 2d.	14. Q. Kt. to B's 2d.
15. Q. Kt. to Q's 2d.	15. P. to K. Kt's 3d.
16. P. to K. Kt's 4th.	16. K. to Kt's 2d.
17. P. to K. R's 4th.	17. R. to K's sq.
18. P. to K. R's 5th.	18. Q. B. to K. B's 2d.
19. P. takes P.	19. Q. B. takes P.

---

* If he had taken the P., Black, by taking the K. B. P. with his B., checking, and when the K. took the B., playing Q. to K. R's 5th (ch.), would have gained a more valuable P. in return, and have deprived his opponent of the privilege of castling.

† This is not advisable. It would be better to take B. with Kt.

‡ The notion of this sacrifice originated with Messrs. Henderson and Williams, of Bristol. during an examination of the present opening.

KING'S BISHOP'S OPENING.   127

20. Q. R. to K. Kt's sq.	20. Q. Kt. to K's 3d.
21. Q. Kt. to Q. B's 4th.	21. B. to Q. B's 2d.
22. P. to K's 5th.	22. K. Kt. to Q's 4th.
23. B. to K. R's 6th (ch.)	23. K. to B's 2d.
24. K. to Kt's 3d.	24. P. to Q. Kt's 4th.
25. Kt. to K's 3d.	25. Kt. takes Kt.
26. B. takes Kt.	26. P. to Q. B's 4th.
27. P. to K. B's 4th.	27. P. takes P.
28. P. takes P.	28. Q. B. to Q's 6th.
29. P. to K. B's 5th.	

Black resigns.

THE KING'S KNIGHT'S DEFENCE IN KING'S BISHOP'S OPENING

GAME THE FIRST.

WHITE.	BLACK.
1. P. to K's 4th.	1 P. to K's 4th.
2. K. B. to Q. B's 4th.	2. K. Kt. to B's 3d.
3. P. to Q's 4th.	3. P. takes P.
4. P. to K's 5th.	4 P. to Q's 4th.
5. B. to Q. Kt's 3d.	5. Kt. to K's 5th.
6. K. Kt. to K's 2d.	6. P. to Q. B's 4th.
7. P. to K. B's 3d.	7. Kt. to K. Kt's 4th.
8. Kt. to K. B's 4th.	8. P. to Q. B's 5th.
9. B. to R's 4th (ch.)	9. Q. Kt. to B's 3d.
10. B. takes Kt. (ch.)	10. P. takes B.
11. Q. takes doubled P	11. Kt. to K's 3d.
12. Kt. takes Kt.	12. K. B. P. takes Kt.
13. Castles.	13. P. to Q. B's 4th.
14. Q. to K. B's 2d.	

Black has the advantage.

GAME THE SECOND.

WHITE.	BLACK.
1. P. to K's 4th.	1. P. to K's 4th.
2. K. B. to Q. B's 4th.	2. K. Kt. to B's 3d.
3. P. to Q's 3d.	3. K. B. to Q. B's 4th
4. K. Kt. to B's 3d.	4. P. to Q's 3d.

5. P. to Q. B's 3d.   5. Castles.
6. P. to Q. R's 4th.   6. P. to Q. R's 4th
   The game is even.

GAME THE THIRD.

WHITE.	BLACK.
1. P. to K's 4th.	1 P. to K's 4th.
2. K. B. to Q. B's 4th.	2. K. Kt. to B's 3d.
3. P. to K. B's 4th.	3. P. to Q's 4th.
4. P. takes Q. P.	4. P. takes B. P.
5. P. to Q's 4th.	5. B. to K. Kt.'s 5th
6. K. Kt. to B's 3d.	

There is no advantage on either side.

GAME THE FOURTH.

WHITE.	BLACK.
1 P. to K's 4th.	1. P. to K's 4th.
2. B. to Q. B's 4th.	2. K. Kt. to B's 3d.
3. K. Kt. to B's 3d.	3. Kt. takes K. P.
4. P. to Q's 3d.	4. Kt. to Q's 3d.
5. Kt. takes K. P.	5. Kt. takes B.
6. Kt. takes Kt.	6. P. to Q's 4th.
7. Kt. to K's 5th.	7. K. B. to Q's 3d.
8. P. to Q's 4th.	8. Castles.
9. Castles.	9. P. to K. B's 3d.
10. Kt. to K. B's 3d.	

Neither party can boast of advantage.

COUNTER GAMBIT IN THE KING'S BISHOP'S OPENING
GAME THE FIRST.

WHITE.	BLACK.
1. P. to K's 4th.	1. P. to K's 4th
2. K. B. to Q. B's 4th.	2. P. to K. B's 4th.

You have now the choice of refusing or accepting the gambit; the former is the more judicious mode of operating, and the consequences arising from it will be shown in this game, while the result of your accepting the gambit shall be considered in the next.

3. P. to Q's 3d.	3. K. Kt. to B's 3d
4. P. to K. B's 4th.	4. K. P. takes P.
5. Q. B. takes P.	5. P. takes K. P.
6. Q. P. takes P.	6. Q. to K's 2d.
7. P. to K's 5th.	7. P. to Q's 3d.
8. Q. to K'r 2d.	8. P. takes P.
9. B. takes P.	9. P. to Q. B's 3d.
10. K. Kt. to B's 3d.	

You have a better developed opening.

Variation I.

Beginning at White's 3d move.

WHITE.	BLACK.
1. P. to K's 4th.	1. P. to K's 4th.
2. K. B. to Q. B's 4th.	2. P. to K. B's 4th.
3. P. to Q's 4th.	3. P. takes Q. P. (best)
4. Q. takes P.	4. Q. Kt. to B's 3d.
5. Q. to K's 3d.	5. P. takes P.
6. Q. takes P. (ch.)	6. Q. to K's 2d.

The game is even.

Variation II.

Beginning also at White's 3d move.

WHITE.	BLACK.
1. P. to K's 4th.	1. P. to K's 4th.
2. K. B. to Q. B's 4th.	2. P. to K. B's 4th.
3. B. takes K. Kt.	3. R. takes B.
4 P. takes P.	4. P. to Q's 4th.
5. Q. to K. R's 5th. (ch.)	5. P. to K. Kt's 3d.
6. P. takes P.	6. R. takes P.
7. K. Kt. to B's 3d.	7. Q. Kt. to B's 3d.
8. Q. takes K. R. P.	8. Q. to K. B's 3d.
9. P. to Q's 3d.	9. K. B. to Q. B's 4th
10. B. to K's 3d.	10. B. takes B.
11. P. takes B.	11. R. takes K. Kt. P

The positions are equal.

GAME THE SECOND.

WHITE.	BLACK.
1. P. to K's 4th.	1. P. to K's 4th
2. K. B. to Q. B's 4th.	2. P. to K. B's 4th.
3. P. takes P.	3. K. Kt. to B's 3d.
4. P. to Q's 4th.	4. P. takes P.
5. Q. takes P.	5. P. to Q's 4th.
6. K. B. to Q's 3d.	6. Q. Kt. to B's 3d.
7. Q. to K's 3d (ch.)	7. K. to B's 2d.
8. K. Kt. to K's 2d.	8. B. to Q. Kt's 5th (ch.)
9. P. to Q. B's 3d.	9. R. to K's sq.
10. Q. to K. Kt's 3d.	10. K. B. to Q's 3d.

His game is better developed.

THE QUEEN'S BISHOP'S PAWN'S DEFENCE IN THE KING'S BISHOP'S OPENING.

WHITE.	BLACK.
1. P. to K's 4th.	1. P. to K's 4th.
2. K. B. to Q. B's 4th	2. P. to Q. B's 3d.
3. Q. to K's 2d.	3. K. Kt. to B's 3d.
4. P. to K. B's 4th.	4. P. to Q's 3d.
5. P. takes P.	5. P. takes P.
6. K. Kt. to B's 3d.	6. K. B. to Q's 3d.
7. P. to Q's 4th.	7. P. takes P.
8. P. to K's 5th.	8. Castles.
9. Castles.	9. K. B. to Q. B's 4th
10. Q. to her 3d.	10. Kt. to Q's 4th.
11. Kt. to his 5th.	11. P. to K. Kt's 3d.
12. Kt. to K's 4th.	12. B. to K's 2d.
13. B. takes Kt.	13. P. takes B.
14. Kt. to B's 6th (ch.)	14. B. takes Kt.
15. P. takes B.	

You have a fine game.

VARIATION,
Beginning at White's 3d move

WHITE.	BLACK.
1 P. to K's 4th.	1. P. to K's 4th

KING'S BISHOP'S OPENING.

2. K. B. to Q. B's 4th.   2. P. to Q. B's 3d.
3. P. to Q's 4th.   3. K. Kt. to B's 3d.
4. P. takes K. P.   4. Q. to Q. R's 4th (ch.)
5. P. to Q. B's 3d.   5. Q. takes K. P.
6. B. to Q's 3d.   6. K. B. to Q. B's 4th.
7. P. to K. B's 4th.   7 Q. to K's 2d.
8. P. to K's 5th.

The game is in your favor.

GAMES

ILLUSTRATIVE OF THE PRECEDING ANALYSES.

GAME I.—Between Messrs. Stanley and Rousseau.

WHITE. (Mr. S.)	BLACK. (Mr. R.)
1. P. to K's 4th.	1. P. to K's 4th.
2. K. B. to Q. B's 4th.	2. K. Kt. to B's 3d.
3. Q. Kt. to B's 3d.	3. K. B. to Q. B's 4th.
4. K. Kt. to B's 3d.	4. P. to Q's 3d.
5. P. to K. R's 3d.	5. Castles.
6. P. to Q's 3d.	6. Q. B. to K's 3d.
7. K. B. to Q. Kt's 3d.	7. Q. Kt. to B's 3d.
8. Q. Kt. to K's 2d.	8. Q. to K's 2d.
9. Q. Kt. to K. Kt's 3d.	9. Q. Kt. to Q's 5th.
10. Kt. takes Kt.	10. B. takes Kt.
11. P. to Q. B's 3d.*	11. B. to Q. Kt's 3d.
12. Castles.	12. P. to Q's 4th.†
13. Q. B. to K. Kt's 5th.	13. P. to Q. B's 3d.
14. Kt. to K. R's 5th.	14. P. takes K. P.
15. P. takes P.	15. B. takes B.
16. Q. to K. B's 3d.‡	16. Q. B. to his 5th.
17. B. takes Kt.	17. Q. to K's 3d.
18. Kt. takes K. Kt. P	18. Q. B. to K's 7th.
19. Kt. takes Q.	19. B. takes Q.
20. Kt. takes R.	

Black surrenders.

---

* White gains a move by this exchange of Pieces.
† P. to K. R's 3d would have been better play.
‡ This is very finely played, and is an example to young players of the importance of gaining time at chess. Had White paused in his attack to recover the lost Bishop, the adversary might have succeeded in dislodging one or other of the Pieces by which he is beleaguered, or in bringing his own forces to the rescue, and then have ultimately retrieved the game.

GAME II.—Between Messrs. Horwitz and Schulten

WHITE. (Mr. S.)   BLACK. (Mr. H.)
1. P. to K's 4th.   1. P. to K's 4th.
2. K. B. to Q. B's 4th.   2. K. Kt. to B's 3d.
3. Q. Kt. to B's 3d.   3. P. to Q. Kt's 4th.
4. B. takes Kt. P.   4. B. to Q. B's 4th.
5. P. to Q's 3d.   5. P. to Q. B's 3d.
6. B. to Q. B's 4th.   6. Q. to her Kt's 3d.
7. Q. to K's 2d.   7. P. to Q's 4th.
8. P. takes P.   8. Castles.
9. Q. Kt. to K's 4th.   9. Kt. takes Kt.
10. P. takes Kt.   10. B. takes K. B. P. (ch.)*
11. Q. takes B.   11. Q. to Kt's 5th (ch.)
12. Q. B. to Q's 2d.   12. Q. takes K. B.
13. Q. to K. B's 3d.   13. P. to K. B's 4th.
14. P. takes K. B. P.   14. B. takes P.
15. Q. to her Kt's 3d.

And Black mated by force in three moves.†

GAME III.—Between Dr. Bledow and Von Bilguer.

WHITE. (Dr. B.)   BLACK. (Von B.)
1. P. to K's 4th.   1. P. to K's 4th.
2. K. B. to Q. B's 4th.   2. P. to K. B's 4th.
3. P. to Q's 3d.   3. K. Kt. to B's 3d.
4. K. Kt. to B's 3d.   4. P. takes K. P.
5. P. takes P.   5. Kt. takes P.
6. Q. to her 5th.   6. Kt. to Q's 3d.
7. Kt. takes K. P.   7. P. to Q. B's 3d.
8. Q. to K. B's 7th.   8. Kt. takes Q.
9. B. takes Kt. (ch.)   9. K. to his 2d.
10. Q. B. to K. Kt's 5th (ch.)   10. K. to Q's 3d.
11. B. takes Q.   11. K. takes Kt.
12. P. to K. B's 4th (ch.)   12. K. to his B's 4th.
13. Q. B. to K. Kt's 5th.   13. K. B. checks.
14. P. to Q. B's 3d.   14. K. R. to B's sq.
15. K. B. to Q. Kt's 3d.   15. P. to K. R's 3d.
16. K. B. to Q. B's 2d (ch.)   16. K. to Kt's 5th.
17. K. B. to Q's sq. (ch.)   17. K. to B's 4th.
18. P. to K. Kt's 4th (ch.)   18. K. to Kt's 3d.
19. B. to Q. B's 2d (ch.)   19. K. to B's 2d.
20. Q. B. to K. R's 4th.   20. K. B. to K's 2d.
21. Q. B. to K. Kt's 3d.   21. P. to Q's 4th.
22. P. to K. B's 5th   22. Kt. to Q's 2d.
23. Kt. to Q's 2d.   23. K. B. to his 3d.

---

* Black plays capitally now to the end.
† It is rarely in actual play one sees so pretty a mate

KING'S BISHOP'S OPENING.

24. Kt. to K. B's 3d.
25. K. to his B's 2d.
26. K. R. to K's sq.
27. P. to Q. Kt's 4th.
28. R. takes Kt.*
29. B. to Q. Kt's 3d (ch.)
30. B. to Q's 6th (ch.)
31. Kt. to K's 5th.
32. P. to K. B's 6th.‡*
33. K. to Kt's sq.

24. R. to K's sq. (ch.)
25. Kt. to Q. B's 4th.
26. Q. B. to Q's 2d.
27. Kt. to K's 5th (ch.)
28. P. takes R.
29. K. to B's sq.
30. B. to K's 2d.
31. P. to K. Kt's 4th.†
32. P. to K's 6th (ch.)

Black resigns.

GAME IV.—Played between two Amateurs.

WHITE.	BLACK.
1. P. to K's 4th.	1. P. to K's 4th.
2. B. to Q. B's 4th.	2. P. to Q. B's 3d.
3. Q. to K's 2d.	3. Q. to Q. B's 2d.
4. P. to Q. B's 3d.	4. K. Kt. to B's 3d.
5. P. to K. B's 4th.	5. P. to Q's 3d.
6. P. to K. B's 5th.	6. P. to Q's 4th.
7. P. takes P.	7. P. takes P.
8. B. checks.	8. B. to Q's 2d.
9. B. takes B. (ch.)	9. Q. Kt. takes B.
10. P. to Q's 4th.	10. P. to K's 5th.
11. K. Kt. to R's 3d.	11. Castles.
12. Castles.	12. B. to Q's 3d.
13. Kt. to K. B's 4th.	13. P. to K. R's 3d.
14. Q. to K. B's 2d.	14. K. Kt. to his 5th.
15. Q. to K's 2d.	15. P. to K. R's 4th.
16. Kt. takes Q. P.	16. B. takes K. R. P. (ch)
17. K. to R's sq.	17. Q. to her 3d.
18. Q. takes K. P.	18. K. R. to K's sq.
19. Q. to K. B's 3d.	19. P. to K. Kt's 3d.
20. B. to K. Kt's 5th.	20. P. to K. B's 3d.
21. B. to Q's 2d.	21. P. to K. Kt's 4th.
22. Q. Kt. to R's 3d.	22. P. to Q. R's 4th.
23. Q. Kt. to Q. B's 4th.	23. Q. to her B's 3d.
24. Q. Kt. takes P.	24. Q. to Kt's 4th.
25. P. to Q. B's 4th.	25. Q. to R's 5th.
26. K. Kt. to Q. Kt's 6th (ch.)	26. Kt. takes Kt.
27. Q. takes P.	

Mate.

---

* The terminating moves are admirably played by Dr. Bledow.
† It is quite evident that on taking the B., mate would have followed next move.
‡ Beautifully played.

Queen's Bishop's Pawn's Opening.

GAME THE FIRST.

WHITE.	BLACK.
1. P. to K's 4th.	1. P. to K's 4th.
2. P. to Q. B's 3d.	2. P. to Q's 4th (best)
3. K. Kt. to B's 3d	3. P. takes K. P.
4. Kt. takes K. P.	4. K. B. to Q's 3d.
5. Kt. to Q. B's 4th.	5. Q. B. to K's 3d.
6. P. to Q's 4th.	6. P. takes P. in passing
7. B. takes P.	

The positions are equal.

VARIATION,
Beginning at Black's 3d move.

WHITE.	BLACK.
1. P. to K's 4th.	1. P. to K's 4th.
2. P. to Q. B's 3d.	2. P. to Q's 4th (best.)
3. K Kt. to B's 3d.	3. K. Kt. to B's 3d.
4. P. to Q's 4th.	4. Kt. takes P.
5. Kt. takes P.	5. K. B. to Q's 3d.
6. K. Kt. to Q's 3d.	6. P. to Q. B's 4th.
7. P. takes P.	7. Kt. takes P.
8. Q. B. to K's 3d.	8. Kt. takes Kt. (ch.)
9. B. takes Kt.	9. Q. Kt. to B's 3d.
10 Castles.	10. Castles.

Neither party has the advantage.

GAME THE SECOND.

WHITE.	BLACK.
1. P. to K's 4th.	1. P. to K's 4th.
2. P. to Q. B's 3d	2. K. Kt. to B's 3d.
3. P. to Q's 4th.	3. K. Kt. takes K. P.
4. Q. P. takes P.	4. P. to Q's 4th (best)
5. Q. B. to K's 3d.	

The game is quite even.

GAMES

ILLUSTRATIVE OF THE QUEEN'S BISHOP'S PAWN'S OPENING.

GAME I.—Between Captain Evans and an Amateur.

WHITE. (Capt. E.)	BLACK. (Mr. P.)
1. P. to K's 4th.	1. P. to K's 4th.
2. P. to Q. B's 3d.	2. K. Kt. to B's 3d.
3. P. to Q's 4th.	3. P. takes P.
4. P. to K's 5th.	4. Kt. to K's 5th.
5. Q. to K's 2d.	5. Kt. to his 4th.
6. P. takes P.	6. B. to Q. Kt's 5th (ch.)
7. Q. Kt. to B's 3d.	7. Q. Kt. to B's 3d.
8. Q. to her 3d.	8. P. to Q's 4th.
9. P. to K. B's 4th.	9. Kt. to K's 5th.
10. K. Kt. to B's 3d.	10. Q. B. to K. B's 4th.
11. Q. to K's 3d.	11. Castles.
12. P. to Q. R's 3d.	12. B. to Q. R's 4th.
13. P. to Q. Kt's 4th.	13. B. to Q. Kt's 3d.
14. Q. B. to Kt's 2d.	14. Q. B. to Kt's 5th.
15. Q. Kt. to Q. R's 4th.	15. B. takes K. Kt.
16. Q. Kt. takes B.	16. B. takes K. Kt. P.
17. B. takes B.	17. Q. to K. R's 5th (ch.)
18. K. to his 2d.	18. Q. R. P. takes Kt.
19. B. takes Kt.	19. P. takes B.
20. Q. takes P.	20. Q. to Kt's 5th (ch.)
21. Q. to K. B's 3d.	21. Q. to K. B's 4th.
22. Q. R. to Q. B's sq.	22. Q. Kt. takes Q. Kt. P.
23. K. R. to K. Kt's sq.*	23. Q. Kt. to B's 3d.
24. K. R. to Kt's 5th.	24. Q. to her 2d.
25. P. to Q's 5th.	25. Kt. to K's 2d.
26. K. R. takes K. Kt. P. (ch.)	26. K. to R's sq.
27. Q. to her 3d.	27. Kt. to K. Kt's 3d.
28. R. takes Kt.	28. Q. R. to K's sq.
29. K. to B's 2d.†	29. R. to K's 3d.
30. R. to K. Kt's 3d.	30. R. to Q's sq.
31. P. takes R.	31. Q. to K's 2d.‡
32. P. takes P.	

Black surrenders.

GAME II.—Between Messrs. Cochrane and Staunton.

WHITE. (Mr. S.)	BLACK. (Mr. C.)
1. P. to K's 4th.	1. P. to K's 4th.

---

* Black played ingeniously in offering to give up the Kt. If White had taken it, he must have been subjected to an embarrassing attack for some little time.

† Had he played on the P. (dis. ch.), he could not take the Q. until his King was removed.

‡ Taking the Q. would have been fatal to him.

2. P. to Q. B's 3d.	2. P. to Q's 4th.
3. K. Kt. to B's 3d.	3. K. Kt. to B's 3d.
4. K. Kt. takes P.	4. K. Kt. takes P.
5. P. to Q's 4th.	5. K. B. to Q's 3d.
6. Q. Kt. to Q's 2d.	6. Castles.
7. Q. Kt. takes K. Kt	7. P. takes Kt.
8. Q. B. to K. B's 4th	8. B. takes Kt.
9. Q. B. takes B.	9. Q. Kt. to B's 3d.
10. K. B. to Q. B's 4th.	10. Q. B. to K's 3d.
11. K. B. to Q. Kt's 5th.	11. Q. Kt. to K's 2d.
12. Castles.	12. P. to Q. B's 3d.
13. K. B. to Q. R's 4th.	13. Q. Kt. to K. Kt's 3d.
14. Q. B. to K. Kt's 3d.	14. P. to K. B's 4th.
15. P. to K. B's 4th.	15. P. takes P. in passing
16. R. takes P.	16. P. to K. B's 5th.
17. K. B. to Q. Kt's 3d.*	17. Q. to her 3d.
18. Q. B. to K. B's 2d.	18. K. to R's sq.
19. K. B. takes B.	19. Q. takes B.
20. Q. to her 3d.	20. Q. R. to K's sq.
21. K. R. to K. R's 3d.	21. Q. to K. B's 4th.
22. Q. to K. B's 3d.	22. Q. R. to K's 5th.
23. K. R. to his 5th.	23. Q. to K's 3d.
24. P. to Q. B's 4th.	24. K. R. to K's sq.
25. P. to Q. Kt's 3d.	25. Q. to K. B's 3d.
26. Q. R. to K. B's sq.	26. Q. R. to K's 7th.
27. P. to Q. R's 4th.	27. Q. R. to his 7th.
28. P. to Q's 5th.	28. Q. R. to his 8th.
29. Q. B. takes Q. R. P.†	29. K. R. to K's 8th.
30. R. takes R.	30. R. takes R. (ch.)
31. K. to B's 2d.	31. Q. to her R's 8th.‡
32. Q. to her 3d.	32. R. to K. Kt's 8th.
33. Q. to K's 2d.	33. Kt. to K's 2d.
34. P. to Q's 6th.	

And wins.

GAME III.—Between Capt. Evans and M. St. Amant

WHITE. (Capt. E.)	BLACK. (M. St. A.)
1. P. to K's 4th.	1. P. to K's 4th.
2. P. to Q. B's 3d.	2. P. to Q. B's 4th.
3. K. Kt. to B's 3d.	3. Q. Kt. to B's 3d.
4. K. B. to Q. B's 4th.	4. K. Kt. to B's 3d.
5. P. to Q's 4th.	5. Q. B. P. takes P.
6. K. Kt. to Kt's 5th.§	6. P. to Q's 4th.
7. P. takes P.	7. K. Kt. takes P.
8. K. Kt. takes K. B. P.	8. K. takes Kt.

* But for this move of resource, Black would evidently have gained "the exchange," at least.
† An important outlet for his King.
‡ Black has now a very menacing position.
§ We have here a position almost identical with the leading one of the "Two Knights' Game."

KING'S BISHOP'S OPENING.

9. Q. to K. B's 3d (ch.)   9. K. to his 3d.
10. Castles.   10. Q. Kt. to R's 4th.
11. Q. B. to K. Kt's 5th.   11. Q. to her 3d.
12. P. to K. Kt's 4th.   12. Q. to her 2d.
13. K. B. to Q's 3d.   13. Q. to K. B's 2d.
14. B. to K. B's 4th (ch.)   14. K. to Q's 3d.
15. P. takes Q. P.   15. Q. B. takes B.
16. P. takes P. (ch.)   16. K. takes P.
17. P. takes B.   17. Q. Kt. to B's 3d.
18. K. R. to K's sq. (ch.)   18. K. to Q's 3d.
19. R. to K's 6th (ch.)   19. K. to Q. B's 4th.
20. Q. B. to K's 3d (ch.)   20. K. Kt. takes B.
21. Q. takes K. Kt. (ch.)   21. K. to Kt's 4th.
22. Q. to her 3d (ch.)   22. K. to Kt's 3d.
23. Q. to her Kt's 3d (ch.)   23. K. to B's 2d.
24. R. takes Kt. (ch.) and wins.

GAME IV.—Between M. St. Amant and Mr. G. Walker

WHITE. (Mr. W.)   BLACK. (M. St. A.)
1. P. to K's 4th.   1. P. to K's 4th.
2. P. to Q. B's 3d.   2. P. to Q's 4th.
3. P. takes P.   3. Q. takes P.
4. K. Kt. to B's 3d.   4. K. B. to Q. B's 4th.
5. P. to Q. Kt's 3d.   5. Q. B. to K. Kt's 5th.
6. K. B. to K's 2d.   6. P. to K's 5th.
7. Kt. to Q's 4th.   7. B. takes B.
8. Kt. takes B.   8. Q. Kt. to B's 3d.
9. Castles.   9. Q. Kt. to K's 4th.
10. Kt. to K. B's 4th.   10. Q. to her 3d.
11. P. to Q's 4th.   11. P. takes P. in passing.
12. K. R. to K's sq.   12. Castles.
13. Q. Kt. to Q's 2d.   13. P. to K. B's 4th.
14. P. to Q. R's 4th.   14. P. to Q. R's 4th.
15. P. to Q. Kt's 4th.   15. P. takes P.
16. P. takes P.   16. B. to Q's 5th.
17. Q. R. to Kt's sq.   17. K. Kt. to B's 3d.
18. Kt. to Q. Kt's 3d.   18. K. Kt. to Kt's 5th.
19. Kt. takes B.   19. Q. takes Kt.
20. B. to K's 3d.   20. Q. to her 3d.
21. B. to Q. B's 5th.   21. Q. to K. R's 3d.
22. Kt. to K. R's 3d.   22. K. R. to K's sq.
23. P. to Q. R's 5th.   23. P. to Q's 7th.
24. R. to K. B's sq.   24. Kt. to Q's 6th.
25. P. to Q. R's 6th.   25. P. takes P.
26. Q. to K. B's 3d.   26. K. R. to K's 5th.
27. Q. takes P. (ch.)   27. Q. to K's 3d.
28. Q. takes Q. (ch.)   28. R. takes Q.
29. Kt. to K. Kt's 5th.   29. R. to K's 8th.
30. B. to K's 3d.   30. Kt. takes B.
31. P. takes Kt.   31. R. takes R. (ch.)
32. K. takes R.   32. Kt. to Q. B's 8th.

And Black wins.

CHAPTER IV.

THE KING'S GAMBIT.

This opening comprises every variety of the game in which the first player, after 1. P. to K's 4th has been played on both sides, commences the attack by moving 2. P. to K. B's 4th. Should the second player take this Pawn with his King's Pawn, he is said to accept the gambit.

This gambit has many modifications, the names appropriated to which will be found in their proper places in the following pages.

THE KING'S GAMBIT PROPER, OR KING'S KNIGHT'S GAMBIT.

GAME THE FIRST.

WHITE.	BLACK.
1. P. to K's 4th.	1. P. to K's 4th.
2. P. to K. B's 4th.	2. P. takes P.
3. K. Kt. to B's 3d.	3. P. to K. Kt's 4th.
4. K. B. to Q. B's 4th.	4. B. to K. Kt's 2d (best)
5. P. to Q's 4th.	5. P. to Q's 3d.
6. P. to Q. B's 3d.	6. P. to K. Kt.'s 5th (best)
7. Kt. to his sq.	7. Q. to K. R's 5th (ch)
8. K. to B's sq.	8. K. B. to K. R's 3d.
9. Q. to her Kt.'s 3d.	9. Q. to K. R's 4th.

You can bring no Piece into action with advantage, while the field is all before him where to choose.

KING'S GAMBIT.

GAME THE SECOND.

WHITE.	BLACK.
1. P. to K's 4th.	1. P. to K's 4th.
2. P. to K. B's 4th.	2. P. takes P.
3. K. Kt. to B's 3d.	3. P. to K. Kt's 4th.
4. K. B. to Q. B's 4th.	4. B. to K. Kt's 2d.
5. P. to K. R's 4th.	5. P. to K. R's 3d (best)
6. P. to Q's 4th.	6. P. to Q's 3d.
7. P. to Q. B's 3d.	7. P. to K. Kt's 5th.
8. Q. B. takes P.	8. P. takes Kt.
9. Q. takes P.	9. Q. B. to K's 3d.
10. Q. Kt. to Q's 2d.	10. K. Kt. to K's 2d.
11. P. to K. R's 5th.	11. B. takes B.
12. Kt. takes B.	12. P. to Q. Kt's 4th.
13. Kt. to K's 3d.	13. Q. Kt. to B's 3d.

You have no adequate compensation for the Piece you are minus.

VARIATION I.

Beginning at White's 7th move.

WHITE.	BLACK.
1. P. to K's 4th.	1. P. to K's 4th.
2. P. to K. B's 4th.	2. P. takes P.
3. K. Kt. to B's 3d.	3. P. to K. Kt's 4th
4. K. B. to Q. B's 4th.	4. B. to K. Kt's 2d
5. P. to K. R's 4th.	5. P. to K. R's 3d.
6. P. to Q's 4th.	6. P. to Q's 3d.
7. Q. Kt. to B's 3d.	7. P. to Q. B's 3d.
8. P. takes K. Kt. P.	8. P. takes P.
9. R. takes R.	9. B. takes R.
10. K. Kt. to K's 5th.	10. P. takes Kt.
11. Q. to K. R's 5th.	11. Q. to K. B's 3d.
12. P. takes K. P.	12. Q. to K. Kt's 2d.
13. P. to K's 6th.	13. B. takes P. (best)
14. B. takes B.	14. K. Kt. to B's 3d.
15. B. takes K. B. P. (ch.)	15. K. to his 2d.
16. Q to K. Kt's 6th.	16. Q. takes B.

The advantage is all on Black's side.

GAME THE THIRD.

WHITE.	BLACK.
1. P. to K's 4th.	1. P. to K's 4th.
2. P. to K. B's 4th.	2. P. takes P.
3. K. Kt. to B's 3d.	3. P. to K. Kt's 4th.
4. B. to Q. B's 4th.	4. B. to K. Kt's 2d.
5. Castles.	5. P. to Q's 3d (best)
6. P. to Q's 4th.	6. P. to K. R's 3d.
7. P. to Q. B's 3d.	7. Q. B. to K's 3d.
8. B. takes B.	8. P. takes B.
9. Q. to her Kt's 3d.	9. Q. to her B's sq.
10. P. to K. R's 4th	10. P. to K. Kt's 5th.
11. Kt. to K. R's 2d.	11. P. to K. Kt's 6th.

He has a Pawn more and a strong position.

GAMES

ILLUSTRATIVE OF THE FOREGOING ANALYSES.

GAME I.—Between V. H. der Laza and Dr. Bledow.

WHITE. (V. H. d. L.)	BLACK. (Dr. B.)
1. P. to K's 4th.	1. P. to K's 4th.
2. P. to K. B's 4th.	2. P. takes P.
3. K. Kt. to B's 3d.	3. P. to K. Kt's 4th.
4. K. B. to Q. B's 4th.	4. K. B. to Kt's 2d.
5. P. to Q's 4th.	5. Q. to K's 2d.*
6. Castles.	6. P. to K. R's 3d.
7. Q. Kt. to B's 3d.	7. P. to Q. B's 3d.
8. P. to K's 5th.	8. Q. to her Kt's 5th.
9. Q. Kt. to K's 4th.	9. K. B. to his sq.
10. Q. to K's 2d.†	10. P. to K. Kt's 5th.
11. Kt. to Q's 6th (ch.)	11. B. takes Kt.
12. P. takes B. (disc. ch.)	12. K. to Q's sq.
13. Kt. to K's 5th.	13. R. to R's 2d.
14. P. to Q. B's 3d.	14. P. to K. B's 6th.
15. Q. to K's 4th.	15. K. Kt. to B's 3d.
16. Q. takes R.	16. Kt. takes Q.

And White gave checkmate in six moves.

---

* The proper move is 5. P. to Q's 3d.
† This little game is excellently played by White.

KING'S GAMBIT.

GAME II.—Between V. H. der Laza and Mr. H. of Berlin

WHITE. (V. H. d. L.)	BLACK. (Mr. H.)
1. P. to K's 4th.	1. P. to K's 4th.
2. P. to K. B's 4th.	2. P. takes P.
3. K. Kt. to B's 3d.	3. P. to K. Kt's 4th.
4. K. B. to Q. B's 4th.	4. B. to K. Kt's 2d.
5. Castles.	5. P. to K. R's 3d.
6. P. to Q's 4th.	6. P. to Q's 3d.
7. P. to Q. B's 3d.	7. P. to Q. B's 3d.
8. Q. to her Kt's 3d.*	8. Q. to K's 2d.
9. P. to K. Kt's 3d.	9. P. to K. Kt's 5th.
10. Q. B. takes P.	10. P. takes Kt.
11. R. takes P.	11. Q. B. to K's 3d.
12. P. to Q's 5th.	12. Q. B. to K. Kt's 5th.
13. P. takes Q. B. P.	13. B. takes R.
14. P. takes Kt. P.	14. Q. takes K. P.
15. P. takes R. (becoming a Q.)	15. Q. takes Q.
16. B. takes K. B. P. (ch.)	16. K. to B's sq.
17. B. takes Kt.	17. R. takes B.
18. B. takes Q. P. (ch.)	18. K. to K's sq.

White mates in three moves.†

GAME III.—Between Mr. Popert and an eminent Polish player.

WHITE. (Mr. Z.)	BLACK. (Mr. P.)
1. P. to K's 4th.	1. P. to K's 4th.
2. P. to K. B's 4th.	2. P. takes P.
3. K. Kt. to B's 3d.	3. P. to K. Kt's 4th.
4. B. to Q. B's 4th.	4. B. to Q. Kt's 2d.
5. P. to Q's 4th.	5. P. to Q's 3d.
6. Castles.	6. P. to K. R's 3d.
7. P. to K. Kt's 3d.	7. P. to K's Kt's 5th.
8. K. Kt. to R's 4th.	8. P. to K. B's 6th.
9. Q. B. to K's 3d.	9. Q. Kt. to B's 3d.
10. P. to Q. B's 3d.	10. K. B. to B's 3d.
11. K. Kt. to K. B's 5th.	11. Q. B. takes Kt.
12. P. takes B.	12. K. Kt. to K's 2d.
13. Q. to her Kt's 3d.	13. P. to Q's 4th.
14. K. B. to Q's 3d.	14. Q. to her 2d.
15. Q. to her B's 2d.	15. P. to K. R's 4th.
16. Kt. to Q's 2d.	16. P. to K. R's 5th.
17. Q. B. to K. B's 4th.	17. Castles on Q's side.
18. P. to Q. R's 4th.	18. P. takes K. Kt. P.
19. Q. B. takes K. Kt's P.	19. K. R. to his 4th.

* Having now your Q. P. protected, and an opening for your Queen, you can advantageously advance the K. Kt's P., and sacrifice your Kt., as in the Muzio Gambit.

† A brilliant and amusing little skirmish.

20. P. to Q. Kt's 4th.	20. K. Kt. takes K. B. P.
21. B. takes Kt.	21. Q. takes B.
22. Q. to her Kt's 2d.	22. B. to K. R's 5th.
23. B. takes B.	23. R. takes B.
24. P. to Q. R's 5th.	24. R. takes K. R. P.
25. K. takes R.	

Black mates in three moves.

The Cunningham Gambit.

GAME THE FIRST.

WHITE.	BLACK.
1. P. to K's 4th.	1. P. to K's 4th.
2. P. to K. B's 4th.	2. P. takes P.
3. K. Kt. to B's 3d.	3. K. B. to K's 2d.

Black's 3d move commences the variation known as the "Cunningham Gambit."

4. K. B. to Q. B's 4th.	4. B. to R's 5th (ch)
5. K. to B's sq.	5. K. B. to his 3d.
6. P. to K's 5th.	6. B. to K's 2d.
7. P. to Q's 4th.	7. P. to Q's 4th.
8. K. B. to K's 2d.	8. P. to K. Kt's 4th.
9. P. to K. R's 4th.	9. P. to K. Kt's 5th.
10. K. Kt to K. R's 2d.	10. P. to K. R's 4th.
11. Q. B. takes P.	11. K. B. takes K. R. P.
12. P. to K. Kt's 3d.	12. B. to K. Kt's 4th.
13. Kt. takes K. Kt. P.	

You must win.

GAME THE SECOND.

WHITE.	BLACK.
1. P. to K's 4th.	1. P. to K's 4th.
2. P. to K. B's 4th.	2. P. takes P.
3. K. Kt. to B's 3d.	3. B. to K's 2d.
4. K. B. to Q. B's 4th.	4. B. to K. R's 5th (ch.)
5. P. to K. Kt's 3d.	5. P. takes P.
6. Castles.	6. P. takes P. (ch.)
7. K. to R's sq.	7. K. B. to his 3d.
8. K. Kt. to K's 5th.	8. B. takes Kt. (best)

KING'S GAMBIT.

9. Q. to K. R's 5th.	9. Q. to K's 2d (best)
10 R. takes K. B. P.	10. Q. to her B's 4th
11 R. to K. B's 8th (dble. ch.)	11. K. to his 2d.
12. P. to Q's 4th.	12. Q. takes P. (best)
13. Q. B. checks.	13. K. to Q's 3d (best)
14 Q. Kt. to Q's 2d.	14. K. Kt. to B's 3d.
15. Q. to K. B's 7th.	15. Kt. takes K. P.
16. Q. B. to K's 3d.	16. K. Kt. to his 6th (ch.)
17. K. to Kt's 2d.	17. Q. takes B.
18. Q. to her 5th (ch.)	18. K. to his 2d.
19 Q. to K. B's 7th (ch.)	19. K. to Q's 3d.

Drawn game.

VARIATION,
Beginning at Black's 7th move.

WHITE.	BLACK.
	7. P. to Q's 4th.
8. B. takes P.	8. K. Kt. to B's 3d.
9. B. takes K. B. P. (ch.)	9. K. takes B.
10. Kt. takes K. B.	10. K. R. to B's sq.
11. P. to Q's 4th.	11. K. to Kt.'s sq.
12. Q. B. to K. Kt's 5th.	12. K. Kt. takes K. P.
13 B. takes Q.	13. R. takes R. (ch.)
14. Q. takes R.	14. Kt. to his 6th (ch.)
15 K. takes P.	15. Kt. takes Q (ch.)

He has the better game.

ANOTHER VARIATION.

WHITE.	BLACK.
	7. B. to K's 2d.
8 B. takes B. P. (ch.)	8. K. takes B.
9. Kt. to K's 5th. (dble. ch.)	9. K. to his 3d (best)
10. Q. to K. Kt's 4th (ch.)	10. K. takes Kt.
11. Q. to K. B's 5th (ch.)	11. K. to Q's 3d.
12. Q. to her 5th.	

And wins.

GAME

ILLUSTRATIVE OF THE CUNNINGHAM GAMBIT

Between two members of the Berlin Chess Club.

WHITE. (V. H. d. L.)	BLACK. (M. J.)
1. P. to K's 4th.	1. P. to K's 4th.
2. P. to K. B's 4th.	2. P. takes P.
3. K. Kt. to B's 3d.	3. K. B. to K's 2d.
4. K. B. to Q. B's 4th.	4. B. to K. R's 5th (ch.)
5. P. to K. Kt's 3d.*	5. P. takes P.
6. Castles.	6. P. takes P. (ch.)
7. K. to R's sq.	7. K. B. to B's 3d.
8. Kt. to K's 5th.	8. B. takes Kt.
9. Q. to K. R's 5th.	9. Q. to K's 2d.
10. R. takes K. B. P.	10. Q. to her B's 4th.
11. R. to K. B's 8th (dble ch.)	11. K. to his 2d.
12. P. to Q's 4th.	12. Q. takes P.†
13. B. to K. Kt's 5th (ch.)	13. K. Kt. to B's 3d.‡
14. B. takes Kt. (ch.)	14. P. takes B.
15. Q. to K. B's 7th (ch.)	15. K. to Q's 3d.
16. Q. Kt. to B's 3d.	16. R. takes R.
17. Q. takes R. (ch.)	17. K. to B's 3d.
18. Q. to her Kt's 4th.	18. P. to Q's 4th.
19. B. to Kt's 5th (ch.)	19. K. to Kt's 3d.
20. Kt. mates.	

THE SALVIO GAMBIT

GAME THE FIRST.

WHITE.	BLACK.
1. P. to K's 4th.	1. P. to K's 4th.
2. P. to K. B's 4th.	2. P. takes P.
3. K. Kt. to B's 3d.	3. P. to K. Kt's 4th.
4. K. B. to Q. B's 4th.	4. P. to K. Kt's 5th.
5. Kt. to K's 5th.	5. Q. to K. R's 5th (ch)
6. K. to B's sq.	6. K. Kt. to B's 3d.

It is this move of Black that constitutes the Salvio defence.

7. Q. to K's sq. (best)	7. Q. takes Q. (ch., best)
8. K. takes Q.	8. Kt. takes K. P.
9. B. takes K. B. P. (ch.)	9. K. to his 2d (best).

---

* The correct reply is 5. K. to B's sq.
† The best move.
‡ K. to Q's 3d is the proper play.

KING'S GAMBIT. 145

10. B. to K. R's 5th.   10. P. to K. Kt's 6th.
11. P. to K. R's 3d.   11 P. to Q's 3d.
12. K. Kt. to Q's 3d.   12 K. B. to R's 3d.
13. Q. Kt. to B's 3d.   13 Kt. takes Kt.
14. Q. P. takes Kt.   14. R. to K. B's sq.
15. R. to K. B's sq.   15. Q. B. to K. B's 4th
16. Kt. takes P.   16. B. takes Kt.
17. B. takes B.   17. K. R. to K. Kt's sq
18. B. takes Q. P. (ch.)   18. P. takes B.
19. R. takes B.   19. K. R. to Kt's 2d.

You have a Pawn more and an advantage in position.

GAME THE SECOND.

WHITE.   BLACK.
1. P. to K's 4th.   1. P. to K's 4th.
2. P. to K. B's 4th.   2. P takes P.
3. K. Kt. to B's 3d   3. P. to K. Kt's 4th.
4. B. to Q B's 4th.   4. P. to K. Kt's 5th.
5. Kt. to K's 5th.   5. Q. to K. R's 5th (ch.)
6. K. to B's sq.   6. K. Kt. to R's 3d.
7. P. to Q's 4th.   7. P. to K. B's 6th.
8. P. takes P.   8. P. to Q's 3d.
9 Kt. to Q's 3d.   9. K. Kt. P. takes P.
10. K. Kt. to K. B's 2d.   10. Q. B. to K. R's 6th (ch.)
11. Kt. takes B.   11. Q. takes Kt. (ch.)
12. K. to B's 2d.   12. Q. to Kt's 7th (ch.)
13. K. to his 3d.   13. Kt. to his 5th (ch.)
14. K. to B's 4th.   14. B. to R's 3d (ch.)

And he mates you in two moves.

VARIATION,

Beginning from White's 8th move.

WHITE.   BLACK.
1. P. to K's 4th.   1. P. to K's 4th
2. P. to K. B's 4th.   2. P. takes P.
3 K. Kt. to B's 3d.   3. P. to K Kt's 4th

4. B. to Q. B's 4th.	4. P. to K. Kt's 5th.
5. Kt. to K's 5th.	5. Q. to K. R's 5th (ch)
6. K. to B's sq.	6. K. Kt. to R's 3d.
7. P. to Q's 4th.	7. P. to K. B's 6th.
8. Q. B. to K. B's 4th	8. P. takes P. (ch.)
9. K. takes P.	9. P. to Q's 3d.
10. B. takes K. Kt.	10. B. takes B.
11. Kt. to Q's 3d.	11. Q. to R's 6th (ch.)
12. K. to B's 2d.	12. Q. to K's 6th (ch.)
13. K. to B's sq.	13. P. to Kt's 6th.

He has a fine attack

THE COCHRANE GAMBIT.

GAME THE FIRST.

WHITE.	BLACK.
1. P. to K's 4th.	1. P. to K's 4th.
2. P. to K. B's 4th.	2. P. takes P.
3. K. Kt. to B's 3d.	3. P. to K. Kt's 4th.
4. B. to Q. B's 4th.	4. P. to K. Kt's 5th.
5. Kt. to K's 5th.	5. Q. to K. R's 5th (ch.)
6. K. to B's sq.	6. P. to K. B's 6th.

In the previous Gambit you will remember Salvio advances this P. one move later, that is, after his K. Kt. is moved to B's 3d, or R's 3d sq.

7. P. to Q's 4th (best)	7. P. takes K. Kt. P (ch., best.)
8. K. takes P.	8. Q. to R's 6th (ch.)
9. K. to Kt's sq.	9. K. Kt. to R's 3d.
10. Q. to her 3d.	10. Q. takes Q.
11. P. takes Q.	11. P. to Q's 3d.
12. B. takes Kt.	12. B. takes B.
13. Kt. takes K. B. P	13. B. to K's 6th (ch.)
14. K. to Kt's 2d.	14. R. to B's sq.
15 R. to B's sq	15. B. takes Q P

He ought to win.

KING'S GAMBIT.

GAME THE SECOND.

	WHITE.	BLACK.
1	P. to K's 4th.	1. P. to K's 4th
2.	P. to K. B's 4th	2. P. takes P.
3	K. Kt. to B's 3d.	3. P. to K. Kt's 4th.
4	B. to Q. B's 4th	4. P. to K. Kt's 5th.
5	Kt. to K's 5th.	5. Q. to K. R's 5th (ch)
6	K. to B's sq.	6. P. to K. B's 6th.
7	B. takes K. B. P. (ch.)	7. K. to his 2d.
8	P. takes P.	8. P. to Q's 3d.
9.	B. takes Kt.	9. P. takes Kt.
10	B. to Q. B's 4th	10. P. takes P.
11	Q. takes P.	11. B. to K. R's 6th (ch.)
12	K. to Kt's sq.	12. Q. to K's 8th (ch.)
13	B. to B's sq.	13. R. checks.

And wins.

GAME THE THIRD.

	WHITE.	BLACK.
1.	P. to K's 4th	1. P. to K's 4th
2.	P. to K. B's 4th.	2. P. takes P.
3.	K. Kt. to B's 3d.	3. P. to K. Kt's 4th.
4.	B. to Q. B's 4th.	4. P. to K. Kt's 5th.
5.	Kt. to K's 5th.	5. Q. to K. R's 5th (ch.)
6.	K. to B's sq.	6. P. to K. B's 6th.
7.	P. to K. Kt's 3d.	7. Q. to R's 6th (ch.)
8.	K. to B's 2d (best)	8. K. Kt. to B's 3d.
9.	P. to Q's 3d.	9. P. to Q's 3d.
10.	Kt. takes K. B. P.	10. P. to Q's 4th.
11.	Kt. takes R.	11. Q. to Kt's 7th (ch.)
12.	K. to his 3d.	12. Q. Kt. to B's 3d.
13.	Kt. to B's 7th.	13. K. takes Kt.
14.	B. takes Q. P. (ch.)	14. Kt. takes B.
15.	P. takes Kt.	15. B. to K. R's 3d (ch.)

And then P. to K B's 7th, winning.

Variation I.

Beginning at White's 9th move.

WHITE.	BLACK.
9. K. to his 3d.	9. B. to K. R's 3d (ch.)
10. K. to Q's 3d.	10. P. to Q's 3d.
11. Kt. takes K. B. P.	11. P. to Q's 4th.
12. B. takes Q. P.	12. Kt. takes B.
13. Kt. takes B.	13. Kt. to Q. Kt's 5th (ch)
14. K. to B's 4th.	14. Q. takes Kt.
15. K. takes Kt.	15. Q. Kt. to R's 3d (ch)
16 K. to B's 3d.	16. Q. to her B's 3d (ch.)
17. K. to Q's 3d.	17. Kt. to his 5th (ch.)
18. K to K's 3d.	18. Kt. takes Q. B. P. (ch.)

Black must win.

Variation II.

Beginning at White's 9th move.

WHITE.	BLACK.
9. Q. Kt. to B's 3d.	9. Q. to Kt's 7th (ch.)
10. K. to his 3d.	10. B. to K. R's 3d (ch.)
11. K. to Q's 3d.	11. Q. Kt. to B's 3d.
12. Kt. takes K. B. P.	12. Q. Kt. to his 5th (ch.)
13. K. to Q's 4th.	13. Q. to B's 7th (ch.)
14. K. to his 5th.	14. P. to Q's 3d (ch.)
15. K. takes Kt.	15. Q. to her 5th (ch.)

And Black wins.

GAME THE FOURTH.

WHITE.	BLACK.
1. P. to K's 4th.	1. P. to K's 4th.
2. P. to K B's 4th.	2. P. takes P.
3. K. Kt. to B's 3d.	3. P. to K. Kt's 4th.
4. B. to Q. B's 4th.	4. P. to K. Kt's 5th.
5. Kt. to K's 5th.	5. Q. to K. R's 5th (ch)
6 K. to B's sq.	6. P. to K. B's 6th.
7. K. Kt. P. takes P.	7. K. Kt. to B's 3d.
8. P. to Q's 4th.	8. P. to Q's 3d.

KING'S GAMBIT

9. Kt. takes K. Kt. P.	9. Q to R's 6th (ch.)
10. K. to his sq.	10. Kt. takes Kt.
11. P. takes Kt.	11. B. to K's 2d.
12. R. to B's sq.	12. B. checks.
13. K. to Q's 2d.	13. Q. B. takes P.
14. B. to K's 2d.	14. K. B. to Kt's 4th (ch.)
15. K. to his sq.	15. Q. to R's 5th (ch.)
16. R. to K. B's 2d.	16. K. B. takes Q. B.
17. Q. takes B.	17. Q. B. takes K. B.
18. K. takes B.	18. Q. takes K. P. (ch.)
19. Q. to K's 3d.	19. Q. takes Q. (ch.)

He has a Pawn more and no inferiority of position.

Variation I.

Beginning at White's 8th move.

8. B. takes K. B. P. (ch.)	8. K. to his 2d.
9. B. to Q. B's 4th.	9. P. to Q's 3d.
10. Kt. to Q's 3d.	10. P. takes P.
11. Kt. to K. B's 2d.	11. Q. B. to K. R's 6th (ch.)
12. Kt. takes B.	12. Q. takes Kt. (ch.)
13. K. to his sq.	13. Kt. takes K. P

His attack is irresistible.

Variation II.

Beginning at White's 8th move

WHITE.	BLACK.
8. Kt. takes K. Kt. P.	8. Kt. takes Kt.
9. P. takes Kt.	9. Q. to R's 6th (ch.)
10. K. to his sq.	10. P. to Q's 4th.
11. B. to K's 2d.	11. Q. to R's 5th (ch)
12. K. to B's sq.	12. P. to K. R's 4th.

He has an excellent game.

Variation III.

Beginning at White's 8th move.

WHITE.	BLACK.
8 Q. to K's 2d.	8. P. to Q's 3d.

9. Kt. takes K. B. P.	9. P. takes P.
10. Q. to K. B's 2d.	10. Q. B. to R's 6th (ch.)
12 K. to his sq.	12. Q. takes K. P. (ch.)
13. K. to Q's sq.	13. Q. takes B.

He must win.

VARIATION IV.
Beginning at White's 8th move.

WHITE.	BLACK.
8. P. to K. R's 3d.	8 P. takes K. R. P.
9. Q. to K's sq.	9. Q. to K. Kt's 4th.
10. Kt. to his 4th.	10. Kt. takes Kt.
11. P. takes Kt.	11. Q. takes P.
12. Q. to K's 2d.	12. P. to K. R's 4th.
13. Q. Kt. to B's 3d.	13. R. to K. Kt's sq.
14. K. to his sq.	14. B. to K's 2d.
15. Kt. to Q's 5th.	15. Q. to R's 5th (ch.)
16. K. to Q's sq.	16. P. to Q. B's 3d.
17. Kt. to Q. B's 7th (ch.)	17 K. to Q's sq.
18. Kt. takes Q. R.	18. P. to Q's 4th.
19. Q. to K's sq.	19. P. takes B.

And wins.

An attentive consideration of the foregoing examples will lead you to the conclusion, I think, that the Salvio defence, or that of Cochrane, which varies from it in the transposition of Black's 6th and 7th moves, is a safe and trustworthy method of opposing the King's Gambit, and that the danger to be apprehended by the second player, in advancing his Pawn to K. Kt's 5th on the 4th move, is not that his opponent should play the Kt. to K's 5th, and admit of the Salvio or Cochrane defence, but that he should leave his Kt. to be taken, and adopt the powerful and almost irresistible attack of the Muzio Gambit

GAMES

ILLUSTRATING THE SALVIO AND COCHRANE GAMBITS

GAME I.—Between V. H. der Laza and H——d of Berlin.

WHITE. (Mr. H.)	BLACK. (V. H. d. L.)
1. P. to K's 4th.	1. P. to K's 4th.
2. P. to K. B's 4th.	2. P. takes P.
3. K. Kt. to B's 3d.	3. P. to K. Kt's 4th.
4. K. B. to Q. B's 4th.	4. P. to K. Kt's 5th.
5. Kt. to K's 5th.	5. Q. to R's 5th (ch.)
6. K. to B's sq.	6. K. Kt. to R's 3d.
7. P. to Q's 4th.	7. P. to K. B's 6th.
8. P. to K. Kt's 3d.	8. Q. to R's 6th (ch.)
9. K. to B's 2d.	9. Q. to K. Kt's 7th (ch.)
10. K. to his 3d.	10. P. to K. B's 3d.
11. Kt. to Q's 3d.	11. K. Kt. to B's 2d.
12. Kt. to K. B's 4th.	12. K. B. to K. R's 3d.
13. K. to Q's 3d.	13. B. takes Kt.
14. Q. B. takes B.	14. P. to Q. B's 3d.
15. Q. Kt. to B's 3d.	15. Castles.
16. Q. B. to Q's 6th.	16. P. to Q. Kt's 4th.
17. B. takes Kt. (ch.)	17. R. takes B.
18. P. to K. R's 3d.	18. P. to Q. Kt's 5th.
19. B. takes Q. Kt. P.	19. Q. B. to R's 3d (ch.)
20. K. to his 3d.	20. Q. takes K. Kt. P.
21. Q. to K. Kt's sq.	21. Q. to her B's 2d.
22. Q. takes P. (ch.)	22. R. to K. Kt's 2d.
23. Q. takes doubled P., and wins.	

GAME II.—From Mr. Cochrane's *Treatise*.

WHITE.	BLACK.
1. P. to K's 4th.	1. P. to K's 4th.
2. P. to K. B's 4th.	2. P. takes P.
3. K. Kt. to B's 3d.	3. P. to K. Kt's 4th.
4. K. B. to Q. B's 4th.	4. P. to Kt's 5th.
5. Kt. to K's 5th.	5. Q. checks.
6. K. to B's sq.	6. P. to K. B's 6th.
7. Q. to K's sq.	7. P. takes P. (ch.)
8. K. takes P.	8. Q. to K. R's 6th (ch.)
9. K. to his B's 2d.	9. K. B. to Kt's 2d.
10. P. to Q's 4th.	10. P. to Q's 3d.
11. B. takes B. P. (ch.)	11. K. to his 2d.
12. B. takes K. Kt.	12. R. takes B.
13. K. Kt. to Q. B's 4th.	13. Q. to K. B's 6th (ch.)
14. K. to Kt's sq.	14. B. takes Q. P. (ch.)
15. B. to K's 3d.	15. P. to K. Kt's 6th.
16. P. to K. R's 3d.	16. P. to Kt's 7th.
17. K. R. to his 2d.	17. Q. B. takes K. R. P.
18. Q. Kt. to Q's 2d.	18. Q. to K. B's 8th (ch.)
19. Kt. takes Q.	19. P. takes Kt.

Becoming a Q., giving check, double check, and mate.

152 CHESS HANDBOOK.

The Muzio Gambit.

In the two defences to the King's Gambit by Salvio and Cochrane just examined, when the second player for his fourth move advances his P. to K. Kt's 5th, attacking the Knight, White replies by moving his Knight to King's 5th, subjecting himself, as was shown, to a counter-attack, from which escape without loss is difficult if not impracticable. From this circumstance, apparently, originated the conception of the "Muzio Gambit," wherein the first player instead of removing the attacked Knight boldly abandons him, and by castling is enabled to bring an almost overwhelming array of forces to the immediate assault of the adverse King.

GAME THE FIRST.

WHITE.	BLACK.
1. P. to K's 4th.	1. P. to K's 4th.
2. P. to K. B's 4th.	2. P. takes P.
3. K. Kt. to B's 3d.	3. P. to K. Kt's 4th.
4. K. B. to Q. B's 4th.	4. P. to K. Kt's 5th.
5. Castles.	5. P. takes Kt.
6. Q. takes P. (best)	6. Q. to K. B's 3d (best)
7. P. to K's 5th.	7. Q. takes K. P.
8. P. to Q's 3d.	8. K. B. to K. R's 3d.
9. Q. B. to Q's 2d.	9. K. Kt. to K's 2d.
10. Q. Kt. to B's 3d.	10. Q. Kt. to B's 3d.
11. Q. R. to K's sq.	11. Q. to B's 4th (ch.)
12. K. to R's sq.	12. Q. Kt. to Q's 5th
13 R. takes Kt. (ch.)	13. K. takes R.
14 Kt. to Q's 5th (ch.)	14. K. to Q's sq.
15. Q. to K. R's 5th.	15. Q. to K. B's sq.
16. Q. to K. R's 4th (ch.)	16. P. to B's 3d.
17. Q. B. takes P.	17. B. takes B.
18. R. takes B.	18. Kt. to Q. B's 3d.
19. R. takes K. B. P.	19. Q. to K's sq.
20. R. to B's 8th (dis. ch.)	20. Kt. to K's 2d.
21. Q. takes Kt.	

Mate.

KING'S GAMBIT.

GAME THE SECOND.

Varying from the preceding at Black's 10th move.

WHITE.	BLACK.
1. P. to K's 4th.	1. P. to K's 4th.
2. P. to K. B's 4th.	2. P. takes P.
3. K. Kt. to B's 3d.	3. P. to K. Kt's 4th.
4. K. B. to Q. B's 4th.	4. P. to K. Kt's 5th.
5. Castles.	5. P. takes Kt.
6. Q. takes P. (best)	6. Q. to K. B's 3d (best)
7. P. to K's 5th.	7. Q. takes K. P.
8 P. to Q's 3d.	8. K. B. to K. R's 3d
9. Q. B. to Q's 2d.	9. K. Kt. to K's 2d.
10. Q. Kt. to B's 3d.	10. P. to Q. B's 3d.
11. Q. R. to K's sq.	11. Q. to her B's 4th (ch.)
12. K. to R's sq.	12. P. to Q's 4th.
13. Q. to K. R's 5th.	13. Q. to her 3d.
14. B. takes Q. P.	14. P. takes B.
15. Kt. takes Q. P.	15. Q. Kt. to B's 3d.
16. Q. B. to his 3d.	16. Q. to K. Kt's 3d.
17. R. takes Kt. (ch.)	17. K. to B's sq.
18. R. to K's 8th (ch.)	18. K. takes R.
19. Kt. to K. B's 6th (ch.)	19. K. to B's sq.
20. Q. to her B's 5th (ch.)	20. Kt. to K's 2d (best)
21. R. to K's sq.	21. Q. B. to K's 3d.
22. Kt. to Q's 7th (ch.)	22. Q. B. takes Kt.
23. Q. takes Kt. (ch.)	23. K. to Kt's sq.
24. Q. takes B.	24. Q. R. to K. B's sq.
25 Q. takes Q. Kt. P.	

And the game is about even.

I think the attack, in a majority of the variations which arise in this game, may be strengthened by your interposing the K. R. at move 12, instead of retreating the K

VARIATION.

Beginning at Black's 19th move.

WHITE.	BLACK.
	19. K. to Q's sq.
20. Q. to her 5th (ch.)	20. K. to Q. B's 2d.

21. B. to K's 5th (ch.) 21. Kt. takes B.
22. Q. takes Kt. (ch.)   22. K. to B's 3d (best)
23. Q. to her 5th (ch.) 23. K. to Kt's 3d.
24. Q. to her 6th (ch.) 24. K. to R's 4th.
25. Q. to her B's 5th (ch.) 25. K. to R's 3d.
26. Q. to B's 4th (ch.) 26. P. to Q. Kt's 4th.
27. Q. to B's 6th (ch.) 27. K. to R's 4th.
28. P. to Q. R's 4th.

And he cannot possibly save the game.

GAME THE THIRD.

Varying from the former at White's 8th move.

WHITE.	BLACK.
1. P. to K's 4th.	1. P. to K's 4th.
2. P. to K. B's 4th.	2. P. takes P.
3. K. Kt. to B's 3d.	3. P. to K. Kt's 4th.
4. K. B. to Q. B's 4th.	4. P. to K. Kt's 5th.
5. Castles.	5. P. takes Kt.
6. Q. takes P. (best)	6. Q. to K. B's 3d (best)
7. P. to K's 5th.	7. Q. takes K. P.
8. P. to Q. Kt's 3d.	8. Q. takes R. (best)
9. Q. Kt. to B's 3d.	9. K. B. to Q. B's 4th (ch.)
10. K. to R's sq.	10. K. Kt. to K's 2d.
11. P. to Q's 4th.	11. B. takes Q. P.
12. B. takes K. B. P. (ch.)	12. K. to Q's sq.
13. B. to Q's 2d.	13. Q. takes R. (ch.)
14. Q. takes Q.	14. R. to K. B's sq.
15. Q. takes P.	15. B. takes Kt.
16. B. takes B.	16. P. to Q's 3d.

Black has the advantage.

GAME THE FOURTH.

WHITE.	BLACK.
1. P. to K's 4th.	1. P. to K's 4th.
2. P. to K. B's 4th	2. P. takes P.
3. K Kt. to B's 3d.	3. P. to K. Kt's 4th

KING'S GAMBIT.

WHITE	BLACK
4. B. to Q. B's 4th.	4. P. to K. Kt's 5th.
5. Castles.	5. P. takes Kt.
6. Q. takes P.	6. K. B. to K. R's 3d.
7. P. to Q's 4th.	7. Q. Kt. to B's 3d.
8. Q. Kt. to B's 3d.	8. Kt. takes Q. P.
9. Q. to K. R's 5th.	9. Q. Kt. to K's 3d.
10. Q. B. takes P.	10. B. takes B.
11. R. takes B.	11. Q. to K's 2d.
12. B. takes Kt.	12. Q. P. takes B.
13. Q. R. to K. B's sq.	

You must win.

VARIATION I.

Beginning at Black's 6th move.

WHITE.	BLACK.
1. P. to K's 4th.	1. P. to K's 4th.
2. P. to K. B's 4th.	2. P. takes P.
3. K. Kt. to B's 3d.	3. P. to K. Kt's 4th.
4. K. B. to Q. B's 4th.	4. P. to K. Kt's 5th
5. Castles.	5. P. takes Kt.
6. Q. takes P.	6. P. to Q's 3d.
7. P. to Q's 4th.	7. B. to K. R's 3d.
8. Q. B. takes P.	8. B. takes B.
9. Q. takes B.	9. Q. to K's 2d.
10. B. takes K. B. P. (ch.)	10. K. to Q's sq.
11. P. to K's 5th.	

With a capital opening.

VARIATION II.

Beginning at Black's 6th move.

WHITE.	BLACK.
1. P. to K's 4th.	1. P. to K's 4th.
2. P. to K. B's 4th.	2. P. takes P.
3. K. Kt. to B's 3d.	3. P. to K. Kt's 4th.
4. K. B. to Q. B's 4th	4. P. to K. Kt's 5th.
5. Castles.	5. P. takes Kt.
6. Q. takes P.	6. Q. to K's 2d.
7. P. to Q's 4th.	7. Q. Kt. to B's 3d

8. Q. takes P.   8. Kt. takes Q. P.
9. B. takes K. B. P. (ch.)   9. K. to Q's sq.
10. Q. Kt. to B's 3d.   10. K. Kt. to R's 3d.
11. Q. B. to K's 3d.   11. Q. Kt. to K's 3d.
12. K. B. takes Kt.   12. Q. takes B.
13. Q Kt. to Q's 5th.   13. P. to Q's 3d.
14. Q. to K. R's 4th (ch.)

You ought to win.

GAME THE FIFTH.

KOCH AND GHULAM KASSIM'S ATTACK.

WHITE.   BLACK.
1. P. to K's 4th.   1. P. to K's 4th.
2. P. to K. B's 4th.   2. P. takes P.
3. K. Kt. to B's 3d.   3. P. to K. Kt's 4th.
4. K. B. to Q. B's 4th.   4. P. to K. Kt's 5th
5. P. to Q's 4th.   5. P. takes Kt.

White's 5th move characterizes the game known as "Koch and Ghulam Kassim's Attack."

6. Q. takes P.   6. P. to Q's 4th.
7. K. B. takes Q. P.   7. P. to Q. B's 3d.
8. B. to Q. Kt's 3d.   8. Q. takes Q. P.
9. Q. B. takes P.   9. K. Kt. to B's 3d.
10. Q. Kt to Q's 2d.   10. Q. B. to K. Kt's 5th
11. Q. to K. Kt's 3d.   11. K. Kt. takes P.
12. Q. Kt. takes Kt.   12. Q. takes Kt. (ch.)
13. K. to Q's 2d.

You have the better game.

VARIATION I.

Beginning at White's 8th move.

8. B. takes K. B. P. (ch.)   8. K. takes B.
9. Q. B. takes P.   9. K. Kt. to B's 3d.
10. P. to Q. B's 3d.   10. Q. B. to K. Kt's 5th

I prefer Black's game.

KING'S GAMBIT

VARIATION II.

Beginning at Black's 6th move.

WHITE.	BLACK.
1. P. to K's 4th.	1. P. to K's 4th.
2. P. to K. B's 4th.	2. P. takes P.
3. K Kt. to B's 3d.	3. P. to K. Kt's 4th.
4. B to Q. B's 4th.	4. P. to K. Kt's 5th.
5. P. to Q's 4th.	5. P. takes Kt.
6. Q. takes P.	6. P. to Q's 3d.
7. Castles.	7. Q. to K. B's 3d.
8. Q. Kt. to R's 3d.	8. Q. takes Q. P. (ch.)
9. K. to R's sq.	9. K. B. to R's 3d.
10. Q. B. takes P.	10. Q. to K. B's 3d.
11. Q. to K's 3d.	11. Q. to K. Kt's 3d.
12. P. to K's 5th.	12. B. takes B.
13 R. takes B.	13. B. to K's 3d.
14. P. takes Q. P.	

You have a capital attack.

GAME THE SIXTH.

McDONNELL'S ATTACK.

WHITE.	BLACK.
1. P. to K's 4th.	1. P. to K's 4th.
2. P. to K. B s 4th.	2. P. takes P.
3. K. Kt. to B's 3d.	3. P. to K. Kt's 4th
4. K. B. to Q. B's 4th.	4. P. to K. Kt's 5th.
5. Q. Kt. to B's 3d.	5. P. takes Kt.
6. Q. takes P.	6. P. to Q's 4th.
7. B. takes Q. P.	7. P. to Q. B's 3d.
8. B. to Q. Kt's 3d.	8. Q. B. to K's 3d.
9. B. takes B.	9. P. takes B.
10. Q. to K. R's 5th (ch.)	10. K. to Q's 2d.
11. P. to Q's 4th.	11. Q. to K. B's 3d
12. P. to K's 5th.	12. Q. to K. B's 4th.
13. Q. to K. B's 3d.	13. K. B. to Q. Kt's 5th
14. Q. B. takes P.	14. K. Kt. to K's 2d.

15. Castles on K's side.	15. B. takes Kt.
16. P. takes B.	16. Q. Kt. to R's 3d.

The game is in his favor.

Our examination of this Gambit would be imperfect without some notice of a variation in the opening, where the first player, instead of abandoning the Knight at his 5th move, sacrifices his Bishop by taking the K. B. Pawn, checking. This attack is not, strictly speaking, a part of the Muzio Gambit, but it is so intimately associated with it that I think it better to consider them both under the same head.

GAME THE SEVENTH.

WHITE.	BLACK.
1. P. to K's 4th.	1. P. to K's 4th.
2. P. to K. B's 4th.	2. P. takes P.
3. K. Kt. to B's 3d.	3. P. to K. Kt's 4th.
4. B. to Q. B's 4th.	4. P. to K. Kt's 5th.
5. B. takes K. B. P. (ch.)	5. K. takes B.
6. Kt. to K's 5th (ch.)	6. K. to his sq.
7. Q. takes P.	7. K. Kt. to B's 3d.
8. Q. takes K. B. P.	8. P. to Q's 3d.
9. Kt. to Q. B's 4th.	9. Q. Kt. to B's 3d.
10. Castles.	10. B. to K. Kt's 2d.
11. P. to Q's 3d.	11. Q. B. to K's 3d.
12. Q. to K. Kt's 3d.	12. Q. to K's 2d.

Your attack is exhausted

GAMES

ILLUSTRATIVE OF THE MUZIO GAMBIT.

GAME I.—Between Mr. Lewis and an Amateur of great skill.

WHITE. (Mr. L.)	BLACK. (Mr. —)
1. P. to K's 4th.	1. P. to K's 4th.
2. P. to K. B's 4th.	2. P. takes P.
3. K. Kt. to B's 3d.	3. P. to K. Kt's 4th.

KING'S GAMBIT.

4. K. B. to Q. B's 4th.	4. P. to K. Kt's 5th.
5. Castles.	5. P. takes Kt.
6. Q. takes P.	6. K. B. to R's 3d.
7. P. to Q's 4th.	7. Q. to K's 2d.
8. Q. B. takes P.	8. Q. Kt. to B's 3d.
9. Q. B. takes K. B.	9. Kt. takes B.
10. Q. to K. R's 5th.	10. Q. to K. B's sq.
11. K. R. to B's 6th.	11. Q. to K. Kt's 2d.
12. Q. takes Kt.	12. Q. takes Q.
13. K. R. takes Q.	13. Q. Kt. takes Q. P.
14. Q. Kt. to Q. R's 3d.	14. P. to Q. B's 3d.
15. K. R. to Q's 6th.	15. Kt. to K's 3d.
16. Q. R. to Q's sq.	16. K. R. to K. Kt's sq.
17. K. B. takes Kt.	17. K. B. P. takes B.
18. Kt. to Q. B's 4th.	18. K. R. to K. Kt's 4th.
19. K. to B's 2d.	19. K. to his 2d.
20. Kt. to K's 3d.	20. P. to Q. R's 4th.
21. K. to his B's 3d.	21. P. to Q. Kt's 4th.
22. Kt. to K. Kt's 4th.	22. Q. R. to his 2d.
23. K. to B's 4th.	23. K. R. to Q. B's 4th.
24. P. to Q. B's 3d.	24. P. to Q. Kt's 5th.
25. P. takes P.	25. P. takes P.
26. Kt. to K's 5th.	26. K. R. to Q. B's 7th.
27. P. to Q. R's 4th.	27. R. takes Q. Kt. P.
28. K. R. takes Q. B. P.	28. R. to K. B's 7th (ch.)
29. K. to his 3d.	29. R. to K. B's sq.
30. Q. R. to Q. B's sq.	30. B. to Q. R's 3d.
31. K. R. to Q. B's 7th.	31. R. takes R.
32. R. takes R.	32. K. to Q's 3d.
33. R. to Q. R's 7th.	33. K. takes Kt.
34. R. takes B.	34. R. to Q. Kt's sq.
35. R. to Q. R's 5th (ch.)	35. P. to Q's 4th.
36. P. takes P.	36. P. takes P.
37. K. to Q's 3d.	37. R. to Q. B's sq.
38. R. to Q. Kt's 5th.	38. R. to Q. B's 6th (ch.)
39. K. to Q's 2d.	39. R. to Q. B's 5th.
40. P. to Q. R's 5th.	40. R. to K. B's 5th.
41. P. to Q. R's 6th.	41. R. to K. B's 7th (ch.)
42. K. to Q's 3d.	42. R. to Q. R's 7th.
43. R. takes Q. Kt. P.	43. R. takes Q. R. P.

Drawn game.

GAME II.—Between Mr. Szen, of Hungary, and V. H. der Laza, of the Berlin Chess Club.

WHITE. (V. H. d. L.)	BLACK. (Mr. S.)
1. P. to K's 4th.	1. P. to K's 4th.
2. P. to K. B's 4th.	2. P. takes P.
3. K. Kt. to B's 3d.	3. P. to Kt's 4th.
4. B. to Q. B's 4th.	4. P. to K. Kt's 5th.
5. Castles.	5. P. takes Kt.

6. Q. takes P.
7. P. to K's 5th.
8. P. to Q's 3d.
9. Kt. to Q. B's 3d.
10. Q. B. to Q's 2d.
11. Q. R. to K's sq.
12. K. to R's sq.
13. Kt. to K's 4th.
14. Q. B. to his 3d.
15. Kt. to Q's 6th.
16. R. takes Kt.†
17. R. takes K. B. P.
18. B. takes R. (ch.)
19. P. takes B.
20. Q. takes K. B. P.
21. R. takes Q.
22. B. to Q. Kt's 3d.
23. B. takes Kt.
24. R. to B's 7th (ch.)
25. R. to K's 7th.
26. R. to K's 8th (ch.)
27. R. takes B.

6. Q. to K. B's 3d.
7. Q. takes K. P.
8. K. B. to K. R's 3d.
9. K. Kt. to K's 2d.
10. Castles.*
11. Q. to Q. B's 4th (ch.)
12. P. to Q. B's 3d.
13. Q. to K. B's 4th.
14. B. to K. Kt's 2d.
15. Q. to K. Kt's 4th.
16. B. takes Q. B.‡
17. R. takes R.
18. K. to Kt's 2d.
19. Kt. to Q. R's 3d.
20. Q. takes Q.
21. Kt. to Q. B's 2d.
22. Kt. to Q's 4th.
23. P. takes B.
24. K. to Kt's sq.
25. P. to Q. Kt's 3d.
26. K. to Kt's 2d.

And wins.

GAME III.—Between two Berlin players.

WHITE.	BLACK.
1. P. to K's 4th.	1. P. to K's 4th.
2. P. to K. B's 4th.	2. P. takes P.
3. K. Kt. to B's 3d.	3. P. to K. Kt's 4th.
4. K. B. to Q. B's 4th.	4. P. to K. Kt's 5th.
5. Castles.	5. P. takes Kt.
6. Q. takes P.	6. Q. to K. B's 3d.
7. P. to K's 5th.	7. Q. takes P.
8. P. to Q's 3d.	8. K. B. to R's 3d.
9. Q. B. to Q's 2d.	9. K. Kt. to K's 2d.
10. Q. Kt. to B's 3d.	10. P. to Q. B's 3d.
11. Q. R. to K's sq.	11. Q. to B's 4th (ch.)
12. K. to R's sq.	12. P. to Q's 4th.
13. Q. to K. R's 5th.	13. Q. to her 3d.
14. K. B. takes Q. P.	14. Castles.
15. K. B. to Q. Kt's 3d.	15. Q. to K. Kt's 3d.
16. Q. to Q. B's 5th.	16. K. Kt. to K. B's 4th.
17. Q. B. takes P.	17. K. B. takes B.
18. K. R. takes B	18. K. Kt. to his 2d.
19. Kt. to K's 4th.	19. K. Kt. to K's 3d.

* Not considered so strong a move as 10 P. to Q. B's 3d.
† Well played.
‡ Had he taken R. with Q., White would have won a Piece by at once playing Kt. to K. B's 5th

KING'S GAMBIT.

20. B. takes Kt.
21. Kt. to B's 6th (ch.)
22. R. takes B.
23. Kt. to R's 5th (ch.)
24. R. takes R.
25. R. to B's 6th (ch.)
26. Q. mates.

20. Q. B. takes B
21. K. to Kt's 2d.
22. P. takes R.
23. K. to R's 3d.
24. Q. takes Kt.
25. K. to Kt's 2d.

GAME IV.—Between La Bourdonnais and McDonnell

WHITE. (Mr. McD.)
1. P. to K's 4th.
2. P. to K. B's 4th.
3. K. Kt. to B's 3d.
4. K. B. to Q. B's 4th.
5. Q. Kt. to B's 3d.
6. Q. takes P.
7. P. to Q's 4th.
8. Castles.
9. B. takes K. B. P. (ch.)
10. Q. to K. R's 5th (ch.)
11. Q. B. takes P.
12. K. R. takes B.
13. Q. to K. Kt's 5th (ch.)
14. Q. R. to K. B's sq.
15. K. R. takes Kt.
16. Q. Kt. to Q's 5th.
17. K. to R's sq.
18. K. R. takes Kt.
19. Kt. to B's 6th (ch.)

BLACK. (M. La B.)
1. P. to K's 4th.
2. P. takes P.
3. P. to K. Kt's 4th.
4. P. to K. Kt's 5th.
5. P. takes Kt.
6. K. B. to K. R's 3d.
7. Q. Kt. to B's 3d.
8. Q. Kt. takes Q. P.
9. K. takes B.
10. K. to his Kt's 2d.
11. B. takes B.
12. K. Kt. to B's 3d.
13. K. to B's 2d.
14. K. to his sq.
15. Q. to K's 2d.
16. Q. to her B's 4th.
17. Kt. to K's 3d.
18. P. takes R.

And wins the Queen.

GAME V.—From Ghulam Kassim.

WHITE.
1. P. to K's 4th.
2. P. to K. B's 4th.
3. K. Kt. to B's 3d.
4. B. to Q. B's 4th.
5. P. to Q's 4th.
6. Q. takes P.
7. B. takes P.
8. Castles.
9. P. takes Kt.
10. Q. to K's 4th (ch.)
11. B. takes P.
12. Q. to B's 3d.
13. Kt. to Q's 2d.
14. Q. to B's 2d.
15. Q. R. to K's sq.
16. Kt. to K's 4th.

BLACK.
1. P. to K's 4th.
2. P. takes P.
3. P. to K. Kt's 4th.
4. P. to K. Kt's 5th.
5. P. takes Kt.
6. P. to Q's 4th.
7. K. Kt. to B's 3d.
8. Kt. takes B.
9. Q. to B's 3d.
10. K. to Q's sq.
11. Q. to K's 2d.
12. R. to Kt's sq.
13. B. to K. Kt's 5th.
14. Kt. to Q's 2d.
15. Q. to B's 3d.
16. Q. to K. Kt's 3d.

17. P. to Q. B's 4th.	17. K. B. to Q's 3a.
18. B. takes B.	18. P. takes B.
19. P. to Q. B's 5th.	19. P. takes P.
20. P. takes P.	20. K. R. to K's sq.
21. Kt. to Q's 6th.	21. R. takes R.
22. Q. takes R.	22. K. to Q. B's 2d.
23. Q. to her Kt's 4th.	23. K. to Q's sq.

White must win.

GAME VI.—Mr. Staunton gives his Queen's Rook

(Remove White's Q. R. from the Board.)

WHITE. (Mr. S.)	BLACK. (Mr. —.)
1. P. to K's 4th.	1. P. to K's 4th.
2. P. to K. B's 4th.	2. P. takes P.
3. K. Kt. to B's 3d.	3. P. to K. Kt's 4th.
4. K. B. to Q. B's 4th.	4. P. to K. Kt's 5th.
5. B. takes K. B. P. (ch.)	5. K. takes B.
6. Kt. to K's 5th (ch.)	6. K. to his sq.
7. Q. takes P.	7. K. Kt. to B's 3d.
8. Q. takes P.	8. P. to Q's 3d.
9. K. Kt. to B's 3d.	9. Q. Kt. to B's 3d.
10. P. to Q's 4th.	10. Q. to K's 2d.
11. Castles.	11. Q. B. to Q's 2d.
12. P. to K's 5th.	12. P. takes P.
13. P. takes P.	13. K. Kt. to Q's 4th.
14. Q. to K's 4th.	14. Q. B. to K's 3d.
15. Q. B. to K. Kt's 5th.	15. Q. to her B's 4th (ch.)
16. K. to R's sq.	16. Q. Kt. to his 5th.
17. P. to Q. B's 4th.	17. K. Kt. to Q. Kt's 3d.
18. P. to Q. Kt's 3d.	18. K. B. to K's 2d.
19. K. Kt. to Q's 4th.	19. Q. B. to K. Kt's sq.
20. B. takes K. B.	20. Q. takes B.
21. K. Kt. to K. B's 5th.	21. Q. to her 2d.
22. Q. to K. R's 4th.	22. Q. R. to Q's sq.
23. Q. to K. B's 6th.	

And wins.

THE ALLGAIER GAMBIT.

GAME THE FIRST.

WHITE.	BLACK.
1. P. to K's 4th.	1. P. to K's 4th.
2. P. to K. B's 4th.	2. P. takes P.
3. K. Kt. to B's 3d.	3. P. to K. Kt's 4th.
4. P. to K. R's 4th.	4. P. to K. Kt's 5th (best)

White's 4th move constitutes the Allgaier Gambit.

KING'S GAMBIT.

5. Kt. to Kt's 5th.   5. P. to K. R's 3d.
6. Kt. takes K. B. P 6. K. takes Kt.
7. Q. takes P.   7. K. Kt. to B's 3d.
8. Q. takes K. B. P. 8. K. B. to Q's 3d (best)
9. B. to Q. B's 4th (ch.) 9. K. to Kt's 2d (best)
10. Q. to K. B's 5th. 10. B. to Kt's 6th (ch.)
11. K. to B's sq.   11. K. R. to B's sq.

Black has a winning position.

VARIATION,
Beginning at Black's 5th move.

WHITE.	BLACK.
1. P. to K's 4th.	1. P. to K's 4th.
2. P. to K. B's 4th.	2. P. takes P.
3. K. Kt. to B's 3d.	3. P. to K. Kt's 4th.
4. P. to K. R's 4th.	4. P. to K. Kt's 5th.
5. Kt. to Kt's 5th.	5. P. to K. R's 4th.
6. K. B. to Q. B's 4th.	6. K. Kt. to R's 3d.
7. P. to Q's 4th.	7. P. to K. B's 3d.
8. Q. B. takes P.	8. P. takes Kt.
9. P. takes P.	9. Kt. to B's 2d.
10. P. to K. Kt's 6th.	10. Kt. to Q's 3d.
11. Q. B. takes Kt.	11. P. takes B.
12. B. to B's 7th (ch.)	12. K. to his 2d.
13. Castles.	13. Q. to her R's 4th
14. B. to Q's 5th.	14. K. to his sq.
15. Q. to her B's sq.	15. K. to Q's sq.
16. Q. to K. Kt's 5th (ch.)	16. B. to K's 2d.
17. P. to K. Kt's 7th.	

And you win with ease.

GAME THE SECOND.

WHITE.	BLACK.
1. P. to K's 4th.	1. P. to K's 4th
2. P. to K. B's 4th.	2. P. takes P.
3. K. Kt. to B's 3d.	3. P. to K. Kt's 4th
4. P. to K. R's 4th	4. P. to K. Kt's 5th.
5. Kt. to K's 5th	5. P. to K. R's 4th (best)

6. K. B. to Q. B's 4th.   6. K. Kt. to R's 3d
7. P. to Q's 4th.   7. P. to Q's 3d.
8. Kt. to Q's 3d.   8. P. to K. B's 6th.
9. P. to K. Kt's 3d.   9. P. to Q's 4th.
10. B. takes Q. P.   10. P. to Q. B's 3d.
11. B. to Q. Kt's 3d.   11. Q. takes Q. P

He has decidedly the better game.

GAME THE THIRD.

WHITE.   BLACK.
1. P. to K's 4th.   1. P. to K's 4th
2. P. to K. B's 4th.   2. P. takes P.
3. K. Kt. to B's 3d.   3. P. to K. Kt's 4th.
4. P. to K. R's 4th.   4. P to K. Kt's 5th.
5. Kt. to K's 5th.   5. P to K. R's 4th.
6. K. B. to Q. B's 4th.   6. R to K. R's 2d.
7. P. to Q's 4th.   7. P. to K. B's 6th(best)
8. P. to K. Kt's 3d.   8. Q. Kt. to B's 3d.
9. Kt. takes Kt.   9. Q P. takes Kt.
10. Q. B. to K. B's 4th.   10. Q. to K's 2d.
11. Q. Kt. to B's 3d.   11. Q. B. to K's 3d.
12. P. to Q's 5th.   12. Castles on Q's side.

He has a little better game, but the advantage is not nearly so decisive as in the second game.

THE KING'S ROOK'S PAWN GAMBIT.

GAME THE FIRST.

WHITE.   BLACK.
1. P. to K's 4th.   1. P. to K's 4th.
2. P. to K. B's 4th.   2. P takes P.
3. P. to K. R's 4th.   3. K. B. to K's 2d (best)

White's 3d move gives the title to this Gambit.

4. Q. to K. Kt's 4th.   4. P. to Q's 4th (best)
5 Q. takes doubled P.   5. P. takes P.
6 Q. takes K. P.   6. K. Kt. to B's 3d
7 Q. to K B's 3d.   7. Castles.

KING'S GAMBIT.

8. K. B. to Q. B's 4th.	8. Q. B. to K. Kt's 5th.
9. Q. takes Q. Kt. P.	9. Q. to her 3d.
10. Q. to her Kt's 3d.	10. Q. Kt. to B's 3d.
11 Q. to her 3d.	11. Q. Kt. to Q's 5th.
12. P. to Q. B's 3d.	12. Q. to K's 4th (ch.)
13. K. to B's sq.	13. Q. Kt. to K. B's 4th.

Black has a winning game.

VARIATION,
Beginning at Black's 3d move.

WHITE.	BLACK.
1. P. to K's 4th.	1. P. to K's 4th.
2. P. to K. B's 4th.	2. P. takes P.
3. P. to K. R's 4th.	3. P. to Q's 4th.
4. P. takes P.	4. Q. takes P.
5. Q. to K's 2d (ch.)	5. Q. B. to K's 3d.
6. Q. Kt. to B's 3d.	6. Q. to her 2d.
7. P. to Q's 3d.	7. K. B. to Q's 3d.
8. K. Kt. to R's 3d.	8. Q. Kt. to B's 3d.
9. Q. Kt. to his 5th.	9. Castles on Q's side
10. Kt. takes B. (ch.)	10. P. takes Kt.
11. Kt. takes P.	11. B. to K. Kt's 5th
12. Q. to her 2d.	12. R. to K's sq. (ch.)

And he has the better game.

GAMES
ILLUSTRATIVE OF THE ALLGAIER GAMBIT.

GAME I.—Between Messrs. Anderssen and Kipping, at the Manchester Chess Meeting,

WHITE. (Mr. A.)	BLACK. (Mr. K.)
1. P. to K's 4th.	1. P. to K's 4th.
2. P. to K. B's 4th.	2. P. takes P.
3. Kt. to K. B's 3d.	3. P. to K. Kt's 4th.
4. P. to K. R's 4th.	4. P. to K. Kt's 5th.
5. Kt. to K's 5th.	5. P. to K. R's 4th.
6. B. to Q. B's 4th.	6. R. to K. R's 2d.
7. B. takes P. (ch.)	7. R. takes B.
8. Kt. takes R.	8. K. takes Kt.
9. P. to Q's 4th.	9. P. to Q's 3d.

10. B. takes P.   10. K. B. to K's 2d.
11. Castles.   11. K. to Kt's 2d.
12. P. to K. Kt's 3d.   12. Q. B. to K's 3d.
13. Q. to Q's 3d.   13. Q. Kt. to Q's 2d.
14. Kt. to Q. B's 3d.   14. P. to Q. B's 4th.
15. Kt. to K's 2d.   15. Q. B. to K. B's 2d.
16. K. R. to K. B's 2d.   16. Q. B. to K. Kt's 3d.
17. Q. R. to K. B's sq.   17. Q. Kt. to K. B's 3d.
18. P. takes Q. B. P.   18. B. takes K. P.
19. Q. to K's 3d.   19. P. takes Q. B. P.
20. B. to K's 5th.   20. Q. to Q's 4th.
21. Q. to K. Kt's 5th (ch.)   21. K. to K. R's 2d
22. Kt. to Q. B's 3d.   22. Q. to Q. B's 3d.
23. B. takes Kt.   23. B. takes B.
24. R. takes B.

And Black resigns.

GAME II.—Between Mr. Cochrane and Capt. Evans

WHITE. (Mr. C.)   BLACK. (Capt. E.)
1. P. to K's 4th.   1. P. to K's 4th.
2. P. to K. B's 4th.   2. P. takes P.
3. K. Kt. to B's 3d.   3. P. to K. Kt's 4th.
4. P. to K. R's 4th.   4. P. to K. Kt's 5th.
5. Kt. to K's 5th.   5. P. to K. R's 4th.
6. K. B. to Q. B's 4th.   6. K. R. to his 2d.
7. Kt. takes K. B. P.   7. R. takes Kt.
8. B. takes R. (ch.)   8. K. takes B.
9. P. to Q's 4th.   9. B. to K. R's 3d.*
10. B. takes P.   10. B. takes B.
11. Castles.   11. Q. takes K. R. P.
12. R. takes B. (ch.)   12. K. Kt. to B's 3d.
13. P. to K's 5th.   13. P. to Q's 4th.
14. R. takes Kt. (ch.)   14. K. to Kt's 2d.
15 Q. to her 2d.   15. Q. Kt. to Q's 2d.
16. Q. to K. R's 6th (ch.)

And Black resigns.

The King's Bishop's Gambit

GAME THE FIRST.

WHITE.   BLACK.
1. P. to K's 4th.   1. P. to K's 4th.
2. P. to K. B's 4th.   2. P. takes P

---

* This is the error which loses Black's game. The correct move is
9. P. to K. B's 6th.

KING'S GAMBIT.

3. K. B. to Q. B's 4th.   3. Q. to K. R's 5th (ch.)

White's 3d move gives the name to this Gambit.

White	Black
4. K. to B's sq.	4. P. to K. Kt's 4th.
5. Q. Kt to B's 3d.	5. K. B. to K. Kt's 2d.
6. K. Kt. to B's 3d.	6. Q. to K. R's 4th.
7. P. to K. R's 4th.	7. P. to K. R's 3d.
8. P. to Q's 4th.	8. P. to Q's 3d.
9. P. to K's 5th.	9. P. takes P.
10. Q. Kt. to Q's 5th.	10. K. to Q's sq.
11. P. takes P.	11 B. to Q's 2d.
12. K. to his Kt's sq.	12. Q. to K. Kt's 3d.
13. P. takes P.	13. P. takes P.
14. R. takes R.	14. B. takes R.
15. K. Kt. takes P.	15. Q. takes K. Kt.
16. Q. B. takes P.	16. Q. to K. Kt's 3d (best'
17. P. to K's 6th.	17. P. takes P.
18. Kt. takes Q. B. P.	18. P. to K's 4th.
19. Kt. takes Q. R.	19. P. takes B.
20. B. takes K. Kt.	20. Q. takes B.
21. Q. to her 6th.	21. Q. Kt. to R's 3d.
22. R. to Q's sq.	22. Q. to K. B's 2d.
23. P. to Q. Kt's 4th	23. Q. to K's 2d.
24. Q. takes K. B. P.	24. Q. takes Q. Kt. P.
25. Q. to K. B's 7th.	25. Q. to K's 2d.
26. Q. to K. Kt's 8th (ch.)	26. Q. to K's sq.
27. Q. to K. Kt's 5th (ch.)	27. K. to Q. B's sq.

And Black is getting into safe quarters.

VARIATION I.

Beginning at White's 6th move.

WHITE	BLACK.
6. P. to Q's 4th.	6. P. to Q's 3d.
7. P. to K's 5th.	7. P. takes P.
8. Q. Kt. to Q's 5th.	8. K. to Q's sq.
9. P. takes P.	9. B. to Q's 2d.
10. K. Kt. to B's 3d	10. Q. to K. R's 4th
11. Q. R. to Q's 2d.	11. K. Kt. to K's 2d

12. Q. B. to his 3d.   12. K. R. to K's sq
13. Kt. takes Kt.   13. R. takes Kt
14. Q. to her 5th.
      The game is about equal.

VARIATION II.

Beginning at White's 6th move.

WHITE.	BLACK.
6. P. to K. Kt's 3d.	6. P. takes P.
7. K. to Kt's 2d.	7. Q. to K. R's 3d.
8. P. takes P.	8. Q. to K. Kt's 3d.

He has the advantage.

GAME THE SECOND.

WHITE.	BLACK.
1. P. to K's 4th.	1. P. to K's 4th.
2. P. to K. B's 4th.	2. P. takes P.
3. B. to Q. B's 4th.	3. Q. checks.
4. K. to B's sq.	4. P. to K. Kt's 4th.
5. K. Kt. to B's 3d.	5. Q. to K. R's 4th.
6. P. to K. R's 4th.	6. K. B. to K. Kt's 2d
7. P. to Q's 4th.	7. P. to K. R's 3d.
8. P. to K's 5th.	8. K. Kt. to K's 2d.
9. Q. Kt. to B's 3d.	9. K. Kt. to B's 4th.
10. Q. Kt. to K's 4th.	10. P. to Q's 3d.
11. K. P. takes P.	11. Q. B. P. takes P.
12. Q. to K's 2d.	12. K. to Q's sq.
13. P. to Q. B's 3d.	13. K. R. to K's sq.
14. K. to Kt's sq.	14. P. to K. Kt's 5th.
15. K. Kt. to Q's 2d.	15. P. to K. B's 6th.
16. Q. to her 3d.	16. P. takes K. Kt. P.
17. K. takes P.	17. P. to Q's 4th.
18. K. B. takes P.	18. Kt. takes K. R. P. (ch.)

And he has the better game.

VARIATION I.

Beginning at White's 7th move.

7. K. to Kt's sq.   7 B. to Q's 5th (ch.)

KING'S GAMBIT.

WHITE	BLACK
8. K. to R's 2d.	8. P. to K. Kt's 5th.
9. Kt. takes B.	9. P. to Kt's 6th (ch.)
10. K. to R's 3d.	10. P. to Q's 4th (dis. ch.)
11. Kt. to K. B's 5th.	11. Q. takes Q.
12. R. takes Q.	12. Kt. to K. R's 3d.
13. P. to K. R's 5th.	13. P. takes K. P.
14. K. to R's 4th.	14. Kt. takes Kt. (ch.)
15. K. to Kt's 5th.	15. P. to K. B's 6th.
16. K. to B's 4th.	16. P. to K. B's 7th.

Black wins.

VARIATION II.

Beginning at White's 7th move.

WHITE.	BLACK.
7. K. R. to his 2d.	7. P. to K. Kt's 5th.
8. K. Kt. to Kt's 5th.	8. K. Kt. to R's 3d.
9. P. to Q's 4th.	9. P. to Q's 4th.
10. K. B. takes Q. P.(best)	10. P. to K. Kt's 6th.
11. B. takes K. B. P. (ch.)	11. Q. takes B.
12. Kt. takes Q.	12. Q. B. to K. Kt's 5th.
13. Q. to K's sq.	13. P. takes R.
14. K. to B's 2d.	14. K. B. takes Q. P. (ch.)

And Black wins.

VARIATION III.

Beginning also at White's 7th move.

WHITE.	BLACK.
7. B. to K's 2d.	7. P. to K. Kt's 5th.
8. Kt. to K's sq.	8. K. Kt to B's 3d.
9. Q. Kt. to B's 3d.	9. Q. to K. Kt's 3d.
10. P. to Q's 3d.	10. Kt. to K. R's 4th.
11. Kt. to Q's 5th.	11. Kt. to Kt's 6th (ch.)
12. K. to Kt's sq.	12. K. B. checks.
13. K. to R's 2d.	13. Kt. takes B.

He ought to win.

GAME THE THIRD.

WHITE.	BLACK.
1. P. to K's 4th.	1. P. to K's 4th.
2. P. to K. B's 4th.	2. P. takes P.
3. B. to Q. B's 4th.	3. Q. to K. R's 5th (ch.)
4. K. to B's sq.	4. P. to K. Kt's 4th.
5. Q. to K. B's 3d.	5. Q. Kt. to B's 3d.
6. P. to K. Kt's 3d.	6. Q. to K. R's 3d.
7. P. takes P.	7. P. takes P.
8. P. to Q's 3d.	8. Q. Kt. to Q's 5th
9. Q. to K. B's 2d.	9. K. B. to Q. B's 4th.
10. Q. B. takes P.	10. Q. Kt. takes Q. B. P
11. B. takes Q.	11. B. takes Q.
12. Q. B. to K. Kt's 7th.	12. K. B. to Q's 5th.

Black maintains his Pawn

VARIATION,
Beginning at Black's 5th move.

WHITE.	BLACK.
1. P. to K's 4th.	1. P. to K's 4th.
2. P. to K. B's 4th.	2. P. takes P.
3. B. to Q. B's 4th.	3. Q. checks.
4. K. to B's sq.	4. P. to K. Kt's 4th
5. Q. to K. B's 3d.	5. P. to Q's 3d.
6. P. to K. Kt's 3d.	6. Q. to K. Kt's 5th.
7. P. to Q's 4th.	7. Q. takes Q.
8. Kt. takes Q.	8. K. B. to K. R's 3d
9. P. takes P.	9. P. takes P.
10. Q. Kt. to B's 3d.	10. Q. B. checks.
11. K. to B's 2d.	11. K. Kt. to K's 2d.
12. Q. Kt. to K's 2d.	12. K. Kt. to his 3d.
13. K. Kt. to K's sq.	

Followed by 14. K. Kt to Q's 3d, winning the P., with a good situation.

IN the previous games we have followed out, at some length, the most prominent variations which occur when both the attack and defence in this opening are conducted upon the principles recommended by the best authorities, and the result would seem to prove that against every system of attack in the King's Bishop's Gambit at present known, the defence, though difficult and complex in the extreme, is satisfactory.

It yet remains for us to consider what are the probable deviations from the several standard methods of defence, and in what manner these should be turned to advantage by the opening player.

GAME THE FIRST.

WHITE.	BLACK.
1. P. to K's 4th.	1. P. to K's 4th.
2. P. to K. B's 4th.	2. P. takes P.
3. B. to Q. B's 4th.	3. P. to K. Kt's 4th.
4. P. to K. R's 4th.	4. B. to K. Kt's 2d.
5. P. to Q's 4th.	5. P. to K. R's 3d.
6. P. takes P.	6. P. takes P.
7. R. takes R.	7. B. takes R.
8. Q. to K. R's 5th.	8. Q. to K. B's 3d.
9. P. to K's 5th.	9. Q. to K. Kt's 2d.
10. K. Kt. to K. R's 3d.	

You have the better game.

GAME THE SECOND.

WHITE.	BLACK.
1. P. to K's 4th.	1. P. to K's 4th.
2. P. to K. B's 4th.	2. P. takes P
3. B. to Q. B's 4th.	3. P. to K. B's 4th.
4. Q. to K's 2d.	4 Q. checks.
5. K. to Q's sq. (best)	5. P. takes K. P.
6. Q. takes P. (ch.)	6 B. to K's 2d.
7. P. to Q's 4th.	7. K. Kt. to B's 3d.
8. Q. takes K. B. P.	8. Q. takes Q.

Even game.

VARIATION,
Beginning at White's 4th move.

WHITE.	BLACK.
4. Q Kt. to B's 3d.	4. Q to K. R's 5th (ch)
5. K. to B's sq.	5. K. Kt. to B's 3d, or (A.)
6. K. Kt. to B's 3d	6. Q. to K. R's 4th.
7. P. to K's 5th.	7. K. Kt. to K's 5th.
8. Q. Kt. to Q's 5th.	8. K. Kt. to his 6th (ch.)
9. K. to K. Kt's sq.	9. K. Kt. takes R.
10. Kt. takes Q. B. P. (ch.)	10. K. to Q's sq.
11. Q. Kt. takes Q. R.	11. K. Kt. to his 6th
12. P. takes K. Kt.	12. P. takes P.
13. P. to Q's 4th.	13. K. B. to K's 2d.
14. Q. B. to K. B's 4th	14. Q. to K. Kt's 5th.
15. Kt. to K. Kt's 5th.	15. Q. takes Q. B.
16. Kt. to K. B's 7th (ch.)	16. K. to his sq.
17. Q. to her 3d.	17. K. B. to Q's sq.
18. K. Kt. to Q's 6th (ch.)	18. K. to B's sq.
19. Q. R. to K. B's sq.	

And you will checkmate in a few moves.

(A.)

	5. P. takes K. P.
6. Q. Kt. takes P.	6. P. to Q. B's 3d.
7. Q. to K's 2d.	7. K. to Q's sq.
8. K. Kt. to K. B's 3d.	8. Q. to K's 2d.
9. Q. Kt. to K. Kt's 5th.	9. Q. takes Q. (ch.)
10. B takes Q.	10. K. to his sq.
11. K. Kt. to K's 5th.	11. K. B. to K's 2d
12. K. Kt. to K. B's 7th.	12. B. takes Q. Kt.
13. Kt takes B.	13. P. to K. R's 3d.
14. B. to K. R's 5th (ch.)	14. K. to K's 2d.
15. Kt. to K. B's 7th.	15. K. Kt. to B's 3d.
16. Kt. takes R.	16. Kt. takes B.
17. Kt. to Kt's 6th (ch.)	17. K. to B's 3d.
18. Kt. to K. R's 4th.	18. P. to K. Kt's 4th.
19. Kt. to K. B's 3d.	

You have the better game.

KING'S GAMBIT.

GAME THE THIRD.

WHITE.	BLACK.
1. P. to K's 4th.	1. P. to K's 4th.
2. P. to K. B's 4th.	2. P. takes P.
3. B. to Q. B's 4th.	3. P. to Q's 4th.
4. B. takes P.	4. K. Kt. to B's 3d.
5. Q. to K's 2d.	5. Kt. takes B.
6. P. takes Kt (dis. ch.)	6. B. to K's 2d.
7. Q. to K. B's 3d.	7. B. to K. R's 5th (ch.)
8. P. to K. Kt's 3d.	8. P. takes P.
9. P. takes P.	9. B. to K Kt's 4th.
10. Q. Kt. to B's 3d.	

Even game.

VARIATION,

Beginning at White's 5th move.

WHITE.	BLACK.
1. P. to K's 4th.	1. P. to K's 4th.
2. P. to K. B's 4th.	2. P. takes P.
3. B. to Q. B's 4th.	3. P. to Q's 4th.
4. B. takes P.	4. K. Kt. to B's 3d.
5. Q. Kt. to B's 3d.	5. K. B. to Q. Kt's 5th.
6. K. Kt. to K's 2d.	6. B. takes Q. Kt.
7. Q. P. takes B.	7. P. to Q. B's 3d.
8. B. to Q. B's 4th.	8. Q. takes Q. (ch.)
9. K. takes Q.	9. Kt. takes K. P.
10. K. to his sq.	

The game is about even, since Black must eventually lose the gambit Pawn.

GAME THE FOURTH.

WHITE.	BLACK.
1. P. to K's 4th.	1. P. to K's 4th.
2. P. to K. B's 4th.	2. P. takes P.
3. B. to Q. B's 4th.	3. P. to Q. B's 3d.
4. P. to Q's 4th.	4. P. to Q's 4th.
5. P takes P.	5. P. takes P.
6. K. B checks.	6. Q. Kt. to B's 3d.

7. Q. B. takes P.   7. Q. to her Kt's 3d.
8. Q. to K's 2d (ch.)   8. Q. B. to K's 3d
9. P. to Q. B's 3d.   9. Castles on Q's side
10. K. Kt. to B's 3d.

The game is equal.

GAME THE FIFTH.

Having gone through the probable variations which Black may adopt instead of checking with the Q., at his 3d move, we have now to consider those at his command, (after giving the check,) when he does not play the usual move of 4. P. to K. Kt's 4th.

WHITE.	BLACK.
1. P. to K's 4th.	1. P. to K's 4th.
2. P. to K. B's 4th.	2. P. takes P.
3. B. to Q. B's 4th.	3. Q. checks.
4. K. to B's sq.	4. B. to Q. B's 4th.
5. P. to Q's 4th.	5. B. to Q. Kt's 3d.
6. K. Kt. to B's 3d.	6. Q. to K's 2d.
7. Q. B. takes P.	7. Q. takes K. P.
8. B. takes K. B. P. (ch.)	8. K. to B's sq.
9. Q. B. to K. Kt's 3d.	9. K. Kt. to R's 3d.
10. Q. Kt. to B's 3d.	10. Q. to K's 2d.
11. K. B. to Q. Kt's 3d	11. P. to Q. B's 3d.
12. Q. to her 2d.	12. P. to Q's 4th.
13. Q. R. to K's sq.	

You have the better game.

GAME THE SIXTH.

WHITE.	BLACK.
1. P. to K's 4th.	1. P. to K's 4th.
2. P. to K. B's 4th.	2. P. takes P.
3. B. to Q. B's 4th.	3. Q. checks.
4. K. to B's sq.	4. K. Kt. to B's 3d.
5. K. Kt. to B's 3d.	5. Q. to K. R's 4th.
6. P. to K. R's 4th.	6. P. to K. Kt's 4th
7. Q. Kt. to B's 3d.	7. P. to K. R's 3d.

KING'S GAMBIT.

8. P. to K's 5th.
9. K B. to K's 2d.
10. Kt. to K. R's 2d.
11. P. to Q's 4th.

8. Kt. to his sq.
9. P. to Kt's 5th
10. Q. takes K. P.

You have the advantage.

GAME THE SEVENTH.

WHITE.	BLACK.
1. P. to K's 4th.	1. P. to K's 4th.
2. P. to K. B's 4th.	2. P. takes P.
3. B. to Q. B's 4th.	3. Q. checks.
4. K. to B's sq.	4. Q. to K. B's 3d.
5. Q. Kt. to B's 3d	5. P. to Q. B's 3d.
6. P. to Q's 4th.	6. P. to Q's 3d.
7. K. Kt. to B's 3d.	7. P. to K. Kt's 4th
8. P. to K. R's 4th.	8. P. to K. R's 3d.
9. P. to K's 5th.	9. P. takes P.
10. P. takes P.	10. Q. to K. Kt's 2d.
11. Q. to her 4th.	11. B. to K. Kt's 5th.
12. P. takes Kt. P.	12. P. takes P.
13. R. takes R.	13. Q. takes R.
14. Kt. takes K. Kt. P.	14. Q. to K. R's 8th (ch.)
15. Q. to K. Kt's sq.	15. Q. takes Q. (ch.)
16. K. takes Q.	

You have the superiority.

VARIATION,
Beginning at Black's 5th move.

WHITE.	BLACK.
1. P. to K's 4th.	1. P. to K's 4th.
2. P. to K. B's 4th.	2. P. takes P.
3. B. to Q B's 4th.	3. Q. checks.
4. K. to B's sq.	4. Q. to K. B's 3d.
5. Q. Kt. to B's 3d.	5. K. Kt. to K's 2d.
6. P. to Q's 4th.	6. P. to Q's 3d.
7. K Kt. to B's 3d.	7. P. to K. Kt's 4th
8. P. to K. R's 4th.	8. P. to K. R's 3d.
9 P. to K's 5th.	9. Q. to K. Kt's 2d

10. K. R. P. takes P.   10. K. R. P. takes P
11. R. takes R.   11. Q. takes R.
12. Q. Kt. to K's 4th. 12. P. takes K. P.
13. P. takes P.   13. Q. to K. R's 8th (ch)
14. K. Kt. to his sq.   14. Q. Kt. to Q's 2d.
15. Q. Kt. takes P.   15. Q. Kt. takes K. P.
16. Q. to K's 2d.

You have the better position.

GAME THE EIGHTH.

WHITE.	BLACK.
1. P. to K's 4th.	1. P. to K's 4th.
2. P. to K. B's 4th.	2. P. takes P.
3. B. to Q. B's 4th.	3. Q. checks.
4. K. to B's sq.	4. P. to Q's 3d.
5. Q. to K. B's 3d.	5. P. to K. Kt's 4th.
6. P. to K. Kt's 3d.	6. Q. to K. Kt's 5th
7. P. to Q's 3d.	7. K. B. to R's 3d.
8. Q. takes Q.	8. B. takes Q.
9. P. to K. R's 4th.	9. P. takes R. P
10. Q. B. takes P.	

Even game.

VARIATION,

Beginning at White's 5th move.

WHITE.	BLACK.
1. P. to K's 4th.	1. P. to K's 4th.
2. P. to K. B's 4th.	2. P. takes P.
3. B. to Q. B's 4th.	3. Q. checks.
4. K. to B's sq.	4. P. to Q's 3d.
5. P. to Q's 4th.	5. Q. B. to K's 3d.
6. Q. to her 3d.	6. B. takes B.
7. Q. takes B.	7. P. to Q. B's 3d.
8. Q. to her Kt's 3d.	8. P. to Q. Kt's 3d.
9. Q. to K. R's 3d.	9. Q. takes Q.
10. Kt. takes Q.	10. K. Kt. to B's 3d.
11. Q. Kt. to B's 3d.	11. Q. Kt. to Q's 2d.

The game is even.

GAMES

ILLUSTRATIVE OF THE KING'S BISHOP'S GAMBIT

GAME I.—Between La Bourdannais and McDonnell.

WHITE. (Mr. McD.)	BLACK. (M. La B.)
1. P. to K's 4th.	1. P. to K's 4th.
2. P. to K. B's 4th.	2. P. takes P.
3. B. to Q. B's 4th.*	3. Q. checks.
4. K. to B's sq.	4. P. to K. Kt's 4th.
5. Q. Kt. to B's 3d.	5. K. B. to Kt's 2d.
6. P. to Q's 4th.	6. P. to Q's 3d.
7. K. B. to K's 2d.	7. Q. Kt. to B's 3d.
8. P. to K's 5th.	8. K. Kt. to K's 2d.
9. Q. Kt. to his 5th.	9. Castles.
10. Q. Kt. takes Q. B. P.	10. Q. R. to Q. Kt's sq.
11. K. Kt. to B's 3d.	11. Q. to K. R's 3d.
12. P. takes P.	12. K. Kt. to K. B's 4th.
13. P. to Q. B's 3d.	13. K. Kt. to his 6th (ch.)
14. P. takes Kt.	14. Q. takes R. (ch.)
15. K. to B's 2d.	15. P. takes P. (ch.)
16. K. takes P.	16. Q. takes Q.
17. B. takes Q.	17. P. to K. R's 3d.
18. P. to Q. Kt's 3d.	18. P. to Q. Kt's 4th.
19. Q. B. to K's 3d.	19. P. to K. B's 4th.
20. P. to Q's 5th.	20. P. to K. B's 5th (ch.)
21. K. to R's 2d.	21. P. takes B.
22. P. takes Kt.	22. P. to K. Kt's 5th.
23. K. Kt. to Q's 4th.	23. B. to K's 4th (ch.)
24. K. to Kt's sq.	24. K. B. takes Q. P.
25. Q. Kt. takes P.	25. K. B. to Q. B's 4th.
26. P. to Q. Kt's 4th †	26. K. B. to Q. Kt's 3d.
27. Q. Kt. to Q's 6th.	27. K. B. takes K. Kt.
28. P. takes B.	28. Q. R. takes Kt. P.
29. Kt. takes B.	29. K. R. takes Kt.
30. P. to Q's 5th.	30. K. to B's 2d.
31. B. to Q. Kt's 3d.	31. K. to K's 2d.
32. K. to B's sq.	32. Q. R. to K's 5th.
33. K. to his 2d.	33. K. R. to K. B's sq.
34. K. to Q's 3d.	34. Q. R. to K's 4th.
35. R. to K's sq.	35. K. to Q's 3d.‡
36. R. takes P.	36. R. takes R. (ch.)
37. K. takes R.	37. P. to K. R's 4th.
38. K. to his 4th.	38. P. to K. R's 5th.

---

* This was a favorite opening of McDonnell's; he bestowed much time and labor on its analyses, and discovered many skilful methods of diversifying the attack.

† Q. B. to K's 2d would have been better play we believe.

‡ This game is very cleverly played by La Bourdonnais.

39. B. to Q's sq.	39. P. to K. R's 6th.
40. P. takes P.	40. P. takes P.
41. B. to K. B's 3d.	41. P. to K. R's 7th.
42. B. to K. Kt's 2d.	42. R. to K. B's 8th.

Mr. McDonnell resigned.

GAME II.—Between Jose R. Capablanca and Isador Gunsberg, in the St. Petersburg Masters' Tournament, 1914.

WHITE. (Gunsberg.)	BLACK. (Capablanca.)
1. P. to K's 4th.	1. P. to K's 4th.
2. P. to K. B's 4th.	2. P. takes P.
3. B. to B's 4th.	3. K. Kt. to B's 3d.
4. Q. Kt. to B's 3d.	4. B. to Kt's 5th.
5. P. to K's 5th.	5. P. to Q's 4th.
6. B. to Kt's 3d.*	6. Kt. to K's 5th.
7. Kt. to B's 3d.†	7. P. to Q. B's 3d.
8. Q. to K's 2d.	8. B. takes Kt.
9. Q. P. takes B.	9. P. to K. Kt's 4th.
10. Kt. to Q's 2d.‡	10. B. to B's 4th.
11. Kt. takes Kt.	11. B. takes Kt.
12. B. to Q's 2d.	12. Kt. to Q's 2d.
13. P. to B's 4th.	13. Q. to K's 2d.
14. P. takes P.	14. P. takes P.
15. B. to B's 3d.	15. Castles. Q. R.§
16. P. to K's 6th.	16. Kt. to B's 3d.
17. P. takes P.‖	17. Q. takes P.
18. Castles. Q. R.	18. K. R. to K.
19. P. to K. R's 4th.	19. P. to K. R's 3d.
20. P. takes P.	20. P. takes P.
21. R. to R's 6th.	21. R. to K's 3d.
22. B. takes Kt.¶	22. R. takes B.
23. Q. to Kt's 4th (ch.)	23. R. to B's 4th.
24. Q. R. to R.**	24. P. to B's 6th.
25. R. to R's 7th.††	25. P. takes P.
26. R. (R.) to R's 6th.	26. P. to Kt's 8th (Q.) (ch.)
Resigns.	

GAME III.—Between Mr. Perigal and an Amateur.

WHITE. (Mr. P.)	BLACK. (Mr. —)
1. P. to K's 4th.	1. P. to K's 4th.
2. P. to K. B's 4th.	2. P. takes P.

NOTES BY I. GUNSBERG.

* If 6 B. to Kt's 5th (ch.), P. to B's 3d; 7 P. takes Kt., P. takes B.; 8 Q. to K's 2d (ch.), White obtains a good position. But to 6 B. to Kt's 5th (ch.) Black could also reply K. Kt. to Q's 2d.

† If 7 Kt. takes P., Q. to R's 5th (ch.) wins for Black.

‡ P. to K. R's 4th is impossible on account of Kt. to Kt's 6th.

§ If Kt. takes P. 16 Q. to Kt's 5th (ch.), Kt. to B's 3d. 17 Castles Q. R. with advantage.

‖ If 17 Q. to B's 2d, Q. takes P.; 18 B. takes Kt., Q. takes B.; 19 Q. takes R. P.

¶ White should on no account have parted with his Bishop, as the two combined are very strong.

** This is the deciding mistake. White still had a good game by playing 24 R. to Q's 4th. If then Q. to Kt's 2d; 25 R. takes B. would win.

†† There was no reply to Black's move of P. to B's 6th, and by this surprise move the well-fought game becomes hopelessly lost.

KING'S GAMBIT.

3. B. to Q. B's 4th.
4. K. to B's sq.
5. Q. Kt. to B's 3d.
6. P. to K. Kt's 3d.
7. K. to Kt's 2d.
8. K. Kt. to B's 3d.
9. B. takes B. P. (ch.)
10. P. to K. R's 3d.
11. Q. P. takes B.
12. K. R. to K's sq.
13. Q. to her 4th.
14. Q. B. takes K. Kt. P.
15. R. takes R.
16. Q. to K. B's 4th (ch.)
17. K. takes P.
18. Kt. to K's 5th (ch.)
19. B. to R's 6th (ch.)

3. Q. checks.
4. P. to K. Kt's 4th
5. B. to K. Kt's 2d.
6. P. takes P.
7. K. B. takes Kt.*
8. Q. to Kt's 5th.
9. K. to B's sq.†
10. Q. takes K. P.
11. K. takes B.
12. Q. to her B's 3d.
13. K. Kt. to B's 3d.
14. R. to K's sq.
15. Kt. takes R.
16. Kt. to K. B's 3d.
17. Q. to her 3d.
18. K. to Kt's 2d.
19. K. to Kt's sq.

White mates in two moves.

GAME IV.—Played some years ago between one of the best players of the day and Mr. Staunton.

WHITE. (Mr. —)
1. P. to K's 4th.
2. P. to K. B's 4th.
3. B. to Q. B's 4th.
4. P. takes P.‡
5. Q. to K. B's 3d.
6. P. to K. R's 3d.
7. P. to Q. B's 3d.
8. P. takes P.
9. P. to Q's 4th.
10. Q. B. takes P.
11. P. to K. Kt's 3d.
12. Q. B. takes K. B.
13. K. to B's sq.
14. K. B. to Q's 3d.
15. Q. B. to K. R's 2d.
16. Q. to K. B's 4th.
17. Q. Kt. to Q's 2d.
18. P. to Q. B's 4th.
19. Q. to K. Kt's 4th.
20. Q. R. to Q's sq.
21. Q. to K. B's 5th.
22. K. takes B.

BLACK. (Mr. S.)
1. P. to K's 4th.
2. P. takes P.
3. P. to Q's 4th.
4. K. Kt. to B's 3d.
5. K. B. to Q's 3d.
6. Castles.
7. P. to Q. B's 3d.
8. Q. Kt. takes P.
9. K. Kt. to K's 5th.
10. Q. to K. R's 5th (ch.)
11. K. Kt. takes P.
12. Kt. takes R. (dis. ch.)
13. Q. B. to K's 3d.
14. Q. R. to Q's sq
15. Q. B. to Q's 4th.
16. Q. to K. R's 4th.
17. Q. Kt. to K's 2d.
18. Q. Kt. to K. Kt's 3d.
19. Q. to K. R's 3d.
20. Q. to K's 6th.
21. B. to K. Kt's 7th (ch.)
22. Kt. to K. R's 5th (ch.)

And Black wins.

---

* This is not advisable play.
† Taking the Bishop would evidently involve the loss of the Queen.
‡ It is better to take the Pawn with the Bishop.

GAME V.—Between MM. Kieseritzky and Desloges.

WHITE. (M. D.)	BLACK. (M. K.)
1. P. to K's 4th.	1. P. to K's 4th.
2. P. to K. B's 4th.	2. P. takes P.
3. B. to Q. B's 4th.	3. P. to Q. Kt's 4th.
4. B. takes Kt. P.	4. Q. to K. R's 5th (ch.)
5. K. to B's sq.	5. P. to K. Kt's 4th.
6. K. Kt. to B's 3d.	6. Q. to K. R's 4th.
7. K. B. to K's 2d.	7. P. to K. Kt's 5th.
8. Kt. to Q's 4th.	8. P. to Q's 3d.
9. P. to K. R's 3d.	9. K. B. to Kt's 2d.
10. K. Kt. to Q. Kt's 3d.	10. P. to K. B's 6th.
11. P. takes P.	11. P. takes K. R. P.
12. P. to K. B's 4th.	12. Q. to K. R's 5th.
13. P. to Q's 3d.	13. P. to K. R's 7th.
14. K. B. to B's 3d.	14. Q. Kt. to B's 3d.
15. P. to Q's 4th.	15. Q. B. to Q. R's 3d (ch.)
16. K. to Kt's 2d.	16. K. Kt. to R's 3d.
17. R. takes P.	17. Q. to K. B's 3d.
18. Q. B. to K's 3d.	18. K. R. to Kt's sq.
19. Q. to K. R's sq.	19. Kt. takes Q. P.
20. Kt. takes Kt.	20. Q. takes Kt.
21. B. takes Q.	21. B. takes B. (dis. ch.)
22. K. to R's 3d.	22. Q. B. to his sq. (ch.)
23. K. to R's 4th.	23. K. B. to his 3d (ch.)
24. K. to R's 5th.	24. R. to K. Kt's 3d.
25. R. to K. Kt's 2d.	25. Kt. to his sq.
26. P. to K. B's 5th.	26. R. to his 3d (ch.)
27. K. to Kt's 4th.	27. R. takes Q.
28. P. to Q. B's 3d.	28. K. B. to K's 4th.
29. K. B. to K's 2d.	29. Kt. to K. B's 3d (ch.)
30. K. to his B's 3d.	30. Kt. takes K. P.
31. R. to Kt's 8th (ch.)	31. K. to his 2d.
32. R. takes Q. B.	32. Kt. to K. Kt's 4th (ch.)
33. K. to Kt's 4th.	33. P. to K. R's 4th (ch.)
34. K. takes Kt.	34. P. to B's 3d (ch.)
35. K. to Kt's 6th.	35. R. to K. Kt's 8th (ch.)
36. K. to R's 7th.	36. Q. R. takes R.
37. P. to Q. R's 3d.	37. Q. R. to K. Kt's sq.
38. B. to Q. B's 4th.	

And Black mates in three moves.

THE GAMBIT DECLINED.

IF Black does not choose to accept the Gambit, he has several modes of defence, which may be briefly noticed.

KING'S JAMBIT

GAME THE FIRST.

WHITE.	BLACK.
1. P. to K's 4th.	1. P. to K's 4th.
2. P. to K. B's 4th.	2. B. to Q. B's 4th.

This appears to be Black's best move, if he declines taking P. with P.

3. K. Kt. to B's 3d.	3. P. to Q's 3d.
4. P. to Q. B's 3d.	4. B. to K. Kt's 5th.
5. B. to K's 2d (best)	5. B. takes Kt.
6. B. takes B.	6. Q. Kt. to B's 3d.
7. P. to Q. Kt's 4th.	7. B. to Q. Kt's 3d.
8. P. to Q. Kt's 5th.	8. Q. Kt. to K's 2d.
9. P. to Q's 4th.	

And the position is, perhaps, a little in your favor.

VARIATION,

Beginning at White's 5th move.

WHITE.	BLACK.
1. P. to K's 4th.	1. P. to K's 4th.
2. P. to K. B's 4th.	2. B. to Q. B's 4th.
3. K. Kt. to B's 3d.	3. P. to Q's 3d.
4. P. to Q. B's 3d.	4. B. to K. Kt's 5th.
5. P. to Q's 4th.	5. P. takes P.
6. P. takes P.	6. B. takes Kt.
7. P. takes B.	7. Q. to K. R's 5th (ch.)
8. K. to his 2d.	8. B. to Q. Kt's 3d.
9. B. to K's 3d.	9. Kt. to K. B's 3d.
10. Kt. to Q. B's 3d.	10. Kt. to Q. B's 3d.

Equal game

GAME THE SECOND.

WHITE.	BLACK.
1. P. to K's 4th.	1. P. to K's 4th.
2. P. to K. B's 4th.	2. P. to Q's 3d.
3. K. Kt. to B's 3d.	3. B. to K. Kt's 5th
4. B. to Q. B's 4th.	4 Q. Kt. to B's 3d.

5. P. to Q. B's 3d.   5. B. takes Kt.
6. Q. takes B.   6. Kt. to K. B's 3d.

The game is slightly in your favour.

VARIATION,

Beginning at White's 3d move

WHITE.	BLACK.
1. P. to K's 4th.	1. P. to K's 4th.
2. P. to K. B's 4th.	2. P. to Q's 3d.
3. B. to Q. B's 4th.	3. P. takes P.
4. K. Kt. to B's 3d.	4. B. to K's 3d.
5. B. takes B.	5. P. takes B.
6. P. to Q's 4th.	6. P. to K. Kt's 4th.
7. P. to K. R's 4th.	7. P. to K. Kt's 5th.
8. Kt. to K. Kt's 5th.	8. Q. to K. B's 3d.
9. Q. takes P.	

You have the advantage.

GAME THE THIRD.

WHITE.	BLACK.
1. P. to K's 4th.	1. P. to K's 4th.
2. P. to K. B's 4th.	2. P. to Q's 4th.
3. P. takes Q. P.	3. Q. takes P.
4. Q. Kt. to B's 3d.	4. Q. to K's 3d.
5. K. Kt. to B's 3d.	5. P. takes P. (dis. ch.)
6. K. to B's 2d.	6. P. to Q. B's 3d (best)
7. P. to Q's 4th.	7. B. to Q's 3d.
8. B. to Q's 3d.	8. K. Kt. to K's 2d.
9. R. to K's sq.	

You have a fine game.

VARIATION,

Beginning at Black's 3d move.

WHITE.	BLACK.
1. P. to K's 4th.	1. P. to K's 4th.
2. P. to K. B's 4th.	2. P. to Q's 4th.

KING'S GAMBIT.

3. P. takes Q. P.	3. P. takes K. B. P
4 B to Q. Kt's 5th (ch.)	4. B. to Q's 2d.
5. Q. to K's 2d (ch.)	5. Q. to K's 2d.
6. Kt. to Q. B's 3d.	6. Kt. to K. B's 3d
7. B. takes B. (ch.)	7. Q. Kt. takes B.
8. P. to Q's 4th.	8. Castles.
9. Q. takes Q.	9. B. takes Q.
10. B. takes P.	10. Q. Kt. to his 3d.

Equal game.

GAMES

ILLUSTRATIVE OF THE KING'S GAMBIT DECLINED.

GAME I.—Played by Mr. Morphy without seeing the Chessboard or men, against M. Bornemann.

WHITE. (Mr. M.)	BLACK. (M. B.)
1. P. to K's 4th.	1. P. to K's 4th.
2. P. to K. B's 4th.	2. K. B. to Q. B's 4th.
3. K. Kt. to K. B's 3d.	3. P. to Q's 3d.
4. P. to Q. B's 3d.	4. Q. B. to K. Kt's 5th.
5. K. B. to Q. B's 4th.	5. K. Kt. to K. B's 3d.
6. P. takes P.	6. B. takes Kt.
7. Q. takes B.	7. Q. P. takes P.
8. P. to Q's 3d.	8. Q. Kt. to Q. B's 3d.
9. Q. B. to K. Kt's 5th.	9. P. to Q. R's 3d.
10. Q. Kt. to Q's 2d.	10. B. to K's 2d.
11. Castles on Q's side.	11. Q. to Q's 2d.
12. Kt. to K. B's sq.	12. Castles on Q's side.
13. Kt. to K's 3d.	13. P. to K. R's 3d.
14. Q. B. to K. R's 4th.	14. P. to K. Kt's 4th.
15. Q. B. to K. Kt's 3d.	15. Q. R. to K. B's sq.
16. Kt. to Q's 5th.	16. K. Kt. to K's sq.
17. P. to Q's 4th.	17. P. takes Q. P.
18. P. takes P.	18. K. Kt. to Q's 3d.
19. K. B. to Q. Kt's 3d.	19. B. to Q's sq.
20. K. R. to K. B's sq.	20. K. Kt. to Q. Kt's 4th.
21. Q. to K's 3d.	21. P. to K. B's 4th.
22. P. takes P.	22. Q. R. takes P.
23. Kt. to Q. Kt's 6th (ch.)*	23. P. takes Kt.
24. K. B. to K's 6th.	24. Q. R. to Q's 4th.
25. K. R. to K. B's 7th.	25. Q. Kt. to K's 2d.

* A manœuvre altogether unforeseen by M. Bornemann.

26. K. to Q. Kt's sq.
27. Q. R. to Q. B's sq. (ch.)
28. K. B. takes Q. (ch.)
29. P. to Q's 5th.*
30. P. takes Kt.
31. P. takes Q. R. (ch.)

26. K. R. to K's sq.
27. K. Kt. to Q. B's 2d.
28. Q. R. takes B.
29. Q. Kt. to Q. B's 3d.
30. K. R. takes Q.

And Black gives up the battle, after fighting for above nine hours.

GAME II.—Played at the Philadelphia Athenæum, between Messrs. H. P. Montgomery and W. R. McAdam, at odds of Knight.

Remove White Queen's Knight.

WHITE. (Mr. M.)
1. P. to K's 4th.
2. P. to K. B's 4th.
3. K. Kt. to B's 3d.
4. P. to K. R's 3d.
5. P. to Q. B's 3d.
6. Q. to Q. B's 2d.
7. P. to Q. Kt's 4th.
8. P. to Q. Kt's 5th.
9. P. takes P.
10. Kt. takes P.
11. Kt. to K. B's 3d.
12. P. to Q's 3d.
13. B. to K's 2d.
14. Q. B. takes Kt.
15. P. to Q's 4th.
16. P. to K's 5th.
17. K. B. to Q. B's 4th (ch.)
18. P. to K. R's 4th.
19. Q. to K's 2d.
20. B. to Q. Kt's 3d.
21. Kt. to K. Kt's 5th.
22. P. to K. R's 5th.
23. P. to K. R's 6th.
24. P. to K. Kt's 4th.
25. Q. to Q. B's 4th.
26. P. to Q's 5th.
27. R. to Q. B's sq.
28. Q. takes Kt.
29. K. to B's sq.
30. K. takes B.
31. K. to B's sq.
32. Q. to K. Kt's 8th.(ch.)
33. Kt. mates.

BLACK. (Mr. McA.)
1. P. to K's 4th.
2. K. B. to Q. B's 4th.
3. P. to Q's 3d.
4. Q. Kt. to B's 3d.
5. K. Kt. to B's 3d.
6. Castles.
7. B. to Q. Kt's 3d.
8. Q. Kt. to K's 2d.
9. P. takes P.
10. Q. Kt. to K. Kt's 3d.
11. Q. to K's 2d.
12. K. Kt. to Q's 4th.
13. K. Kt. to K's 6th.
14. B. takes B.
15. P. to K. B's 4th.
16. P. to K. B's 5th.
17. K. to R's sq.
18. Q. B. to K. B's 4th.
19. Q. to Q. R's 6th.
20. Kt. to K's 2d.
21. B. to K. Kt's 3d.
22. B. to K. B's 4th.
23. P. to K. Kt's 3d.
24. Q. to Q. R's 4th.
25. Q. B. takes P.
26. Kt. takes P.
27. B. takes R.
28. Q. takes P. (ch.)
29. B. checks.
30. Q. to K's 6th (ch.)
31. B. to Q's 7th.
32. R. takes Q.

---

* Capitally played. Black can take it only at the expense of a piece.

CHAPTER V.

THE QUEEN'S GAMBIT.

GAME THE FIRST.

WHITE.	BLACK.
1. P to Q's 4th.	1. P. to Q's 4th.
2 P. to Q. B's 4th.	2. P. takes P.

These moves form the Queen's Gambit.

WHITE.	BLACK.
3. P. to K's 3d.	3. P. to K's 4th.
4. K. B. takes P.	4. P. takes Q. P.
5. P. takes P.	5. K. Kt. to B's 3d
6. Q. Kt. to B's 3d.	6. K. B. to Q's 3d.
7. K. Kt. to B's 3d.	7. Q. Kt. to B's 3d
8. Castles.	8 Castles.
9. P. to K. R's 3d.	9. P. to K. R's 3d.

The game is equal; but your P. is well placed, and you have still the move.

VARIATION,
Beginning at Black's 3d move.

WHITE.	BLACK.
1. P. to Q's 4th.	1. P. to Q's 4th.
2. P. to Q. B's 4th.	2. P. takes P.
3. P. to K's 3d.	3. P. to Q. B's 4th
4. B. takes P.	4. P. takes Q. P.
5. P. takes P.	5. Q. Kt. to B's 3d.
6. K Kt. to K's 2d.	6. P. to K's 4th.
7. Q. B. to K's 3d.	7. P. takes P.
8. Kt. takes P.	8. Kt. takes Kt.
9. B. takes Kt.	9. Q. to K's 2d (ch.)

WHITE	BLACK
10. K. B. to K's 2d.	10. Q. to her Kt's 5th (ch.)
11. Q. to her 2d.	11. Q. takes Q. (ch.)
12. Kt. takes Q.	12. Kt. to K's 2d.

You have the superiority.

GAME THE SECOND.

WHITE.	BLACK.
1. P. to Q's 4th.	1. P. to Q's 4th.
2. P. to Q. B's 4th.	2. P. takes P.
3. P. to K's 4th.	3. P. to K's 4th.
4. P. to Q's 5th.	4. P. to K. B's 4th.
5. K. B. takes P.	5. K. Kt. to B's 3d.
6. K. Kt. to B's 3d.	6. K. B. to Q's 3d.
7. P. takes P.	7. Q. B. takes P.
8. Castles.	8. Castles.
9. Q. Kt. to B's 3d.	9. Q. Kt. to Q's 2d.

The positions are pretty equal, but you have still an advantage in the move.

GAME THE THIRD.

Before proceeding to the consideration of games wherein Black refuses the gambit, it may be well to give a brief example of a different mode of carrying on the opening in the regular gambit which is at your command, and often adopted.

WHITE.	BLACK.
1 P. to Q's 4th.	1. P. to Q's 4th.
2. P. to Q. B's 4th.	2. P. takes P.
3. Q. Kt. to B's 3d.	3. K. Kt. to B's 3d.
4. P. to K's 3d.	4. P. to K's 4th.
5. K. B. takes P.	5. P. takes P.
6. P. takes P.	6. K. B. to Q's 3d.

The game may be called even.

QUEEN'S GAMBIT.

VARIATION,
Beginning at Black's 3d move.

WHITE.	BLACK.
1. P. to Q's 4th.	1. P. to K's 4th.
2. P. to Q. B's 4th.	2. P. takes P.
3. Q. Kt. to B's 3d.	3. P. to Q. B's 4th.
4. P. to Q's 5th.	4. P. to K's 3d.
5. P. to K's 4th.	5. P. takes P.
6. P. takes P.	6. K. B. to Q's 3d
7. K. B. takes P.	7. K. Kt. to K's 2d.

Equal game.

GAME THE FOURTH.
THE SCHWARTZ DEFENCE.

WHITE.	BLACK.
1. P. to Q's 4th.	1. P. to Q's 4th.
2. P. to Q. B's 4th.	2. P. takes P.
3. P. to K's 4th.	3. P. to K. B's 4th.
4. P. to K's 5th.	4. Q. B. to K's 3d.
5. Q. Kt. to R's 3d	5. Q. Kt. to B's 3d.
6. Q. B. to K's 3d.	6. Q. Kt. to R's 4th
7. Q. to Q. R's 4th (ch.)	7. P. to Q. B's 3d.
8. B. to Q's 2d.	8. Q. takes Q. P.
9. Q. takes Kt.	9. Q. takes Q. Kt. P
10. Q. B. to his 3d.	10. Q. to her Kt's 3d
11. Q. takes Q.	11. P. takes Q.
12. Q. Kt. takes P.	12. P. to Q. Kt's 4th.
13. Q. Kt. to K's 3d.	13. P. to K. B's 5th.
14. Q. Kt. to Q. B's 2d.	14. R. takes P.
15. K. B. to Q's 3d.	15. R. takes R. (ch.)
16. B. takes R.	

You have much the better game.

The Gambit Refused.

This opening is frequently adopted by the best players. The following games show the conduct of offence and defence by celebrated masters:

Between H. N. Pillsbury and Carl Schlechter.

WHITE. (Mr. P.)	BLACK. (Mr. S.)
1. P. to Q's 4th.	1. P. to Q's 4th.
2. P. to Q. B's 4th.	2. P. to K's 3d.
3. Q. Kt. to B's 3d.	3. K. Kt. to B's 3d.
4. B. to Kt's 5th.	4. B. to K's 2d.
5. Kt. to B's 3d.	5. Q. Kt. to Q's 2d.
6. P. to K's 3d.	6. P. to Q. Kt's 3d.
7. R. to B's sq.*	7. B. to Kt's 2d.
8. P. takes P.	8. P. takes P.
9. B. to Q's 3d.	9. Castles.
10. Castles.	10. P. to B's 4th.
11. B. to Q. Kt's sq.†	11. Kt. to K's 5th.‡
12. B. to B's 4th.	12. Kt. takes Kt.
13. R. takes Kt.	13. P. to B's 5th.
14. Kt. to K's 5th.	14. P. to B's 4th.§
15. K. to R's sq.	15. Kt. takes Kt.
16. B. takes Kt.	16. B. to Q's 3d.
17. P. to B's 4th.	17. B. to B's sq.‖

*NOTES BY W. STEINITZ.—White's game has been modelled chiefly after Steinitz's favorite attack. Here, however, 7. P. takes P. is preferable, for if 7. ... P. takes P; 8. B. to Kt's 5th, B. to Kt's 2d; 9. Kt. to K's 5th, with a strong attack.

† As often shown in my annotations in similar positions, it is absolutely injurious to White's game to allow three well-supportable Pawns against two to be established on the Queen's side. The prospect of a King's side attack on which White speculates is quite unreliable in comparison to the disadvantage on the Queen's side to which he is subjected. At any rate, Pawns ought to be exchanged first, and thus Black's centre weakened.

‡ It was better to make sure of his superiority on the Queen's side by P. to B's 5th at once.

§ He had sufficient force on the King's side to ignore any hostile attack in that direction, and systematic operations on the other wing, commencing with P. to Q. Kt's 4th, were most in order.

‖ The combination of this with the next five moves, more especially with the two closely following, is full of high ingenuity, which, however, is wasted on an imaginary danger. For all purposes of defence it was only necessary to advance P. to K. Kt's 3d at the right time,

QUEEN'S GAMBIT.

18. Q. to R's 5th.	18. P. to Q. R's 3d.
19. R. to K. B's 3d.	19. R. to R's 2d.
20. R. to K. R's 3d.	20. P. to Kt's 3d.
21. Q. to R's 6th.	21. B. takes B.
22. B. P. takes B.	22. R. to K. Kt's 2d.
23. R. to K. B's 3d.	23. P. to Q. Kt's 4th.
24. R. to Q. B's sq.	24. Q. to K's 2d.*
25. Q. R. to K. B's sq.	25. R. (B. sq.) to B's 2d.
26. P. to K. R's 4th.	26. B. to K's 3d.
27. P. to K. Kt's 4th.†	27. Q. to Q's 2d.‡
28. P. takes P.	28. P. takes P.
29. Q. to R's 5th.	29. R. to Kt's 3d.
30. B. takes P.	30. B. takes B.
31. R. takes B.	31. R. takes R.
32. R. takes R.	32. P. to Kt's 5th.
33. Q. to B's 3d.	33. P. to B's 6th.
34. P. takes P.	34. P. takes P.
35. R. to B's 8th (ch.)	35. K. to Kt's 2d.
36. R. to Q. Kt's 8th.	36. Q. to K's 2d.
37. Q. to B's 4th.	37. P. to K. R's 4th.
38. P. to K's 6th.§	38. R. takes P.
39. R. to Q. B's 8th.	39. R. to K's 5th.‖
40. R. to B's 7th.	40. R. takes Q.
41. R. takes Q. (ch.)	41. R. to B's 2d.
42. R. to K's 5th.	42. P. to B's 7th.
43. R. to Kt's 5th (ch.)	43. K. to R's 3d.
44. R. to Kt's sq.	44. R. to Q. Kt's 2d.

White resigns.

---

and then to play R. to B's 2d, followed by B. to K. B's sq. eventually. The Queen's wing was still the proper point of attack to which he should have directed his attention more promptly.

* For aggressive purposes on the Queen's side, the Queen was better placed at B's 2d.

† This rash attack and Black's timid reply were only to be accounted for as results of time pressure on both sides.

‡ There was not the slightest danger in capturing the Pawn with a Pawn ahead, while this loses one.

§ A fatal miscalculation. R to Q. B's 8th led to a most probable draw, for if 38. . . . R. to Kt's 5th ; 39. Q. to B's 6th (ch.), &c.

‖ Black seizes his opportunity with scientific exactitude.

Between Frank J. Marshall and D. Janowsky.

WHITE. (Mr. M.)	BLACK. (Mr. J.)
1. P. to Q's 4th.	1. P. to Q's 4th.
2. P. to Q. B's 4th.	2. P. to K's 3d.
3. Kt. to Q. B's 3d.	3. Kt. to K. B's 3d
4. B. to Kt's 5th.	4. Q. Kt. to Q's 2d.
5. Kt. to B's 3d.	5. B. to K's 2d.
6. P. to K's 3d.	6. Castles.
7. R. to B's sq.*	7. R. to K's sq.†
8. B. to Q's 3d.	8. P. takes P.
9. B. takes P.	9. P. to Q. R's 3d‡
10. Castles.§	10. P. to Kt's 4th.
11. B. to Q's 3d.	11. B. to Kt's 2d.
12. Q. to K's 2d.	12. P. to B's 4th.
13. P. takes P.‖	13. Kt. takes P.
14. B. to B's 2d.¶	14. Kt. to Q's 4th.
15. B. takes B.	15. Q. takes B.
16. Kt. takes Kt.	16. B. takes Kt.
17. P. to Q. Kt's 3d.	17. Q. R. to B's sq.
18. P. to K's 4th.	18. B. to Kt's 2d.
19. P. to Q. Kt's 4th.**	19. Kt. to Q's 2d.
20. K. R. to Q's sq.	20. Kt. to B's sq.
21. P. to Q. R's 3d.	21. R. to B's 6th.††
22. B. to Q's 3d.	22. K. R. to B's sq.‡‡

* Marshall abandons his favorite variation 7. Q. to B's 2d.
† Janowsky also changes P. to B's 4th, played in the earlier games
‡ Janowsky's favorite manœuvre, which might have been expected. Therefore Marshall could have played P. takes P. previous to B. to Q's 3d
§ P. to Q. R's 4th would have prevented the Bishop being dislodged; but as he manages eventually to prevent Black from keeping the majority of Pawns on the Queen's side, there is nothing to be said against it—except that he only keeps about an even game.
‖ This is compulsory, because of the threat P. to B's 5th, followed by P. to Kt's 5th.
¶ B. to Kt's sq. might be followed by P. to Kt's 5th, when K. to Q's sq. would take up the place which the K. R. intends to occupy; but the move would have been better, nevertheless.
** It is doubtful whether the advance might not have been dispensed with, because of the threat Kt. to Q's 2d, Kt's 3d, and B's 5th eventually. But Marshall plays still for attack, not content with a draw in an even position.
†† Black has now the better game.
‡‡ Better would have been 22. . . . Q. to B's 2d; 23. Q. to Kt's 2d, K. R. to B's sq.; 24. R. takes Q., Q. takes R., with the command of the open file.

QUEEN'S GAMBIT.

23. R. takes R.	23. R. takes R.
24. Q. to Kt's 2d.	24. R to B's sq.*
25. R. to Q. B's sq.	25. R. to Q's sq.†
26. B. to Kt's sq.	26. Kt. to Q's 2d.‡
27. Q. to Q's 4th.	27. Kt. to B's 3d.
28. Q. to K's 5th.	28. Kt. to Kt's 5th.
29. Q. to B's 4th.	29. Kt. to B's 3d.
30. P. to R's 3d.	30. Kt. to K's sq.
31. Kt. to K's 5th.	31. Kt. to Q's 3d.
32. Kt. to Kt's 4th.	32. Kt. to B's 5th.§
33. P. to K's 5th.	33. K. to R's sq.
34. Kt. to B's 6th.	34. P. takes Kt.‖
35. Q. to R's 4th. ¶	35. Resigns.

---

* NOTES BY L. HOFFER.—Q. to B's 2d could be played here.
† An alternative would be 25. . . Q. to B's 3d ; 26. P. to K's 5th, Q. to Q's sq. ; 27. R. takes R., Q. takes R.; 28. Q. to B's 2d, Q. takes Q.; 29. B. takes Q., Kt. to Q's 2d, winning the K. P.
‡ Q. to Q's 3d or Q. to B's 2d could be played. The text move gives White a chance to bring his Queen effectively into play.
§ Kt. to K's sq. would have been safer.
‖ Marshall did not expect this *complaisance*, and Janowsky would not have obliged him had he seen the fatal 35. Q. to R's 4th. 34. . . Kt. takes K. P. should have been played.
¶ Marshall risked losing the game in trying to win. His boldness was rewarded, but the verdict should be: Don't try it again.

CHAPTER VI.

IRREGULAR OPENINGS.

GAME THE FIRST.
THE FRENCH GAME.

WHITE.	BLACK.
1. P. to K's 4th.	1. P. to K's 3d.

These two moves begin the "French Game."

2. P. to Q's 4th (best)	2. P. to Q's 4th.
3. P. takes P. (best)	3. P. takes P.
4. P. to Q. B's 4th.	4. K. B. checks.
5. B. to Q's 2d.	5. Q. to K's 2d (ch.)
6. Q. to K's 2d.	6. Q. B. to K's 3d.
7. P. takes P.	7. B. takes B. (ch.)
8. Q. Kt. takes B.	8. B. takes P.

The game is equal.

VARIATION,
Beginning at White's 2d move.

WHITE.	BLACK.
1. P. to K's 4th.	1. P. to K's 3d.
2. P. to K. B's 4th.	2. P. to Q's 4th.
3. P. takes P.	3. P. takes P.
4. K. Kt. to B's 3d.	4. P. to Q. B's 4th
5. P. to Q's 4th.	5. Q. Kt. to B's 3d
6. P. to Q. B's 3d.	6. K. Kt. to B's 3d
7. Q. B. to K's 3d.	7. Q. to her Kt's 3d.
8. Q. to her Kt's 3d.	8. Q. Kt. to R's 4th
9. Q. takes Q.	9. P. takes Q.

10. K. B. checks.	10. Q. B. to Q's 2d.
11. B. takes B. (ch.)	11. K. Kt. takes B.

The game is even.

GAME THE SECOND.
THE SICILIAN GAME.

WHITE.	BLACK.
1. P. to K's 4th.	1. P. to Q. B's 4th.

These moves commence the "Sicilian Game." Black's move is considered by Staunton the best reply to White's move, 1. P. to K's 4th.

2. K. Kt. to B's 3d.	2. P. to K's 3d.
3. P. to Q's 4th.	3. P. to Q's 4th.
4. P. takes Q. P.	4. K. P. takes P.
5. P. to Q. B's 4th.	5. P. takes Q. P.
6. P. takes Q. P.	6. Q. takes P.
7. Q. takes P.	7. Q. takes Q.
8. Kt. takes Q.	8. K. B. to Q. B's 4th
9. Kt. to Q. Kt's 3d.	9. B. to Q. Kt's 3d.
10. B. to Q. B's 4th.	10. K. Kt. to B's 3d
11. Castles.	11. Castles.

Equal game.

GAME THE THIRD.

WHITE.	BLACK.
1. P. to K's 4th.	1. P. to Q. B's 4th.
2. P. to Q's 4th.	2. P. takes P.
3. Q. takes P.	3. Q. Kt. to B's 3d.
4. Q. to her sq.	4. K. Kt. to B's 3d.
5. Q. Kt. to B's 3d	5. P. to K's 3d.
6. Q. B. to K. Kt's 5th.	6. K. B. to K's 2d.

The game appears to be equal.

GAME THE FOURTH.

WHITE.	BLACK.
1. P. to K's 4th.	1. P. to Q. B's 4th.

2. P. to K. B's 4th.   2. P. to K's 3d
3. K. Kt. to B's 3d.   3. P. to Q's 4th.
4. P. to K's 5th.   4. Q. Kt. to B's 3d.
5. P. to Q. B's 3d.   5. P. to K. B's 3d.
6. K. B. to Q's 3d.   6. K. Kt. to R's 3d.
7. K. B. to Q. B's 2d.   7. Q. to her Kt's 3d.

Black has the advantage.

VARIATION,
Beginning at Black's 2d move.

WHITE	BLACK.
1. P. to K's 4th.	1. P. to Q. B's 4th.
2. P. to K. B's 4th.	2. Q. Kt. to B's 3d.
3. K. Kt. to B's 3d.	3. P. to K's 3d.
4. B. to K's 2d.	4. P. to Q's 4th.
5. P. to Q's 3d.	5. P. takes P.
6. P. takes P.	6. Q. takes Q. (ch.)
7. B. takes Q.	7. K. Kt. to B's 3d
8. Q. Kt. to B's 3d.	8. Q. B. to Q's 2d.
9. Q. B. to K's 3d.	9. Castles.

The game is even.

GAME THE FIFTH.

WHITE.	BLACK.
1. P. to K's 4th.	1. B. to Q. B's 4th.
2. P. to Q. B's 4th.	2. P. to K's 3d.
3. K. Kt. to B's 3d.	3. Q. Kt. to B's 3d.
4. Q. Kt. to B's 3d.	4. P. to K. Kt's 3d.
5. P. to Q's 3d.	5. B. to K. Kt's 2d
6. B. to K's 2d.	6. K. Kt. to K's 2d

I much prefer his game.

GAME THE SIXTH.
THE WING GAMBIT.

WHITE.	BLACK.
1. P. to K's 4th.	1. P. to Q. B's 4th
2. P. to Q. Kt's 4th.	2. P. takes P.

IRREGULAR OPENINGS.

3. P. to Q's 4th.   3. P. to Q's 4th.
4. P. to K's 5th.   4. Q. B. to K. B's 4th
5. P to Q. R's 3d   5. P. takes P.
6. Q. B. takes P.   6. Q. Kt. to B's 3d.

You have no equivalent for the lost Pawn.

GAME THE SEVENTH.

THE CENTRE COUNTER GAMBIT.

WHITE.   BLACK.
1. P. to K's 4th.   1. P. to Q's 4th.
2. P. takes P. (best)   2. Q. takes P.
3. Q. Kt. to B's 3d.   3. Q. to her sq. (best)
4. P. to Q's 4th.   4. Q. B. to K. B's 4th
5. K. Kt. to B's 3d.   5. P. to K's 3d.
6. K. B. to Q. B's 4th.

You have a better opened game.

VARIATION I.

Beginning at Black's 2d move.

WHITE.   BLACK.
1. P. to K's 4th   1. P. to Q's 4th.
2. P. takes P   2. K. Kt. to B's 3d.
3. B. to Q. Kt's 5th (ch.)   3. B. to Q's 2d.
4. K. B. to Q. B's 4th.   4. P. to Q. Kt's 4th.
5. K. B. to Q. Kt's 3d.   5. Q. B. to K. Kt's 5th
6. P. to K. B's 3d.   6. Q. B. to his sq.
7. Q. to K's 2d.   7. P. to Q. R's 3d.
8. P. to Q. B's 4th.   8. P. to Q. B's 3d.
9. Q. P takes P.   9. Q. Kt. takes P.
10. Q. B. P. takes P.   10. Q. Kt. to Q's 5th.
11. Q. to K's 3d.   11. Q. R. P. takes P.
12. Kt. to K's 2d.   12. Kt. takes Kt.
13. K. takes Kt.   13. Q. B. to Q. R's 3d.
14. K. R. to Q's sq.   14. P. to Q. Kt's 5th (dis ch.)

15. P. to Q's 3d.   15. P. to K's 3d.
16. P. to Q. R's 3d.

You have a good game, and a Pawn superiority.

Variation II.
Beginning at Black's 5th move.

WHITE.	BLACK.
1. P. to K's 4th.	1. P. to Q's 4th.
2. P. takes P.	2. K. Kt. to B's 3d.
3. B. to Q. Kt's 5th (ch.)	3. B. to Q's 2d.
4. B. to Q. B's 4th.	4. P. to Q. Kt's 4th.
5. B. to Q. Kt's 3d.	5. P. to Q. R's 4th.
6. P. to Q. R's 3d.	6. Q. B. to K. Kt's 5th
7. P. to K. B's 3d.	7. B. to his sq.
8. Q. Kt. to B's 3d.	8. Q. B. to Q. R's 3d.
9. P. to Q's 3d.	9. P. to Q. Kt's 5th.
10. Q. R. P. takes P.	10. Q. R. P. takes P.
11. Q. Kt. to R's 4th.	11. Q. B. to Q. Kt's 2d.
12. Q. B. to Q's 2d.	

Black's position is inferior.

GAME THE EIGHTH.
The Fianchetto.

WHITE.	BLACK.
1. P. to K's 4th.	1. P. to Q. Kt's 3d.
2. P. to Q's 4th.	2. Q. B. to Q. Kt's 2d.
3. K. B. to Q's 3d.	3. P. to K's 3d.
4. P. to K. B's 4th	4. P. to Q's 4th.
5. P. to K's 5th.	5. P. to Q. B's 4th
6. P. to Q. B's 3d.	6. K. Kt. to K. R's 3d

The game appears to be equal.

Variation,
Beginning at Black's 3d move.

WHITE.	BLACK.
1. P. to K's 4th.	1. P. to Q. Kt's 3d.
2. P. to Q's 4th.	2. B. to Q. Kt's 2d.

IRREGULAR OPENINGS.

3. B. to Q's 3d.	3. P. to K. Kt's 3d.
4. P. to K. B's 4th.	4. B. to K. Kt's 2d.
5. K. Kt. to B's 3d.	5. P. to Q's 3d.
6. Q. B. to K's 3d.	6. Q. Kt. to Q's 2d.
7. P. to Q. B's 4th.	7. P. to K's 3d.
8. Q. Kt. to B's 3d.	8. K. Kt. to K's 2d.
9. Q. to K's 2d.	9. Castles.
10. Castles on Q's side.	10. P. to K. B's 4th.
11. K. Kt. to his 5th.	11. P. takes K. P.
12. B. takes P.	12. B. takes B.
13. Q. Kt. takes B.	

You have the better game.

GAME THE NINTH.

1. P. to Q's 4th.	1. P to K B's 4th.
2. P. to Q. B's 4th.	2. K Kt. to B's 3d.
3. Q. Kt. to B's 3d.	3. P to Q's 3d.
4. Q. B. to K. B's 4th	4. P to Q. B's 3d.
5. P. to K's 3d.	5. Q to her B's 2d.
6. K. Kt. to B's 3d.	6. K Kt. to K. R's 4th
7. Q. B. to K. Kt's 5th.	7. P to K. R's 3d.
8. B. to K. R's 4th.	8. P to K. Kt's 4th.
9. K. Kt. to Q's 2d.	9. K Kt. to B's 3d.
10. B. to K. Kt's 3d.	10. P to K's 4th

Equal game.

VARIATION I.

Beginning at White's 2d move.

WHITE.	BLACK.
1. P. to Q's 4th.	1. P. to K. B's 4th.
2. P. to K's 4th.	2. P. takes P.
3. Q. Kt. to B's 3d.	3. K. Kt. to B's 3d
4. Q. B. to K. Kt's 5th.	4. P. to Q B's 3d.
5. B. takes Kt.	5. K. P. takes B.
6. Q. Kt. takes K P.	6. P. to Q's 4th.
7. Q. Kt. to K. Kt's 3d.	7. B. to Q's 2d.
8. B. to Q's 3d.	8. Castles.

I prefer your position.

VARIATION II.
Beginning at White's 2d move.

WHITE.	BLACK.
1. P. to Q's 4th.	1. P. to K. B's 4th.
2. P. to K. R's 3d.	2. K. Kt. to B's 3d.
3. P. to K. Kt's 4th.	3. P. to Q's 4th (best)
4. P. to K. Kt's 5th	4. K. Kt. to K's 5th.
5. P. to K. R's 4th.	5. P. to Q. B's 4th.
6. P. to Q. B's 3d.	6. P. to K's 3d.
7. K. Kt. to B's 3d.	7. Q. Kt. to B's 3d.
8. Q. B. to K. B's 4th.	8. K. B. to Q's 3d.
9 B. takes B.	9. Q. takes B.

Even game.

GAME THE TENTH.

WHITE.	BLACK.
1. P. to Q's 4th.	1. P. to Q. B's 4th.
2. P. to Q's 5th.	2. P. to K's 4th.
3. P. to Q. B's 4th.	3. P. to K. B's 4th.
4. Q. Kt. to B's 3d.	4. P. to Q's 3d.

You have the advantage.

GAME THE ELEVENTH.

WHITE.	BLACK.
1. P. to K. B's 4th.	1. P. to Q's 4th.
2. K. Kt. to B's 3d.	2. Q. B. to K. Kt's 5th
3. K. Kt. to K's 5th.	3. B. to K. B's 4th.
4. P. to K. Kt's 4th.	4. P. to K's 3d.
5. P. to K. Kt's 5th.	5. P. to K. B's 3d.
6. Kt. to K. B's 3d.	6. P. takes P.
7. Kt. takes P.	7. K. B. to K's 2d.
8. P. to K. R's 4th.	8. P. to K. R's 3d.
9. Kt. to K. B's 3d.	9. Q. B. to K. Kt's 5th.

Black has the better game, owing to your premature attack at the 4th move.

IRREGULAR OPENINGS.

GAME THE TWELFTH.

WHITE.	BLACK.
1. P. to Q. B's 4th.	1. P. to Q. B's 4th.
2. P. to K. B's 4th.	2. P. to K. B's 4th.
3. P. to Q's 3d	3. K. Kt. to B's 3d.
4. Q. Kt. to B's 3d	4. P. to Q's 3d.
5. P. to K's 4th.	5. Q. Kt. to B's 3d.
6. K. Kt. to B's 3d.	6. P. to K's 4th.
7. B. to Q's 2d.	7. Q. to K's 2d.
8. P. to Q. R's 3d.	8. P. to K. Kt's 3d.
9. P. to K. Kt's 3d.	9. K. B. to Kt's 2d.
10. Q. Kt. to Q's 5th.	10. Kt. takes Kt.
11. Q. B. P. takes Kt.	11. Q. Kt. to Q's 5th.
12. Kt. takes Kt.	12. Q. B. P. takes Kt.

Equal game.

VARIATION,

Beginning at Black's 1st move.

WHITE.	BLACK.
1. P. to Q. B's 4th.	1. P. to K's 4th.
2. Q. Kt. to B's 3d.	2. P. to K. B's 4th
3. P. to K's 3d.	3. K. Kt. to B's 3d.
4. P. to Q's 4th.	4. P. to K's 5th.
5. K. Kt. to R's 3d.	

You have the advantage in position.

FRENCH DEFENCE.

GAME I.—Between Drs. Lasker and Tarrasch.

WHITE. (Dr. L.)	BLACK. (Dr. T.)
1. P. to K's 4th.	1. P. to K's 3d.
2. P. to Q's 4th.	2. P. to Q's 4th.
3. Kt. to Q. B's 3d.	3. Kt. to K. B's 3d.
4. B. to Kt's 5th.	4. B to Kt's 5th.
5. P. takes P.	5. Q. takes P.
6. Kt. to B's 3d.*	6. P. to B's 4th.†
7. B. takes Kt.	7. P. takes B.
8. Q. to Q's 2d.	8. B. takes Kt.
9. Q. takes B.‡	9. Kt. to Q's 2d.

* The best line of play against the McCutcheon defence. It was played in a game Sjöberg *vs.* Giersing, Stockholm, 1906.

† Out of place in this position. Q. Kt. to Q's 2d or Kt. to K's 5th, would be alternatives—the former move in preference.

‡ This excellent move was probably not taken into consideration by Tarrasch when advancing P. to B's 4th.

CHESS HANDBOOK.

10. R. to Q's sq.	10. R. to K. Kt s sq.*
11. P. takes P	11. Q. takes P.
12. Q. to Q's 2d.†	12. Q. to Kt's 3d ‡
13. P. to B's 3d.	13. P. to Q. R's 3d.
14. Q to B's 2d.	14. P. to B's 4th.
15. P. to K. Kt's 3d.	15. Kt. to B's 4th.
16. B to Kt's 2d.	16. Q. to B's 2d.
17. Q. to K's 2d.	17. P. to Kt's 4th.
18. Castles.	18. B. to Kt's 2d.
19. P. to B's 4th.	19. P. to Kt's 5th.
20. Q. to Q's 2d.	20. R. to Kt's sq.
21. Q. to R's 6th.	21. B. takes Kt.
22. B. takes B.	22. Q to K's 4th.
23. K. R. to K's sq.	23. Q. takes P ₰
24. Q. to B's 4th.	24. R. to Q B's sq.
25. Q. to Q's 6th.	25. P. to B's 3d.
26. B. to R's 5th (ch.)	26. R. to Kt's 2d.
27. B. takes R. (ch.)	27. P. takes B.
28. R. takes P. (ch.)	28. Resigns.

GAME II.—Played by Mr. Morphy without seeing the Chess-board or men, against M. Bierwirth.

WHITE. (Mr. M.)	BLACK. (M. B.)
1. P. to K's 4th.	1. P. to K's 3d.
2. P. to Q's 4th.	2. P. to Q. B's 3d.
3. K. B. to Q's 3d.	3. P. to Q's 4th.
4. P. takes P.	4. K. P. takes P.
5. K. Kt. to K. B's 3d.	5. Q. B. to K. Kt's 5th.
6. Castles.	6. K. B. to Q's 3d.
7. P. to K. R's 3d.	7. Q. B. to K. R's 4th.
8. Q. B. to K's 3d.	8. Q. Kt. to Q's 2d.
9. K. R. to K's sq.	9. K. Kt. to K's 2d.
10. Q. Kt. to Q's 2d.	10. Q. B. takes Kt.
11. Kt. takes B.	11. P. to K. R's 3d.
12. Q. to Q's 2d.	12. Q. to Q. B's 2d.
13. P. to Q. B's 4th.	13. P. takes P.
14. K. B. takes P.	14. P. to K. B's 4th.
15. Kt. to K's 5th.	15. Castles on Q's side.
16. K. B. to K's 6th.	16. B. takes Kt.
17. P. takes B.	17. K. to Q. Kt's sq.

* If 10.., P. takes P., then 11. R. takes P., and Black could not challenge the Queen with 11.., Q. to Q. B's 4th, because of 12. R. to Q. B's 4th Nor could 10.., K. to K's 2d be played, because of 11. P. takes P , and 11.., Q. takes B. P. would be answered with 12. R. takes Kt. winning the Queen, and as the continuation in the text is hopeless, there remains the only alternative of 10.., Castles, with a good enough game. all things considered.

† Simply position play. Black's forces are paralyzed, and the King fixed on the middle of the centre.

‡ Q. to B's 2d at once seems comparatively better, and if necessary Castles, and the case is not altogether hopeless.

₰ Not a judicious capture, to say the least.

| This move, or resigning. There is nothing else. The latter course would be more to the purpose, unless a miracle is expected.

18. Q. to Q. B's 3d.*	18. Q. Kt. to Q. Kt's 3d.
19. Q. to Q. R's 3d.	19. Q. Kt. to Q. B's sq.
20. Q. R. to Q. B's sq.	20. P. to K. Kt's 4th.
21. P. to K. B's 4th.	21. P. takes P.
22. Q. B. takes P.	22. Q. R. to Q's 5th.
23. Q. to K's 3d.	23. Q. R. to K's 5th.
24. Q. to K. B's 3d.	24. Q. to Q. Kt's 3d (ch.)
25. K. to K. R's 2d.	25. Q. R. takes R.
26. R. takes R.	26. Q. to Q. Kt's 5th.
27. R. to K's 2d.	27. K. Kt. to K. Kt's 3d.
28. Q. B. to Q's 2d.	28. Q. to Q. Kt's 4th.
29. K. B. takes Kt.	29. R. takes B.
30. B. takes K. R. P.	30. R. to K. R's sq.
31. B. to K. Kt's 7th.	31. R. to K. R's 2d.
32. B. to K. B's 6th.	32. R. to K. B's 2d.
33. Q. to K. R's 5th.	33. Kt. to K. B's 5th.
34. Q. takes R.	

And Black surrenders, after a struggle of nearly nine hours.

GAME III.—Played between Mr. H. P. Montgomery, of Philadelphia, and Mr. Pindar, one of the leading members of the Manchester Chess Club, England.

WHITE. (Mr. P.)	BLACK. (Mr. M.)
1. P. to K's 4th.	1. P. to K's 3d.
2. P. to Q's 4th.	2. P. to Q's 4th.
3. P. takes P.	3. Q. takes P.
4. Q. Kt. to B's 3d.	4. K. B. to Q. Kt's 5th.
5. K. Kt. to B's 3d.	5. K. Kt. to B's 3d.
6. K. B. to Q's 3d.†	6. P. to Q. B's 4th.‡
7. Q. B. to Q's 2d.	7. B. takes Kt.
8. B. takes B.	8. P. to Q. B's 5th.
9. K. B. to K's 2d.	9. K. Kt. to K's 5th.
10. Castles.	10. Kt. takes B.§
11. P. takes Kt.	11. Q. Kt. to Q's 2d.‖
12. Kt. to Q's 2d.	12. Kt. to Kt's 3d.
13. P. to Q. R's 4th.¶	13. P. to Q. R's 4th.

* A very ingenious move. If Black take the Pawn with his Queen, he of course loses her by " B. takes Q. R. P. (ch.), &c.,' and if with the Kt. it costs him at least a Piece.

† A favorite move with several of the strongest of modern players.

‡ If White take P. with P., the Black K. B. is brought into play; and if not, the advance of P. to B's 5th is threatened.

§ Chiefly to double White's Pawns.

‖ Black foresaw the intended attack on the B. P., and by providing for it in this way brought another Piece into action.

¶ White keeps up the attack on the B. P. with a great deal of vigor The move of R. P. two was a very good one.

14. Q. R. to Q. Kt's sq.	14. Q. to Q. B's 3d.*
15. B. to K. B's 3d.	15. Q. to Q. B's 2d.
16. Kt. to K's 4th.	16. Kt. takes Q. R. P
17. Q. to Q's 2d.	17. Castles.
18. Q. R. to Q. Kt's 5th.†	18. P. to K. B's 4th.‡
19. Kt. to K. Kt's 3d.	19. Q. R. to Q. Kt's sq.
20. P. to Q's 5th.	20. Q. to Q's 2d.§
21. R. takes Q. R. P. ‖	21. P. to Q. Kt's 4th.¶
22. Q. to K. B's 4th.¶	22. Q. to Q. Kt's 2d.**
23. Q. P. takes P.	23. Q. to Q. Kt's 3d.
24. P. to K's 7th.	24. K. R. to K's sq.
25. K. R. to K's sq.	25. B. to K's 3d.††
26. R. takes Kt.‡‡	26. P. takes R.
27. Q. to K's 5th.§§	27. K. R. takes P.
28. Kt. takes P.	28. K. R. to K. B's 2d.
29. Kt. to Q's 6th.	29. K. R. to K. B's 3d.
30. Kt. to K's 4th.	30. K. R. to K. B's 4th.
31. Q. to K. Kt's 3d.	31. Q. R. to K. B's sq.‖‖
32. Kt. to K. Kt's 5th.	32. B. to Q's 4th.
33. B. takes B. (ch.)	33. R. takes B.
34. Kt. to K's 6th.	34. Q. takes Kt.¶¶

And Black wins.

SICILIAN DEFENCE.

GAME IV.—Played by Correspondence between New York and Philadelphia.

WHITE. (N. Y.)	BLACK. (Phila.)
1. P. to K's 4th.	1. P. to Q. B's 4th.
2. P. to Q's 4th.	2. P. takes P.
3. K. Kt. to B's 3d.	3. P. to K's 3d.
4. Q. takes P.	4. Q. Kt. to B's 3d.

---

* The best move.

† The R. is well posted—for attack and defence.

‡ Black has now resumed the offensive.

§ Threatening to take Q. if P. takes P., and attacking Q. R. at the same time. There was still another motive for this move, viz.: to induce White to take R. P., foreseeing the R. would be lost subsequently.

‖ To enslave the Rook.

¶ A nexcellent move. In this and the succeeding moves, White played very well. His efforts were directed to saving his R., but, as the result showed, without success.

** Apparently hazardous, but justified by the gain of time.

†† We believe his best move.

‡‡ White was obliged to lose the exchange, although he fought manfully against it.

§§ Another very good move in White.

‖‖ Black's advantage in the exchange begins now to tell on the game.

¶¶ Threatening mate if R. takes Q.

IRREGULAR OPENINGS.

5. Q. to Q's sq.	5. K. B. to Q. B's 4th.
6. K. B. to Q's 3d.	6. K. Kt. to K's 2d.
7. Q. Kt. to B's 3d.	7. P. to Q's 4th.
8. P. takes P.	8. K. Kt. takes P.
9. Q. Kt. to K's 4th.	9. B. to Q. Kt's 3d.
10. B. to Q. Kt's 5th.	10. Castles.
11. K. B. takes Kt.	11. P. takes B.
12. Castles.	12. P. to K. B's 4th.
13. Q. Kt. to K. Kt's 3d	13. Q. to Q. B's 2d.
14. P. to Q. B's 4th.	14. Kt. to K. B's 3d.
15. Q. to Q. B's 2d.	15. P. to Q. B's 4th.
16. P. to Q. Kt's 3d.	16. B. to Q. Kt's 2d.
17. K. Kt. to Kt's 5th.	17. Q. to Q. B's 3d.
18. P. to K. B's 3d.	18. B. to Q. B's 2d.
19. K. R. to K's sq.	19. Q. R. to K's sq.
20. B. to Q. Kt's 2d.	20. P. to K. Kt's 3d.
21. K. R. to K's 2d.	21. P. to K's 4th.
22. Q. R. to K's sq.	22. P. to K's 5th.
23. P. takes P.	23. B. to K. B's 5th.
24. K. Kt. to K. R's 3d	24. B. takes Kt.
25. P. takes B.	25. Kt. takes P.
26. Kt. to Kt's 5th.	26. Kt. takes Kt.
27. Q. to Q. B's 3d.	27. Q. takes K. Kt. P. (ch.)
28. R. takes Q.	28. R. takes R. (ch.)
29. Q. takes R.	29. Kt. to B's 6th (ch.)
30. K. to B's sq.	30. Kt. takes Q.
31. R. to Q's 2d.	31. P. to B's 5th.
32. P. takes P.	32. Kt. to K. Kt's 7th.
33. R. to Q's 7th.	33. R. takes P. (ch.)
34. K. to Kt's sq.	34. B. to K's 5th.
35. R. to K. Kt's 7th (ch.)	35. K. to B's sq.
36. R. takes K. R. P.	36. Kt. to K's 6th.
37. R. to K. R's 8th (ch.)	37. K. to B's 2d.
38. B. to K's 5th.	38. R. to K. B's 8th (ch.)
39. K. to K. R's 2d.	39. Kt. to K. B's 4th.
40. K. to R's 3d.	40. P. to K. Kt's 4th.
41. R. to Q. B's 8th.	

And Philadelphia announces mate in six moves.

GAME V.—Played by Mr. Morphy without seeing the Chess board or men, against M. Preti.

WHITE. (Mr. M.)	BLACK. (Mr. P.)
1. P. to K's 4th.	1. P. to Q. B's 4th.
2. P. to Q's 4th.	2. P. takes P.
3. K. Kt. to K. B's 3d.	3. P. to K's 4th.
4. K. B. to Q. B's 4th.	4. K. B. checks.
5. P. to Q. B's 3d.	5. P. takes P.
6. P. takes P.	6. K. B. to Q. B's 4th.
7. K. Kt. takes K's P.	7. Q. to K. B's 3d.
8. K. B. takes K. B. P. (ch.)	8. K. to B's sq.
9. K. Kt. to Q's 3d.	9. K. B. to Q. Kt's 3d.

10. K. B. to Q. Kt's 3d.	10. P. to Q's 3d.
11. Q. B. to Q. R's 3d.	11. Q. Kt. to Q. B's 3d.
12. Castles.	12. K. Kt. to K. R's 3d.
13. P. to K's 5th.	13. Q. to K. Kt's 3d.
14. K. Kt. to K. B's 4th.	14. Q. to K. Kt's 5th.
15. K. Kt. to K's 6th (ch.)*	15. Q. B. takes Kt.
16. Q. takes Q. P. (ch.)	16. K. to B's 2d.
17. Q. to Q's 7th (ch.)	17. K. to K. Kt's 3d.
18. K. B. takes B.	18. Q. to K. Kt's 4th.
19. K. B. to Q's 5th.	19. Q. Kt. takes K. P.
20. K. B. to K's 4th (ch.)	20. K. Kt. to K. B's 4th.
21. Q. to K's 6th (ch.)	21. Q. to K. B's 3d.
22. K. B. takes Kt. (ch.)	22. K. to K. R's 4th.
23. P. to K. Kt's 4th (ch.)	23. Kt. takes P.
24. K. B. takes Kt. (ch.)	

And Black surrenders.

GAME VI.—Played at the Philadelphia Athenæum, between Mr. Clements and Dr. Lewis.

WHITE. (Mr. C.)	BLACK. (Dr. L.)
1. P. to K's 4th.	1. P. to Q. B's 4th.
2. P. to Q's 4th.	2. P. to K's 3d.†
3. K. Kt. to B's 3d.	3. P. to Q's 4th.
4. K. P. takes P.	4. K. P. takes P.
5. K. B. to Q. Kt's 5th (ch.)	5. Q. Kt. to Q. B's 3d.
6. Castles.	6. K. Kt. to B's 3d.
7. K. Kt. to K's 5th.	7. Q. to Q. Kt's 3d.
8. B. takes Kt. (ch.)	8. P. takes B.
9. R. to K's sq.	9. Q. B. to K's 3d.
10. Q. to K's 2d.‡	10. Q. B. P. takes P.
11. Kt. takes K. B. P.§	11. K. Kt. to K's 5th.
12. Kt. takes R.	12. Castles.
13. Q. to K. B's 3d.	13. K. B. to Q. B's 4th.
14. R. takes Kt.	14. P. takes R.
15. Q. takes P.	15. R. to K's sq.
16. P. to Q. Kt's 4th.	16. Q. B. to Q's 2d.
17. Q. takes R. (ch.)	17. B. takes Q.
18. Kt. P. takes B.	18. Q. takes P.
19. Q. B. to R's 3d.	19. Q. takes B. P.
20. P. to K. R's 3d.	20. P. to Q's 6th.
21. B. to Kt's 4th.	21. Q. to her Kt's 7th.
22. B. to Q. B's 3d.	22. Q. to Q. B's 8th (ch.)
23. K. to R's 2d.	23. P. to Q. B's 4th.

---

* This is more effectual than taking the Queen's Pawn with Queen at once.

† The proper move.

‡ Well played.

§ This move, properly followed up, should have given White the game.

IRREGULAR OPENINGS.

24. B. to Q's 2d.	24. Q. to Q. B's 7th.
25. P. to Q. R's 4th.	25. B. to Q. B's 3d.*
26. Kt. to K. B's 7th.	26. Q. to Q's 8th.
27. Kt. to Q's 6th (ch.)	27. K. to Q's 2d.
28. Kt. to Q. B's 4th.	28. B. to K's 5th.
29. B. to Q. B's 3d.	29. Q. to Q. B's 7th.
30. K. Kt. to Q's 2d.	30. B. to Q's 4th.
31. B. takes P.	31. P. to Q. B's 5th.
32. B. to Q. B's 3d.	32. Q. to Q's 8th.
33. Kt. to R's 3d.	33. Q. to K. R's 4th.
34. Kt. to Q. Kt's 5th.	34. Q. to K. Kt's 3d.
35. P. to K. B's 3d.	35. P. to K. R's 4th.
36. R. to K's sq.	36. P. to K. R's 5th.
37. R. to K's 5th.	37. B. to Q. B's 3d.
38. Kt. takes Q. R. P.	38. B. takes Q. R. P.
39. Kt. takes Q. B. P.	39. B. to Q. Kt's 6th.
40. R. to Q's 5th (ch.)	40. K. to Q. B's 2d.
41. B. to K's 5th (ch.)	41. K. to Q. Kt's 2d.
42. R. to Q's 7th (ch.)	42. K. to R's 3d.
43. R. to Q's 6th (ch.)	43. Q. takes R.
44. B. takes Q.	44. B. takes Kt.
45. B. to Q. Kt's 4th.	45. K. takes Kt.
46. K. to K. Kt's sq.	46. K. to Q. Kt's 3d.
47. B. to Q's 2d.	47. K. to Q. B's 4th.
48. K. to K. B's 2d.	48. K. to Q's 4th.
49. B. to K's sq.	49. K. to K's 4th.
50. K. to K's 3d.	50. K. to K. B's 4th.
51. B. takes P.	51. P. to Q's 7th.†
52. K. takes P.	52. K. to K. B's 5th.
53. K. to K's sq.	53. B. to Q's 6th.
54. K. to K. B's 2d.	54. K. to K. B's 4th.
55. P. to K. Kt's 3d.	55. B. to Q. B's 5th.
56. P. to Kt's 4th (ch.)	56. K. to Kt's 3d.
57. P. to K. B's 4th.	57. B. to Q's 4th.
58. P. to K. B's 5th (ch.)	58. K. to K. Kt's 2d.
59. P. to K. Kt's 5th.	59. B. to K's 5th.
60. P. to K. B's 6th (ch.)	60. K. to Kt's 3d.
61. K. to Kt's 3d.	61. B. to Q's 4th.
62. K. to Kt's 4th.	62. B. to K's 3d (ch.)
63. K. to Kt's 3d.	

And Black draws the game.

---

* Allowing the escape of the Knight.

† From this point, we believe Black can draw the game against White's best possible play. The latter part of the game is well played by Black.

GAME VII.—Played between Mr. James Thompson of New York and Mr. H. P. Montgomery of Philada.

WHITE. (Mr. T.)	BLACK. (Mr. M.)
1. P. to K's 4th.	1. P. to Q. B's 4th.
2. P. to Q. B's 4th.	2. P. to K's 4th.
3. Kt. to Q. B's 3d.	3. P. to K. B's 4th.
4. P. takes P.	4. Kt. to K. B's 3d.
5. Kt. to Q's 5th.	5. P. to Q's 3d.
6. B. to Q's 3d.	6. Kt. to Q. B's 3d.
7. P. to K. Kt's 4th.	7. Kt. takes Kt.
8. P. takes Kt.	8. Kt. to Q's 5th.
9. Kt. to B's 3d.	9. P. to K. R's 4th.
10. P. takes R. P.	10. Kt. takes K. B. P.
11. B. to Q. Kt's 5th (ch.)	11. B. to Q's 2d.
12. B. takes B. (ch.)	12. Q. takes B.
13. Kt. to K. Kt's 5th.	13. Kt. to Q's 5th.
14. P. to Q's 3d.	14. Q. to K. B's 4th.
15. B. to K's 3d.	15. Castles (Q's side.)
16. R. to Q. B's sq.	16. B. to K's 2d.
17. B. takes Kt.	17. K. P. takes B.
18. Kt. to K's 4th.	18. Q. R. to K's sq.
19. R. to K. Kt's sq.	19. B. to K. Kt's 4th.
20. Q. to K's 2d.	20. Q. to B's 5th.
21. R. to Q. B's 2d.	21. B. to B's 3d.
22. P. to K. R's 3d.	22. K. to Kt's sq.
23. P. to Q. Kt's 4th.	23. Q. to K. R's 7th.
24. Q. to K. Kt's 4th.	24. K. R. to K. B's sq.
25. K. to Q's sq.	25. R. takes Kt.
26. P. takes R.	26. P. to Q's 6th
27. R. to Q's 2d.	27. Q. to K's 4th.
28. R. takes Q. P.	28. Q. to Q. R's 8th (ch.)
29. K. to K's 2d.	29. Q. takes R. P. (ch.)
30. K. to B's sq.	30. P. takes Q. Kt. P.
31. Q. to K's 2d.	31. P. to Kt's 6th.
32. R. to Q's sq.	32. P. to Kt's 7th.
33. Q. to Q. B's 2d.	33. B. to Q's 5th.
34. R. to K. Kt's 2d.	34. P. Queens, and wins.

GAME VIII.—Between Dr. Emanuel Lasker and A. A. Alechine, played in the St. Petersburg Masters' Tournament, 1914.

WHITE. (Lasker.)	BLACK. (Alechine.)
1. P. to K's 4th.	1. P. to Q's 4th.
2. P. takes P.	2. Kt. to K. B's 3d.
3. P. to Q's 4th.	3. Kt. takes P.
4. Kt. to K. B's 3d.	4. B. to Kt's 5th.
5. P. to B's 4th.	5. Kt. to Kt's 3d.
6. Kt. to B's 3d.	6. P. to K's 4th.
7. P. to B's 5th.	7. P. takes P.
8. Kt. to K's 4th.	8. K. Kt. to Q's 2d.

9. Q. takes P.	9. Q. to K's 2d.
10. B. to Q. Kt's 5th.	10. Kt. to B's 3d.
11. B. takes Kt.	11. P. takes B.
12. Castles.	12. B. takes Kt.
13. P. takes B.	13. Castles.
14. Q. to R's 4th.	14. Kt. to K's 4th.
15. K. to Kt's 2d.	15. Q. to K's 3d.
16. Q. takes R. P.	16. Q. to B's 4th.
17. Q. to R's 8th (ch.)	17. K. to Q's 2d.
18. R. to Q. (ch.)	18. K. to K's 3d.
19. Q. takes R.	19. Q. takes P. (ch.)
20. K. to Kt.	20. B. to K's 2d.
21. Q. to Q's 4th.	21. Q. to Kt's 5th (ch.)
22. K. to R.	22. Q. to B's 6th (ch.)
23. K. to Kt.	23. Q. to Kt's 5th (ch.)
Drawn.	

GAME IX.—Between Mr. Morphy and Mr. Andersson.

WHITE. (Mr. M.)	BLACK. (Mr. A.)
1. P. to K's 4th.	1. P. to Q's 4th.
2. P. takes P.	2. K. Kt. to B's 3d.
3. P. to Q's 4th.	3. Kt. takes P.
4. P. to Q. B's 4th.	4. Kt. to K. B's 3d.
5. Q. Kt. to B's 3d.	5. Q. B. to K. B's 4th.
6. K. Kt. to B's 3d.	6. P. to K's 3d.
7. Q. B. to K's 3d.	7. K. B. to Q. Kt's 5th.
8. Q. to Q. Kt's 3d.	8. B. takes Kt. (ch.)
9. P. takes B.	9. B. to K's 5th.
10. Kt. to Q's 2d.	10. B. to Q. B's 3d.
11. K. B. to Q's 3d.	11. Q. Kt. to Q's 2d.
12. Q. to Q. B's 2d.	12. P. to K. R's 3d.
13. Castles.	13. Castles.
14. Q. R. to K's sq.	14. P. to Q. Kt's 3d.
15. P. to K. R's 3d.	15. Q. to Q. B's sq.
16. K. to R's 2d.	16. K. to R's sq.
17. K. R. to K. Kt's sq.	17. R. to K. Kt's sq.
18. P. to K. Kt's 4th.	18. P. to K. Kt's 4th.
19. P. to K. B's 4th.	19. Q. to K. B's sq.
20. R. to K. Kt's 3d.	20. Q. R. to Q's sq.
21. Kt. to K. B's 3d.	21. B. takes Kt.
22. R. takes B.	22. Q. to her 3d.
23. K. to Kt's 2d.	23. Kt. to K. R's 4th.
24. P. takes P.	24. P. takes P.
25. P. takes Kt.	25. P. to Kt's 5th.
26. P. takes P.	26. R. takes P. (ch.)
27. K. to B's sq.	27. P. to K. B's 4th.
28. Q. to K. B's 2d.	28. Kt. to K's 4th.
29. P. takes Kt.	29. Q. takes B. (ch.)
30. Q. to K's 2d.	30. Q. to K's 5th.

31. B. to K. B's 2d.	31. Q. to Q. B's 3d.
32. R. to Q's sq.	32. R. takes R. (ch.)
33. Q. takes R.	33. Q. takes Q. B. P. (ch.)
34. Q. to her 3d.	34. Q. takes Q. R. P.
35. R. to K. Kt's 3d.	35. Q. to Q. B's 5th.
36. Q. takes Q.	36. R. takes Q.
37. R. to K. Kt's 6th.	37. R. to Q. B's 3d.
38. P. to Q. B's 4th.	38. P. to Q. R's 4th.
39. K. to his 2d.	39. R. takes P.
40. R. takes P.	40. R. to Q. B's 7th (ch.)
41. K. to B's 3d.	41. P. to Q. R's 5th.
42. R. to K. Kt's 6th.	42. R. to Q. B's 5th.
43. R. to K. Kt's sq.	43. P. to Q. R's 6th.
44. P. to K's 6th.	44. P. to Q. R's 7th.
45. R. to Q. R's sq.	45. R. to K's 5th.
46. R. takes P.	46. R. takes P.
47. K. to B's 4th.	47. R. to Q's 3d.
48. K. takes P.	48. R. to Q's 4th (ch.)
49. K. to Kt's 4th.	49. P. to Q. Kt's 4th.
50. R. to Q. R's 8th (ch.)	50. K. to R's 2d.
51. R. to R's 7th.	51. R. to Q's 2d.
52. B. to K. Kt's 3d.	52. R. to K. Kt's 2d (ch.)
53. K. to R's 4th.	

And Black resigns.

GAME X.—Played at the Philadelphia Athenaeum, between Dr. Jones and Mr. H. P. Montgomery, at the odds of the Pawn and Move.

(Remove Black's King's Bishop's Pawn from the Board.)

WHITE. (Dr. J.)	BLACK. (Mr. M.)
1. P. to K's 4th.	1. P. to Q's 3d.
2. P. to Q's 4th.	2. K. Kt. to B's 3d.
3. K. B. to Q's 3d.	3. Q. Kt. to B's 3d.
4. Q. B. to K's 3d.	4. P. to K's 4th.
5. P. to Q's 5th.	5. Q. Kt. to K's 2d.
6. K. Kt. to K's 2d.	6. Q. Kt. to Kt's 3d.
7. P. to K. R's 3d.	7. Q. Kt. to K. R's 5th.
8 Castles.	8. Q. B. takes K. R. P.
9. P. takes B.	9. Kt. to K. B's 6th (ch.)
10. K. to Kt's 2d.	10. Kt. to R's 5th (ch.)
11. K. to R's sq.	11. Q. to Q's 2d.
12. Kt. to his sq.	12. P. to K. R's 3d.
13. P. to K. B's 4th.	13. P. takes P.
14. B. takes P.	14. Castles.
15. B. to K. R's 2d.	15. K. B. to K's 2d.
16. Q. Kt. to B's 3d.	16. P. to K. Kt's 4th.
17. K. B. to Q. Kt's 5th.	17. P. to Q. B's 3d.
18. P. takes P.	18. P. takes P.
19. B. to K's 2d.	19. P. to K. R's 4th.

20. P. to K's 5th.	20. Kt. to K. R's 2d.
21. B. takes K. R. P.	21. K. to Q. Kt's sq.
22. B. to K. Kt's 4th.	22. Q. to Q. Kt's 2d.
23. B. to K. B's 3d.	23. P. to Q's 4th.
24. Q. to K's 2d.	24. K. R. to K. B's sq
25. Q. to Q's 3d.	25. K. B. to Q. B's 4th
26. Q. Kt. to K's 2d.	26. P. to K. Kt's 5th.
27. B. takes P.	27. Kt. to K. Kt's 4th.
28. Q. to Q. Kt's 3d.	28. B. to Q. Kt's 3d.
29. Q. B. to K. Kt's 3d.	29. Kt. to K. Kt's 3d.
30. K. R. to K. B's 6th.	30. R. takes R.
31. P. takes R. (dis. ch.)	31. K. to Q. R's sq.
32. Q. to her 3d.	32. Kt. to K's 5th.
33. P. to Q. Kt's 3d.	33. Kt. to K's 4th.
34. Q. to her sq.	34. Kt. takes K. B.
35. P. takes Kt.	35. R. to K. R's sq. (ch.)
36. K. to Kt's 2d.	36. Q. to K. R's 2d.
37. Q. to her 3d.	37. Q. to R's 8th (ch.)
38. K. to K. B's sq.	38. R. to K. B's sq.
39. B. to K's 5th.	39. Kt. takes P.
40. B. to Q's 6th.	40. R. to B's 2d.
41. Q. to K. B's 5th.	41. Q. to K. R's sq.
42. K. to Kt's 2d.	42. R. to K. Kt's 2d.
43. B. to K's 5th.	43. Kt. takes P.
44. B. takes R.	44. Kt. to K's 6th (ch.)
45. K. to B's 3d.	45. Q. to R's 8th (ch.)
46. K. to B's 4th.	

And Black wins.

GAME XI.—Between Dr. S. Tartakower, of Vienna, and Rudolph Spielmann, of Munich, 1913.

WHITE. (Tartakower.)	BLACK. (Spielmann.)
1. P. to K. B's 4th.	1. P. to K's 4th.
2. P. takes P.*	2. P. to Q's 3d.
3. P. takes P.	3. B. takes P.
4. K. Kt. to B's 3d.	4. P. to K. Kt's 4th.†
5. P. to Q's 4th.	5. P. to Kt's 5th.
6. Kt. to K's 5th.	6. Q. Kt. to B's 3d.‡
7. Kt. takes Kt.	7. P. takes Kt.
8. P. to K. Kt's 3d.	8. P. to K. R's 4th.
9. B. to Kt's 2d.	9. P. to R's 5th.

* This constitutes the From Gambit, or, more correctly speaking, the From Defense. If White wishes to avoid this he can do so by playing 2 P. to K's 4th, leading to the ordinary Gambit position.

† First played by Lasker against Bird.

‡ The alternative move is B. takes Kt., 7 P. takes B., Q. takes Q. (ch.), 8 K. takes Q., Q. Kt. to B's 3d, 9 Kt. to B's 3d. B. to K's 3d, 10 P. to Kt's 5th.

10. Q. to Q's 3d.*	10. B. to Q's 2d.
11. Kt. to B's 3d.	11. R. to Kt.
12. Castles.	12. P. takes P.
13. P. takes P.	13. P. to Q. B's 4th.
14. B. to B's 4th.	14. B. takes B.†
15. R. takes B.	15. Q. to Kt's 4th.
16. Kt. to K's 4th.	16. Q. to R's 3d.
17. Kt. takes P.	17. Kt. to B's 3d.
18. Kt. takes B.	18. Kt. takes Kt.
19. Q. to K's 4th (ch.)	19. K. to Q.
20. R. takes B. P.	20. R. to K.
21. Q. takes P.	21. Q. to K's 6th (ch.)
22. K. to B.	22. Resigns.

GAME XII.—Between Messrs. Harrwitz and Morphy.

WHITE. (Mr. H.)	BLACK. (Mr. M.)
1. P. to Q's 4th.	1. P. to K. B's 4th.
2. P. to Q. B's 4th.	2. P. to K's 3d.
3. Q. Kt. to Q. B's 3d.	3. K. Kt. to K. B's 3d.
4. Q. B. to K. Kt's 5th.	4. K. B. to K's 2d.
5. P. to K's 3d.	5. Castles.
6. K. B. to Q's 3d.	6. P. to Q. Kt's 3d.
7. K. Kt. to K's 2d.	7. Q. B. to Q. Kt's 2d.
8. Castles.	8. K. Kt. to K. R's 4th.
9. B. takes B.	9. Q. takes B.
10. K. Kt. to Kt's 3d.	10. Kt. takes Kt.
11. K. R. P. takes Kt.	11. P. to Q's 3d.
12. P. to K. B's 4th.	12. Kt. to Q. B's 3d.
13. P. to K. Kt's 4th.	13. Kt. to Q. Kt's 5th.
14. P. takes P.	14. P. takes P.
15. Q. to K's 2d.	15. Q. R. to K's sq.
16. Q. R. to K's sq.	16. Q. to K. R's 5th.
17. B. to Q. Kt's sq.	17. Q. R. to K's 3d.
18. Q. to K. B's 2d.	18. Q. to K. R's 4th.
19. P. to Q's 5th.	19. Q. R. to K. R's 3d.
20. Q. to K. B's 3d.	20. Q. to K. R's 5th.
21. P. to Q. R's 3d.‡	21. Kt. to Q. R's 3d.
22. P. to Q. Kt's 4th.	22. Kt. to Q. Kt's sq.
23. Kt. to K's 2d.	23. Kt. to Q's 2d.
24. Kt. to K. Kt's 3d.	24. P. to K. Kt's 3d.
25. K. to B's 2d.	25. Kt. to K. B's 3d.
26. K. R. to K. R's sq.	26. Kt. to K. Kt's 5th (ch.)
27. K. to Kt's sq.	27. Q. to K. B's 3d.
28. R. takes R.	28. Kt. takes R.
29. Q. to her sq.	29. Kt. to K. Kt's 5th.
30. Q. to her 2d.	30. Q. to K. R's 5th.
31. Kt. to K. B's sq.	31. R. to K's sq.
32. P. to K. Kt's 3d.	32. Q. to K. R's 6th.
33. P. to Q. Kt's 5th.	33. Kt. to K. B's 3d.
34. Q. to K. Kt's 2d.	34. Q. takes Q. (ch.)
35. K. takes Q.	35. P. to Q. R's 3d.

* Showing a masterful restraint. If 10 B. takes P. (ch.), B. to Q's 2d, 11 B. takes R., Q. takes B., 12 R. to Kt., P. takes P., 13 P. takes P., R. to R's 6th, with considerable attacking chances. White's idea of being satisfied with what he has got is a very sound one, and the play is easier to handle—a very important point in matches.

† If R. takes P., 15 B. takes B., P. takes B., 16 P. takes P., P. takes P., 17 Kt. to K's 4th, with a winning attack.

‡ Surely it would have been wiser to play Kt. to K's 2d.

IRREGULAR OPENINGS.

36. P. to Q. R's 4th.	36. P. takes P.
37. Q. R. P. takes P.	37. R. to Q. R's sq.
38. Kt. to Q's 2d.	38. R. to Q. R's 6th.
39. P. to K's 4th.	39. P. takes P.
40. Kt. takes P.	40. Kt. takes Kt.
41. B. takes Kt.	41. R. to Q. B's 6th.
42. B. to K. B's 3d.	42. K. to K. R's 2d.
43. R. to K's 4th.	43. B. to Q. B's sq.
44. B. to K's 2d.	44. B. to K. B's 4th.
45. R. to Q's 4th.	45. P. to K. R's 4th.
46. K. to B's 2d.	46. K. to B's 3d.
47. R. to Q's 2d.	47. B. to Q. B's 7th.
48. K. to K's sq.	48. B. to K's 5th.
49. K. to B's 2d.	49. K. to B's 4th.
50. R. to Q. R's 2d.	50. P. to K. R's 5th.
51. P. takes P.	51. K. takes K. B. P.
52. R. to Q. R's 7th.	52. R. to K. R's 6th.
53. R. takes Q. B. P.	53. R. to K. R's 7th (ch.)
54. K. to K's sq.	54. K. to K's 6th.

And White resigns.

GAME XIII.—Between Mr. Murphy and Mr. Harrwitz

WHITE. (Mr. H.)	BLACK. (Mr. M.)
1. P. to Q's 4th.	1. P. to K's 3d.
2. P. to Q. B's 4th.	2. P. to Q's 4th.
3. Q. Kt. to Q. B's 3d.	3. K. Kt. to K. B's 3d.
4. Q. B. to K. B's 4th.*	4. P. to Q. R's 3d.
5. P. to K's 3d.	5. P. to Q. B's 4th.
6. K. Kt. to K. B's 3d.	6. Q. Kt. to Q. B's 3d.
7. P. to Q. R's 3d.	7. Q. B. P. takes Q. P.
8. K. P. takes P.	8. Q. P. takes P.
9. K. B. takes P.	9. P. to Q. Kt's 4th.
10. K. B. to Q's 3d.	10. Q. B. to Q. Kt's 2d.
11. Castles.	11. K. B. to K's 2d.
12. Q. B. to K's 5th.	12. Castles.
13. Q. to K's 2d.	13. K. Kt. to Q's 4th.
14. Q. B. to K. Kt's 3d.	14. K. to R's sq.
15. K. R. to K's sq.	15. K. B. to K. B's 3d.
16. Q. to K's 4th.	16. P. to Kt's 3d.
17. Q. Kt. takes Kt.	17. Q. takes Kt.
18. Q. takes Q.	18. P. takes Q.
19. Kt. to K's 5th.	19. Q. R. to Q's sq.†
20. Kt. takes Kt.	20. Q. B. takes Kt.
21. Q. R. to Q. B's sq.	21. Q. R. to Q. B's sq.
22. Q. B. to Q's 6th.	22. K. R. to K. Kt's sq.

* A favorite move of Mr. Harrwitz, though decried by the chief authorities.

† Had he taken the Queen's Pawn, White would have won at least the exchange by moving Kt. to Q's 7th.

23. Q. B. to K's 5th.	23. K. to K. Kt's 2d.*
24. P. to K. B's 4th.	24. Q. B. to Q's 2d.
25. K. to K. B's 2d.	25. P. to K. R's 3d.
26. K. to K's 3d.†	26. Q. R. takes R.
27. R. takes R.	27. R. to Q. B's sq.
28. R. to Q. B's 5th.	28. K. B. takes B.
29. K. B. P. takes B.	29. B. to K's 3d.
30. P. to Q. R's 4th.‡	30. P. takes P.
31. B. takes Q. R. P.	31. R. to Q. Kt's sq.
32. R. to Q. Kt's 5th.	32. R. to Q's sq.§
33. R. to Q. Kt's 6th.	33. R. to Q. R's sq.
34. K. to Q's 2d.	34. B. to Q. B's sq.
35. B. takes B.	35. R. takes B.
36. R. to Q. Kt's 5th.	36. R. to Q. R's sq.
37. R. takes Q. P.	37. P. to Q. R's 6th.
38. P. takes P.	38. R. takes P.
39. R. to Q. B's 5th.	39. K. to K's B's sq.
40. K. to K's 2d.	40. K. to K's 2d.
41. P. to Q's 5th.	41. K. to Q's 2d.
42. R. to Q. B's 6th	42. P. to K. R's 4th.
43. R. to K. B's 6th.	43. K. to K's 2d.
44. P. to Q's 6th (ch.)	44. K. to K's sq.
45. P. to K's 6th.	45. P. takes P.
46. R. takes P. (ch.)	46. K. to K. B's 2d.
47. P. to Q's 7th.	47. R. to Q. R's sq.
48. R. to Q's 6th.	48. K. to K's 2d.
49. R. takes P.	49. K. takes P.
50. R. to K. Kt's 5th.	50. R. to K. R's sq.
51. K. to K. B's 3d.	51. K. to K's 3d.
52. K. to K. Kt's 3d.	52. P. to K. R's 5th (ch.)
53. K. to K. Kt's 4th.	53. P. to K. R's 6th.
54. P. to K. Kt's 3d.	54. K. to K. B's 3d.
55. R. to K. R's 5th.	

And Black abandoned the game.

Game XIV.—(*Unclassified.*) Between Mr. Morphy and Mr Anderssen.

WHITE. (Mr. A.)	BLACK. (Mr. M.
1. P. to Q. R's 3d.	1. P. to K's 4th.
2. P. to Q. B's 4th.	2. K. Kt. to B's 3d.
3. Q. Kt. to B's 3d.	3. P. to Q's 4th.
4. P. takes P.	4. Kt. takes P.
5. P. to K's 3d.	5. B. to K's 3d.

---

* Fearing to take the Bishop lest White should obtain an entrance with the Rook.

† All this is exceedingly well played by White.

‡ The *coup juste.* From this point it would not be easy to improve on White's moves.

§ Better, perhaps, to have played the Rook to Q. R's sq. at once

IRREGULAR OPENINGS.

6. K. Kt. to B's 3d.	6. B. to Q's 3d.
7. B. to K's 2d.	7. Castles.
8. P. to Q's 4th.	8. Kt. takes Kt.
9. P. takes Kt.	9. P. to K's 5th.
10. Kt. to Q's 2d.	10. P. to K. B's 4th.
11. P. to K. B's 4th.	11. P. to K. Kt's 4th.
12. B. to Q. B's 4th.	12. B. takes B.
13. Kt. takes B.	13. P takes P.
14. P. takes P.	14. Q. to K's sq.
15. Castles.	15. Q. to Q. B's 3d.
16. Q. to Q. Kt's 3d.	16. Q. to her 4th.
17. R. to Q. Kt's sq.	17. P. to Q. Kt's 3d.
18. Q. to Q. R's 2d.	18. P. to Q. B's 3d.
19. Q. to K's 2d.	19. Kt. to Q's 2d.
20. Kt. to K's 3d.	20. Q. to K's 3d.
21. P. to Q. B's 4th.	21. Kt. to K. B's 3d.
22. R. to Q. Kt's 3d.	22. K. to B's 2d.
23. B. to Q. Kt's 2d.	23. Q. R. to Q. B's sq.
24. K. to R's sq.	24. R. to K. Kt's sq.
25. P. to Q's 5th.	25. P. takes P.
26. P. takes P.	26. Q. to her 2d.
27. Kt. to Q. B's 4th.	27. K. to his 2d.
28. B. takes Kt. (ch.)	28. K. takes B.
29. Q. to Q. Kt's 2d (ch.)	29. K. to B's 2d.
30. R. to K. R's 3d.	30. R. to K. Kt's 2d.
31. Q. to her 4th.	31. K. to Kt's sq.
32. R. to K. R's 6th.	32. B. to B's sq.
33. P. to Q's 6th.	33. R. to K. B's 2d.
34. R. to K. R's 3d.	34. Q. to Q. R's 5th.
35. R. to Q. B's sq.	35. R. to Q. B's 4th.
36. Q. R. to K. Kt's 3d (ch.)	36. B. to K. Kt's 2d.
37. P. to K. R's 3d.	37. K. to R's sq.
38. R. takes B.	38. R. takes R.
39. R. to Q. B's 3d.	39. P. to K's 6th.
40. R. takes P.	40. R. takes Kt.
41. Q. to K. B's 6th.	41. R. to Q. B's 8th (ch.)
42. K. to R's 2d.	42. Q. takes P. (ch.)

And White loses.

GAME XV.—STEINITZ GAMBIT.

Between W. Steinitz and J. W. Zukertort.

WHITE. (Mr. S.)	BLACK. (Mr. Z.)
1. P. to K's 4th.	1. P. to K's 4th.
2. Kt. to Q. B's 3d.	2. Kt. to Q. B's 3d.
3. P. to B's 4th.	3. P. takes P.
4. P. to Q's 4th.	4. Q. to R's 5th (ch.)
5. K. to K's 2d.	5. P. to Q's 4th.*

* The ingenious attack instituted hereby was invented by Zukertort.

6. P. takes P.	6. B. to Kt's 5th (ch.)
7. Kt. to B's 3d.	7. Castles.
8. P. takes Kt.	8. B. to Q. B's 4th.
9. P. takes P. (cl)	9. K. to Kt's sq.
10. Kt. to Kt's 5th *	10. Kt. to B's 3d.
11. K. to Q's 3d.†	11. Q. to R's 4th.
12. K. to B's 3d.	12. B. takes P. (ch.)‡
13. Q. Kt. takes B.	13. Q. to B's 4th (ch.)
14. K. to Kt's 3d.	14. Q. to Kt's 3d (ch.)
15. B. to Kt's 5th.	15. B. takes Kt.
16. Q. takes B.	16. R. takes Kt.
17. Q. to B's 6th.	17. Q. to R's 4th.
18. P. to B's 3d.	18. R. to Q's 3d.
19. Q. to B's 4th.	19. P. to Kt's 4th.
20. K to B's 2d.	20. Resigns.§

* 10. P. takes B., Kt. to B's 3d !; 11. Q. takes R. (ch), obtains three pieces for the Q., but loses the game. Q. to K's sq., here or on the following move, offers the only defence.

† Zukertort's analysis, which filled pages and pages of the *Neue Berliner Schachzeitung*, considered every conceivable move of White's down to P. to Q R's 3d, but this one, upon which, in conjunction with the following K. move, Steinitz rested his gambit. 11. P. to B's 3d has been refuted in an elaborate analysis by Mr. Walter Penn Shipley, of Philadelphia.

‡ Black wins here by,

12. . . .	12. R. to Q. R's 3d.
13. K. to Kt's 3d.	13. P. takes Kt.
14. P. to B's 3d.	14. R. takes P. !
15. P. takes R.	15. Q. to Q's 4th (ch.)
16. K. to B's 2d.	16. B. to B's 4th (ch.)
17. K. to Q's 2d.	17. B. to Kt's 5th (ch.)
18. K. to K's 2d.	18. Kt. to Kt's 5th. !

as played by Messrs. Honegger and Raubitscheck in a consultation game against Steinitz at the Metropolitan Chess Club, 1897. If, instead of K. to Kt's 3d, 13. Kt. takes P. Black wins by R. takes P. ! .

§ White has brought his K. into safety and will remain a piece ahead. Had Black, instead of his last move, pinned the B., the game would have proceeded as follows:

19. . . .	19. R. to Kt's 3d.
20. P. to Q. R's 4th.	20. P. to Q. R's 3d.
21. B. takes P.	21. R. takes P.
22. K. to B's 2d.	22. B. takes B.
23. P. takes P.	23. Q. takes P.
24. B. takes P. (ch.) and wins.	

CHAPTER VII.

ENDINGS OF GAMES

To play with correctness and skill the ends of games, is an important but a very rare accomplishment, except among the very best players. In order to assist the learner as much as possible in this branch of the game, we present a number of end positions, with the proper play necessary in each case. Our selection of positions is necessarily very limited; but those we give will serve to show the careful play that is requisite even when the stronger party feels sure of success, and the danger of defeat if he suffer his vigilance to be relaxed for a moment.

KING AND QUEEN AGAINST KING.

Diagram 1.

WHITE.	BLACK.
1. Q. to Q. R's 7th.	1. K. to Q's sq.
2. Q. to Q. Kt's 8th. Mate.	

KING AND ROOK AGAINST KING.

Diagram 2.

WHITE.	BLACK.
1. R. to K. R's 7th.	1. K. to K. B's sq.
2. K. to K's 2d.	2. K. to K. Kt's sq.
3. R. to Q. R's 7th.	3. K. to K. B's sq.
4. K. to K's 3d.	4. K. to K's sq.
5. K. to K's 4th.	5. K. to Q's sq.
6. K. to Q's 5th.	6. K. to Q. B's sq.
7. K. to Q's 6th.	7. K. to Q. Kt's sq.
8. R. to Q. B's 7th.	8. K. to Q. R's sq.
9. K. to Q. B's 6th.	9. K. to Q. Kt's sq.
10. K. to Q. Kt's 6th.	10. K. to Q. R's sq.
11. R. to Q. B's 8th. Mate.	

Diagram 3.

WHITE.	BLACK.
1. R. to Q. R's 5th, or K. Kt's 5th.	If 1. K. to B's sq.
2. R. to Q. Kt's 5th.	
	If 1. K. to K's sq.
2. R. to K. B's 5th.	2. K. to Q's sq.
3. R. mates at Kt's 8th or K. B's 8th.	

KING AND TWO BISHOPS AGAINST KING

Diagram 4.

WHITE.	BLACK.
1. K. B. to K. R's 3d.	1. K. to Q's sq.
2. Q. B. to K. B's 4th.	2. K. to K's 2d.
3. K. to his 2d.	3. K. to K. B's 3d.
4. K. to K. B's 3d.	4. K. to K's 2d.
5. K. B. to K. B's 5th.	5. K. to K. B's 3d.
6. K. to his Kt's 4th.	6. K. to his 2d.
7. K. to his Kt's 5th.	7. K. to Q's sq.
8. K. to his B's 6th.	8. K. to K's sq.
9. Q. B. to Q. B's 7th.	9. K. to B's sq.
10. K. B. to Q's 7th.	10. K. to Kt's sq.
11. K. to his Kt's 6th.	11. K. to B's sq.
12. Q. B. to Q's 6th (ch.)	12. K. to Kt's sq.
13. K. B. to K's 6th (ch.)	13. K. to R's sq.
14. Q. B. checkmates.	

KING, BISHOP, AND KNIGHT, AGAINST KING.

Diagram 5.

WHITE.	BLACK.
1. Kt. to K. B's 7th (ch.)	1. K. to Kt's sq.
2. B. to K's 4th.	2. K. to B's sq.
3. B. to K. R's 7th.	3. K. to his sq.
4. Kt. to K's 5th.	4. K. to his B's sq.
5. Kt. to Q's 7th (ch.)	5. K. to his sq.
6. K. to his 6th.	6. K. to Q's sq.
7. K. to Q's 6th.	7. K. to his sq. (best)
8. B. to K. Kt's 6th (ch.)	8. K. to Q's sq.
9. Kt. to Q. B's 5th.	9. K. to Q. B's sq.
10. K. B. to his 7th.	10. K. to Q's sq.
11. Kt. to Q. Kt's 7th (ch.)	11. K. to Q. B's sq.
12. K. to Q. B's 6th.	12. K. to Q. Kt's sq.
13. K. to Q. Kt's 6th.	13. K. to Q. B's sq.
14. B. to K's 6th (ch.)	14. K. to Q. Kt's sq.
15. Kt. to Q. B's 5th.	15. K. to Q. R's sq.
16. B. to Q's 7th.	16. K. to Q. Kt's sq.
17. Kt. to Q. R's 6th (ch.)	17. K. to Q. R's sq.
18. B. to Q. B's 6th (checkmate.)	

ENDING OF GAMES 217

No. 1.
BLACK.

WHITE.

No. 2.
BLACK.

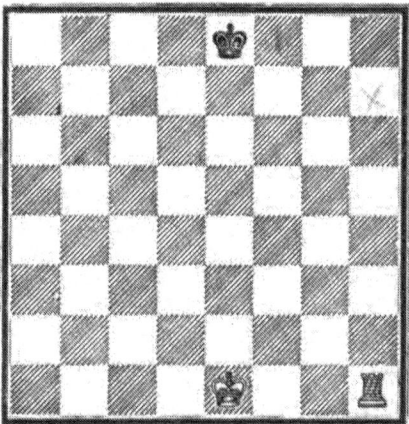

WHITE.

No. 3.
BLACK.

WHITE.

No. 4.
BLACK.

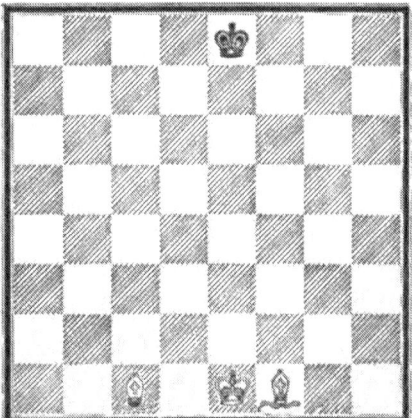

WHITE.

ENDINGS OF GAMES.

KING AND TWO KNIGHTS AGAINST KING.

The two Knights, with the assistance of the King, cannot force checkmate, except in some very rare cases.

KING AND PAWN,—KING, BISHOP, AND PAWN,—AND KING, KNIGHT, AND PAWN,—AGAINST KING.

When one Pawn only is left on the board, supported by its King, and the adverse King is either in front of the Pawn, or within such distance as to be able to intercept it, it becomes a point of great nicety in some cases, to calculate whether or not you have the power of Queening the Pawn, and therefore of winning the game. This frequently depends upon your gaining the opposition, which you cannot always do.

In the next position (see Diagram 6) you have the opposition, and if Black have to play you will win. Thus:—

	1. K. to his sq.
2. P. to K's 7th.	2. K. to his 2d.
3. K. to B's 7th, and	
4. P. Queens.	

But if you move first, the game is drawn; for if you play P. to K's 7th (ch.), Black moves King to his square, and you must either abandon the Pawn or give stalemate. You will find, on trial, that any other mode of play on your part will produce the same result.—from which is deduced this important general rule: That if you can advance the Pawn to its 7th sq., *not giving check*, you will win; but that if the Pawn checks at this point, you will only draw.

In this position (see Diagram 7), you will win either with or without the move; for if Black have to play, he is forced to allow your King to be moved either to B's 7th or Q's 7th sq.; and if you move you gain the opposition, by playing K. to B's 6th or Q's 6th, and then P. to K's 6th. It is evident that this would equally hold good if your Pawn were any number of squares less advanced; so that you invariably win, if you can succeed in placing your King on the sixth square of the file occupied by your Pawn, and in front of it; provided, of course, that the single King cannot attack the Pawn, so as to compel you to retreat in order to support it. It is perhaps scarcely necessary to observe, that if the Pawn be upon either of the Rooks' files, these remarks will not apply—this contingency will be considered hereafter.

Diagram 8.

WHITE.	BLACK.
1. K. to Q's 2d.	1. K. to his 2d.
2. K. to his 3d.	2. K. to his 3d.
3. K. to his 4th.	3. K. to B's 3d.
4. K. to Q's 5th.	4. K. to K's 2d.
5. K. to his 5th.	5. K. to B's 2d.
6. K. to Q's 6th.	

If he play K. to E's 3d, you advance P. to K's 4th, then to K's

5th, and on his afterwards moving K. to his sq., you gain the opposition, as shown before.

6. K. to his sq., or to B's sq.

7. K. to K's 6th.
And then advances Pawn, winning.

Next, suppose Black has the move, and he will draw:—

WHITE.	BLACK.
	1. K. to K's 2d.
2. K. to Q's 2d.	2. K. to his 3d.
3. K. to his 3d.	3. K. to his 4th.
4. K. to Q's 3d.	4. K. to Q's 4th.
5. P. to K's 3d, or to K's 4th (ch.)	5. K. to K's 4th.

And it is clear that, play as you may, you can only draw the game.

The only exception in all the foregoing cases is to be found, as has already been remarked, when the Pawn is upon either of the Rooks' files. In these instances, Black will invariably draw the game when his King can be placed on any part of the file in front of the Pawn, it being quite immaterial at what distance the adverse King and Pawn may be. Even, as in the next example, the player of the single King will draw the game, if he have not the move, against two Pawns in a somewhat similar position. For White being to move, he can only play K. to R's 8th, to which Black must reply by K. to B's sq.; and if White then advance B's Pawn, it will be taken: or if he play R's Pawn, Black returns K. to B's 2d, and his adversary is stalemated. (See Diagram 9.)

Two *united* Pawns, with their King, always win against King alone. Another advantage in having two Pawns thus situated is, that they can always maintain themselves until the arrival of the King to their support; for should one be taken, the other will advance to Queen. In the next position (see Diagram 10), White wins by advancing K. to Kt's 5th, then Queening Rook's Pawn, and upon that being taken, playing K. to R's 6th, or B's 6th, having the opposition.

QUEEN AGAINST A KNIGHT OR BISHOP.

(In all cases, each party is of course understood to have a King in addition to the Pieces named.)

Diagram 11.

WHITE.	BLACK.
1. Q. to her 4th (ch.)	1. K. to his 3d.
2. K. to his 4th.	2. Kt. to K. Kt's 3d.
3. Q. to her Kt's 6th (ch.)	3. K. to B's 2d.
4. K. to B's 5th.	4. Kt. to K's 2d (ch.)
5. K. to Kt's 5th.	5. Kt. to Q's 4th.
6. Q. to her 6th.	6. Kt. to K's 2d.
7. Q. to K. B's (ch.)	7. K. to his sq.
8. Q. to K's 6th.	8 K. to Q's sq.

ENDINGS OF GAMES. 221

No. 5.
BLACK.

WHITE.

No. 6.
BLACK.

WHITE.

CHESS HANDBOOK.

No. 7.
BLACK.

WHITE.

No. 8.
BLACK.

WHITE.

ENDINGS OF GAMES. 223

No. 9.
BLACK.

WHITE.

No. 10.
BLACK.

WHITE.

No. 11.
BLACK.

WHITE.

No. 12.
BLACK.

WHITE.

9. K. to B's 6th.   9. Kt. to Q B's sq.
10. Q. to Q. B's 6th.
             And you must win the Kt.

The Queen also easily wins against a Bishop.

QUEEN AGAINST ROOK.
Diagram 12.

WHITE.	BLACK.
	1. K. to Kt's 6th.
2. K. to K's 6th.	2. R. to Q. B's 7th.
3. K. to Q's 5th.	3. K. to Kt's 7th.
4. K. to Q's 4th.	4. K. to R's 8th.
5. K. to Q's 3d.	5. R. to Kt's 7th.
6. Q. to K. R's 4th (ch.)	6. K. to Kt's 8th.
7. K. to B's 3d.	7. R. to K. R's 7th.
8. Q. to Kt's 5th (ch.)	8. K. to R's 8th.
9. Q. to R's 6th (ch.)	9. K. to Kt's 8th.
10. Q. to Kt's 6th (ch.)	10. K. to R's 7th.
11. Q. to R's 7th (ch.)	11. K. to Kt's 8th.
12. Q. to Kt's 8th (ch.)	

Then takes Rook, and wins.

QUEEN AGAINST ROOK AND PAWN.

With few exceptions, arising from peculiar situations, the Queen wins also against a Rook and Pawn. Diagram 13, illustrating a won game, is from Philidor.

Diagram 13.
White moves and wins.

WHITE.	BLACK.
1. Q. to R's 7th (ch.)	1. K. to K's 3d (best.)
2. Q. to Q. B's 7th.	2. R. to Q. B's 4th.
3. Q. to Q's 8th.*	3. K. to K's 4th.
4. Q. to K's 8th (ch.)	4. K. to Q's 4th.
5. Q. to Q. B's 8th.	5. R. to K's 5th (ch.)
6. K. to K. B's 5th.	6. R. to K's 4th (ch.)
7. K. to K. B's 6th.	7. R. to K's 5th.
8 Q. to K. B's 5th (ch.)	8. R. to K's 4th.
9. Q. to Q's 3d (ch.)	9. K. to Q. B's 4th.
10. Q. to Q's 2d.	10. K. to Q. B's 3d.
11. Q. to Q's 4th.	11. K. to Q's 2d.
12. Q. to Q. B's 4th.	12. R. to Q. B's 4th.
13. Q. to K. B's 7th (ch.)	13. K. to Q. B's 3d.
14. K. to his 7th.	14. R. to K's 4th (ch.)

* This is the position which White must endeavor to gain, in order that he may force the King to his Queen's 4th. in front of the Pawn.

15. K. to Q's 8th.
16. Q. to Q's 7th (ch.)
17. K. to K's 7th.
18. Q. to K. B's 5th (ch.)
19. K. to Q's 7th.
20. Q. to K's 4th (ch.)
21. K. takes P.

15. R. to Q. B's 4th.
16. K. to Q's 4th.
17. R. to Q. B's 3d.
18. K. to Q. B's 5th.
19. R. to Q. B's 4th.
20. K. to Kt's 6th.

And wins.

QUEEN AGAINST TWO BISHOPS.

The Queen usually wins against two of the minor Pieces, at least if they are on different parts of the board, or at a distance from their King. There are, however, many instances in which, by skilful play, the weaker force may draw the game.

The two Bishops will be able to draw when they can assume a position similar to that in Diagram 14, or in other words, such a position in front of their King, that the adverse King cannot approach.

Diagram 14.

White moves first.

WHITE.
1. Q. to Q's 7th (ch.)
2. Q. to K's 6th.
3. K. to K. B's 4th.
4. Q. to Q's 7th (ch.)
5. Q. to K's 8th (ch.)
6. K. to Kt's 4th.
7. Q. to K's 6th.
8. Q. checks at Q's 7th.
9. Q. to K's 8th (ch.)
10. K. to R's 5th.

BLACK.
1. K. to B. or Kt's sq. (best.)
2. K. to Kt's 2d.
3. B. to K. R's 2d.
4. K. to Kt's 3d.
5. K. to Kt's 2d.
6. B. to Kt's 3d.
7. B. to R's 2d.
8. K. to Kt's 3d.
9. K. to Kt's 2d.
10. Q. R. to K. B's 4th.

The game is drawn.

QUEEN AGAINST TWO KNIGHTS.

Two Knights can often draw the game against a Queen.

QUEEN AGAINST KNIGHT AND BISHOP.

A King with Bishop and Knight can in many cases draw the game against a King and Queen.

QUEEN AGAINST QUEEN AND PAWN.

In cases of this kind the game is usually drawn without difficulty, and most generally so by means of a perpetual check, though the same object may sometimes be attained by an exchange of Queens, when your King is able to stop the Pawn. When, however, the Pawn is advanced to its 7th square, and more particularly if defended by its King, the task is one of more difficulty, and many instructive

ENDINGS OF GAMES 227

No. 13.
BLACK.

WHITE.

No. 14.
BLACK.

WHITE.

No. 15.
BLACK.

WHITE.

No. 16.
BLACK.

WHITE.

ENDINGS OF GAMES. 229

No. 17.
BLACK.

WHITE.

No. 18.
BLACK.

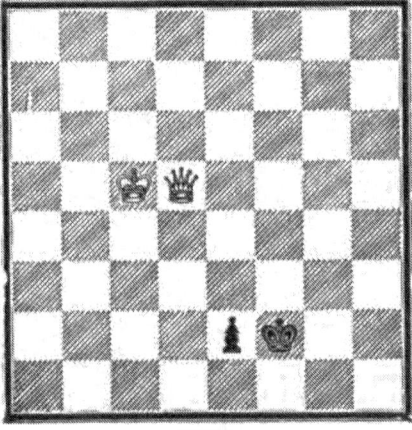

WHITE.

230   CHESS HANDBOOK.

No. 19.
BLACK.

WHITE.

No. 20.
BLACK.

WHITE.

situations occur where the Pawn may be Queened and the game therefore won. We subjoin an example or two of each kind, by way of illustration.

Diagram 15.

WHITE.	BLACK.
1. Q. to K. Kt's 4th (ch.)	1. Q. to K. Kt's 6th.
2. Q. to K's 4th (ch.)	2. K. to Kt's 8th.
3. Q. to Q's 4th.	3. K. to R's 7th.
4. Q. to K. R's 8th (ch.)	4. Q. to R's 6th.
5. Q. to K's 5th (ch.)	5. K. to Kt's 8th.
6. Q. to Kt's 5th (ch.)	6. Q. to Kt's 7th.
7. Q. to K's 3d.	

White will always be able to make a drawn game.

Diagram 16.

WHITE.	BLACK.
	1. Q. to her Kt's 4th.
2. K. moves.	2. K. to Q's 8th.
3. Q. to Q. R's sq. (ch.)	3. P. Queens.

And wins.

Diagram 17.

WHITE.	BLACK.
1. P. Queens (ch.)	1. K. to K. B's 5th.
2. Q. to K. B's 8th (ch.)	2. K. to his 5th.
3. Q. to K's 7th (ch.)	3. K. to K. B's 6th.
4. Q. to K. B's 6th (ch.)	4. K. to his 5th.
5. Q. to K's 6th (ch.)	5. K. to K. B's 6th.
6. Q. to K. B's 5th (ch.)	6. K. to his 7th.
7. Q. to her 3d (ch.)	

Then forces an exchange of Queens, and wins with his remaining Pawn.

QUEEN AGAINST PAWN.

In all ordinary situations, the Queen of course easily stops a single Pawn and wins against it; if, however, the latter has reached its 7th square, and has the support of its King, there are instances in which the game must be drawn. Our first position (see Diagram 18), will show the method of winning, and we shall afterwards point out the exceptions.

Diagram 18.

WHITE.	BLACK.
1. Q. to K. B's 5th (ch.)	1. K. to K. Kt's 7th.
2. Q. to K's 4th (ch.)	2. K. to B's 7th.
3. Q. to K. B's 4th (ch.)	3. K. to Kt's 7th.
4. Q. to K's 3d.	4. K. to B's 8th.
5. Q. to K. B's 3d (ch.)	5. K. to his 8th.
6. K. to Q's 4th.	6. K. to Q's 8th.
7. Q. to her 3d (ch.)	7. K. to his 8th.
8. K. to his 3d.	8. K. to B's 8th.
9. Q. takes P. (ch.) and wins.	

The same mode of procedure can always be adopted, unless the single Pawn should be either on the Bishop's or Rook's file, in which case Black may usually make a drawn game, owing to the power which he then has of making a stalemate. His having this alternative, however, altogether depends upon the distance which the adverse King may chance to be from the scene of action. In the next position (Diagram 19) the game is drawn.

WHITE.	BLACK.
1. Q. to K. Kt's 4th (ch.)	1. K. to R's 8th.
2. Q. to K. B's 3d (ch.)	2. K. to Kt's 8th.
3. Q. to K. Kt's 3d (ch.)	3. K. to R's 8th.

And it is evident, that if White take the Pawn, his adversary is stalemated.

The result is the same when the Pawn is on the Rook's file, as you will at once see by making the experiment.

The next position (see Diagram 20), is a very ingenious exception to this rule, and will well repay your attention.

WHITE.	BLACK.
1. K. to Q. B's 5th (ch.)	1. K. to Q. B's 7th (best)
2. Q. to K. Kt's 2d (ch.)	2. K. to Q. B's 6th.
3. Q. to K. B's sq.	3. K. to Q. Kt's 7th.
4. Q. to K's 2d (ch.)	4. K. to Q. Kt's 6th.
5. Q. to her sq. (ch).	5. K. to Q. Kt's 7th.
6. Q. to her 2d sq. (ch.)	6. K. to Q. Kt's 8th.
7. K. to Q. Kt's 4th.	7. P. Queens.
8. K. to Q. Kt's 3d.	

And wins.

ROOK AGAINST BISHOP.

Diagram 21.

WHITE.	BLACK.
1. B. to Q. Kt's 7th.	1. R. to Q. Kt's 3d.
2. B. to Q's 5th.	2. R. to Q. Kt's 7th.
3. B. to Q. B's 6th.	3. R. to K. B's 7th (ch.)
4. K. to Kt's sq.	4. K. to his 7th.
5. B. to Q's 5th.	5. K. to his 8th.
6. B. to Q. B's 6th.	6. R. to K. B's 3d.
7. B. to Q. Kt's 7th.	7. R. to K. Kt's 3d (ch.)
8. K. to K. R's 2d.	8. K. to K. B's 7th.
9. K. to K. R's 3d, &c.	

And the game is drawn.

Diagram 22.

WHITE.	BLACK.
1. R. to Q. B's 2d.	1. B. to Q. Kt's 6th.
2. R. to B's 8th (ch.)	2. B. to K. Kt's sq.
3. K. to Q's 6th.	3. P. to Q. Kt's 6th.
4. R. to Q. B's 7th.	4. B. to Q's 4th (best)

ENDINGS OF GAMES. 233

No. 21.
BLACK.

WHITE.

No. 22.
BLACK.

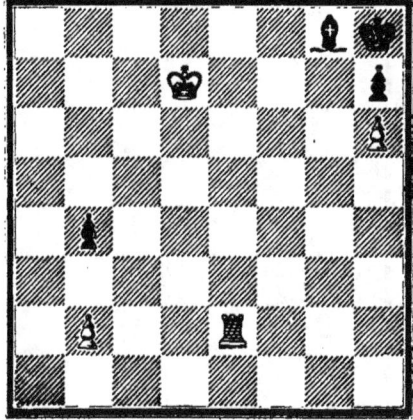

WHITE.

234   CHESS HANDBOOK.

No. 23.
BLACK.

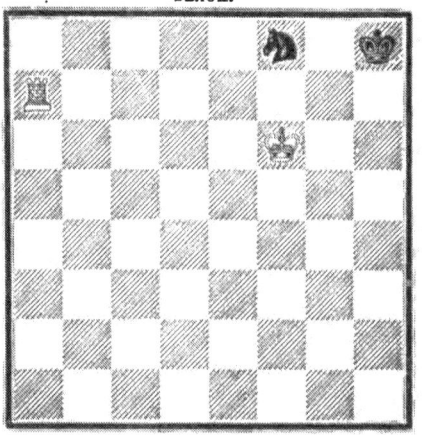

WHITE.

No. 24.
BLACK.

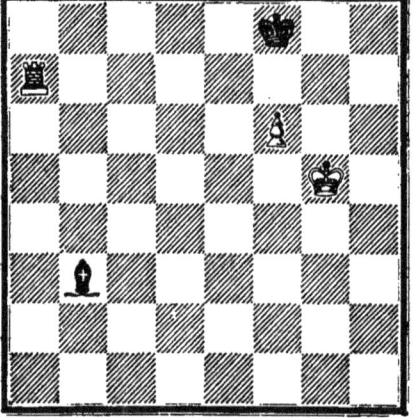

WHITE.

ENDINGS OF GAMES.

WHITE	BLACK
5. K. takes B.	5. K. to Kt's sq.
6. K. to his 6th.	6. K. moves.
7. R. mates.	

ROOK AGAINST KNIGHT.

In ordinary positions, and where the Knight is near to, or cannot be prevented approaching, his King, the weaker party will be able to draw the game. The method of doing so, however, is not very easy, and there are many positions (of which we shall give an example) where the Rook can win.

In the following position (see Diagram 23) White will win either with the move or without it.

WHITE.	BLACK.
	1. Kt. to R's 2d (ch.)
2. K. to K. B's 7th.	2. Kt. to Kt's 4th (ch.)
3. K. to K. Kt's 6th.	

And wins.

ROOK AND PAWN AGAINST BISHOP.

Diagram 24.

WHITE.	BLACK.
1. R. to Q. Kt's 7th.	1. B. to Q. B's 5th.
2. R. to Q. B's 7th.	2. B. to Q. Kt's 4th.
3. K. to B's 5th.	3. B. to K's 7th (best)
4. P. to B's 7th.	4. K. to Kt's 2d (best)
5. K. to his 6th.	5. B. to K. R's 4th (best)
6. R. to Kt's 7th.	6. B. to K. Kt's 3d.
7. P. to B's 8th, becoming a Q. (ch.)	7. K. takes Q.
8. K. to B's 6th.	

And wins.

ROOK AGAINST THREE MINOR PIECES.

Diagram 25.

WHITE.	BLACK.
1. R. to Q. R's 3d (ch.)	1. B. to K's 6th.
2. R. to Q. R's 2d.	2. K. to Kt's 6th.
3. R. to K. R's 2d.	3. B. to K. B's 5th.
4. R. to Q. R's 2d.	4. B. to K. R's 6th.
5. R. to Q. R's 3d (ch.)	5. B. to K's 6th.
6. R. to Q. R's 2d.	6. Kt. to K. B's 7th (ch.)
7. K. to Kt's sq.	7. B. to K. Kt's 7th.
8. R. to K's 2d.	8. Kt. to K. R's 6th (check mate.)

ROOK AND PAWN AGAINST ROOK.

Diagram 26.

WHITE.	BLACK.
1. P. to K's 5th.	1. R. to Q. Kt's 3d.
2. R. to Q. R's 7th.	2. R. to Q. B's 3d.
3. P. to K's 6th.	3. R. to Q. B's 8th.
4. K. to K. B's 6th.	4. R. to K. B's 8th (ch.)

And will draw.

ROOK AGAINST ONE OR MORE PAWNS.

Diagram 27.

White must lose, even with the move.

Suppose:—

WHITE.	BLACK.
1 R. to K's 8th.	1. K. to Q's 2d.
2. K. to his 3d.	2. P. "Queens."

&c., &c.

Diagram 28.

Here White will win the Pawn, and therefore the game.

WHITE.	BLACK.
1. R. to K. Kt's 6th (ch.)	1. K. to Q's 4th.
2. K. to Q's 2d.	2. P. to Q. B's 4th.
3. R. to Q's 6th (ch.)	3. K. to Q. B's 5th.
4. K. to Q. B's 6th.	4. K. to Q. Kt's 5th.
5. K. to Q's 5th.	5. P. to Q. B's 5th.
6. R. to Q. Kt's 6th (ch.)	6. K. to Q. B's 6th
7. R. to Q. B's 6th.	

And white wins.

Diagram 29.

WHITE.	BLACK.
	1. P. to K. B's 6th (ch.)
2. R. takes P.	2. R. P. "Queens" (ch.)
3. K. takes Q.	3. K. takes R.
4. K. to K. Kt's sq.	4. P. to K. Kt's 7th.
5. K. to K. R's 2d.	5. K. to B's 7th, and wins.

Or,

	1. P. to K. B's 6th (ch.)
2. K. to R's sq.	2. P. to K. Kt's 7th (ch.)
3. K. takes R. P.	3. P. takes R., and becomes a Kt. (ch.), and wins.

ROOK AGAINST TWO ROOKS.

Diagram 30.

WHITE.	BLACK.
1. R. to K. R's 5th	. R. takes R.

ENDINGS OF GAMES. 237

No. 25.
BLACK.

WHITE.

No. 26.
BLACK.

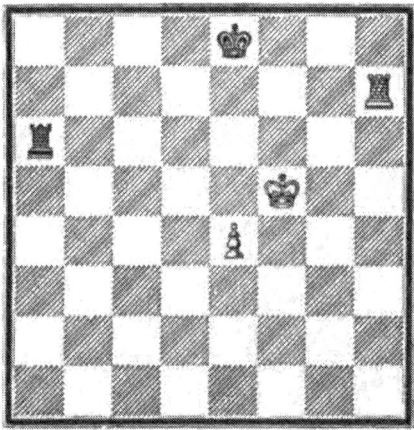

WHITE.

No. 27.
BLACK.

WHITE.

No. 28.
BLACK.

WHITE.

ENDINGS OF GAMES.

No. 29.
BLACK.

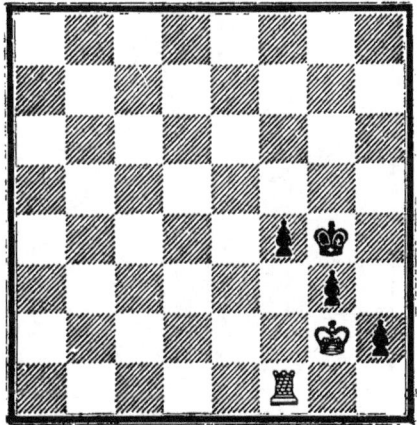

WHITE.

No. 30.
BLACK.

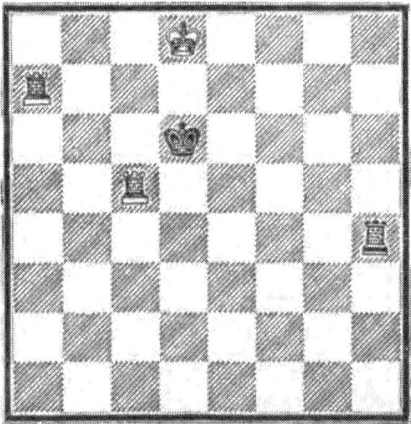

WHITE.

No. 31.
BLACK.

WHITE.

No. 32.
BLACK.

WHITE.

2. R. to Q. R's 6th (ch.)   2. K. moves
3. R. to Q. R's 5th (ch.)   3. K. moves.
4. R. takes R.

And wins.

ROOK AND BISHOP AGAINST ROOK.

Diagram 31.

WHITE.	BLACK.
1. R. to K's 8th (ch.)	1. K. to K. B's sq.
2. K. to K's 7th.	2. R. to K. B's 8th.
3. R. to Q's 7th.	3. R. to K. B's 7th.
4. R. to Q. B's 7th.	4. R. to K. B's 8th.
5. B. to K. B's 6th.	5. R. to K. Kt's 8th (ch.)
6. K. to B's 5th.	6. R. to K. Kt's 7th.
7. B. to K's 5th.	7. R. to Q. R's 7th.
8. R. to K. Kt's 7th (ch.)	8. K. to B's sq.
9. R. to Q's 7th.	9. K. to Kt's sq.
10. K. to B's 6th.	10. R. to Q. R's 3d (ch.)
11. B. to Q's 6th.	11. R. to Q. R's 8th.
12. R. to K. Kt's 7th (ch.)	12. K. to R's sq.
13. R. to K. Kt's 2d.	13. R. to K. B's 8th (ch.)
14. K. to K. Kt's 6th.	14. K. to Kt's sq.
15. B. to Q. B's 5th.	15. R. to K. B's 5th.
16. R. to K. Kt's 5th.	16. R. to Q. R's 5th.
17. K. to B's 6th (dis. ch.)	17. K. to R's 2d.
18. B. to K's 3d.	18. R. to Q. B's 5th.
19. R. to K. Kt's 7th (ch.)	19. K. to R's sq.
20. R. to Q. Kt's 7th.	20. K. to Kt's sq.
21. R. to Q. Kt's 8th (ch.)	21. K. to R's 2d.
22. R. to Q. Kt's 6th.	22. R. to Q. B's 2d.
23. B. to Q's 4th.	23. R. to K. B's 2d (ch.)

This is his only move to draw the game; and now, whether you take the Rook or not, he will succeed in preventing your winning.

ROOK AGAINST ROOK AND KNIGHT.

Diagram 32.

White, with the move, will win the Rook in four moves.

WHITE.	BLACK.
1. Kt. to K's 6th (ch.)	1. K. to Q's 4th.

(If instead he play K. to his 5th, White will check with R. at Kt's 4th.)

2. R. to Q's 8th (ch.)   2. K. to his 5th.
3. R. to Q's 4th (ch.)   3. K. moves.
4. K. takes R.

16

KING AND PAWN AGAINST KING AND PAWN.
Diagram 33.

WHITE.	BLACK.
	1. R. takes P. (ch.)
2. R. takes R.	2. P. to Q's 7th.
3. R. to Q's 5th.	3. K. takes R.
4. P. to Q's 7th.	4. P. Queens.
5. P. Queens (ch.)	

And wins.

KING AND TWO PAWNS AGAINST KING AND PAWN
Diagram 34.

First, suppose White moves:—

WHITE.	BLACK.
1. K. to Q's 4th.	1. K. to Q's 3d.
2. K. to Q's 3d.	2. K. to Q's 2d.
3. K. to K's 3d.	3. K. to K's 2d.
4. K. to Q's 4th.	4. K. to Q's 3d.
5. K. to K's 4th.	5. K. to K's 3d.

And the game must be drawn.

But suppose Black have to play:—

WHITE.	BLACK.
	1. K. to Q's 3d.
2. P. to K. B's 5th.	2. K. to K's 2d.
3. P. to K. B's 6th (ch.)	3. K. to his 3d.
4. K. to Q's 4th.	4. K. to Q's 3d.
5. P. to K. B's 7th.	5. K. to his 2d.
6. K. to his 5th.	6. K. takes P.
7. K. to Q's 6th.	7. K. to B's sq.
8. K. to his 6th.	8. K. to Kt's 2d.
9. K. to his 7th.	9. K. to Kt's sq.
10. K. to B's 6th.	10. K. to R's 2d.
11. K. to B's 7th.	11. K. to R's sq.
12. K. takes P.	12. K. to Kt's sq.
13. K. to B's 6th.	13. K. to R's 2d.
14. K. to B's 7th.	14. K. to R's sq.
15. K. to Kt's 6th.	15. K. to Kt's sq.
16. K. to R's 6th.	16. K. to R's sq.
17. P. to Kt's 6th.	

And wins.

KING AND TWO PAWNS AGAINST KING AND TWO PAWNS.
Diagram 35.

WHITE.	BLACK.
1. K. to his 3d.	1. K. to his 4th.
2. K. to B's 3d.	2. K. to B's 4th.

ENDINGS OF GAMES. 243

3. K. to Kt's 3d.   3. K. to K's 4th.
4. K. to Kt's 4th.   4. K. to B's 3d.
5. K. to Kt's 3d.   5. K. to K's 4th.

And the game is drawn.

If Black move, he plays:—

                1. K. to his 4th.
2. K. to his 3d.   2. K. to Q's 4th.

[Were he to move K. to B's 4th, you would win by 3. K. to Q's 4th.]

3. K. to B's 3d.   3. K. to his 4th.
4. K. to Kt's 3d.   4. K. to his 3d.
5. K. to Kt's 4th.   5. K. to B's 3d.

And by continuing to play thus, Black may always draw the game

KING AND TWO PAWNS AGAINST KING AND THREE PAWNS.

Diagram 36.

With or without the move Black wins.

First, with the move,—

WHITE.	BLACK.
	1. P. to K. Kt's 6th.
2. P. to R's 3d, or (A.)	2. K. to Q's 5th.
3. K. to B's 3d.	3. K. to his 4th.
4. K. to his 2d.	4. K. to his 5th.
5. K. to D's sq.	5. K. to Q's 6th.
6. K. to his sq.	6. K. to K's 6th.
7. K. to B's sq.	7. K. to Q's 7th.
8. K. to Kt's sq.	8. K. to his 7th.
9. K. to R's sq.	9. P. to B's 6th.
10. P. takes P.	10. K. to B's 7th.

Winning.

(A.)

2. P. takes P.	2. R. P. takes P.
3. K. to B's sq.	3. K. to his 6th.
4. K. to his sq.	4. K. to Q's 6th.
5. K. to B's sq.	5. K. to Q's 7th.
6. K. to Kt's sq.	6. K. to his 7th.
7. K. to R's sq.	7. P. to B's 6th.

And wins.

Next, if White move first he must equally lose.

WHITE.	BLACK.
1. K. to B's 2d.	1. P. to Kt's 6th (ch.)
2. K. to Kt's sq.	2. K. to his 6th.
3. K. to R's sq.	3. P. to B's 6th.
4. P. takes B. P.	4. K. to B's 7th, &c.

Winning.

244   CHESS HANDBOOK

No. 33.
BLACK.

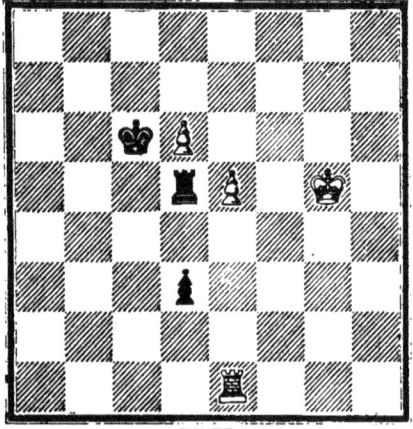

WHITE.

No. 34.
BLACK.

WHITE.

ENDINGS OF GAMES. 241

No. 35.
BLACK.

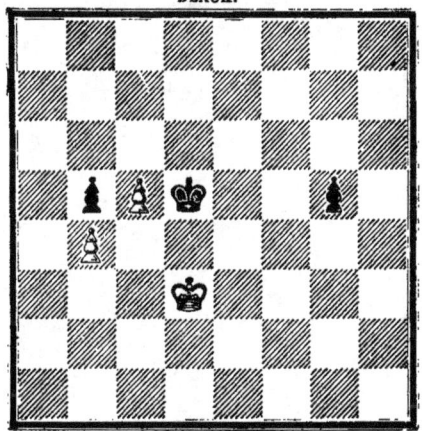

WHITE.

No. 36.
BLACK.

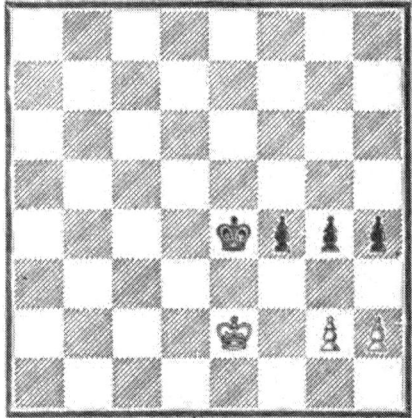

WHITE.

No. 37.
BLACK.

WHITE.

No. 38.
BLACK.

WHITE.

ENDINGS OF GAMES.

KING AGAINST THREE PASSED PAWNS.
Diagram 37.

WHITE.	BLACK.
	1. P. to B's 4th.
2. K. to Kt's 2d.	2. P. to R's 4th.
3. K. to Kt's 3d.	3. P. to Kt's 4th.
4. K. to Kt's 2d.	4. P. to B's 5th.
5. K. to B's 3d.	5. P. to R's 5th.
6. K. to Kt's 4th.	

And wins; because whatever Pawn is moved, the King takes it.

KING AND THREE PASSED PAWNS AGAINST KING AND THREE PASSED PAWNS.
Diagram 38.

WHITE.	BLACK.
	1. K. to Q's 2d.
2. P. to R's 4th.	2. K. to Q. B's 3d.
3. P. to R's 5th.	3. K. to Kt's 4th.
4. P. to Kt's 4th.	4. P. to R's 4th.
5. P. to B's 4th (ch.)	5. K. to R's 3d.
6. P. to B's 5th.	6. K. to Kt's 4th.
7. K. to B's 2d.	7. P. to R's 5th.
8. K. to Kt's 2d.	8. P. to Kt's 4th.
9. K. to R's 3d.	9. P. to B's 4th.
10. K. to R's 2d.	10. P. to B's 5th.
11. K. to Kt's 2d.	11. P. to Kt's 5th.
12. K. to Kt's sq.	12. P. to B's 6th.
13. K. to B's 2d.	13. P. to R's 6th.
14. K. to Kt's 3d.	14. Is obliged to move his King, and one of the White Pawns will Queen.

CHESS PROBLEMS.

PROBLEM 1.

White to play and mate in two moves.

WHITE.

CHESS PROBLEMS.

PROBLEM 2.
White to play and mate in two moves.

WHITE

PROBLEM 3.
White to play and mate in three moves.

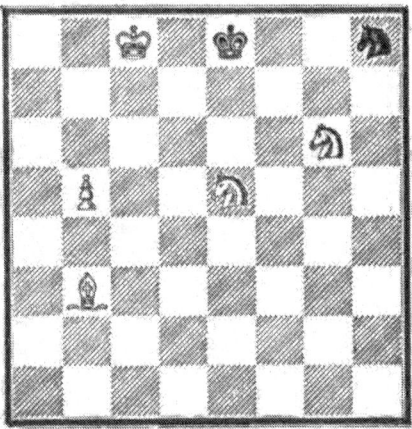

WHITE.

Problem 4.
White to play and mate in three moves

WHITE.

Problem 5.
White to play and mate in four moves.

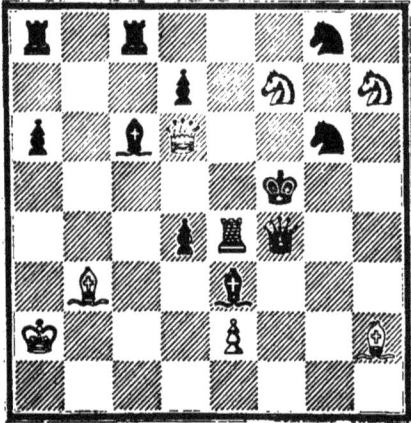

WHITE.

CHESS PROBLEMS.

PROBLEM 6.
White to play and mate in three moves.

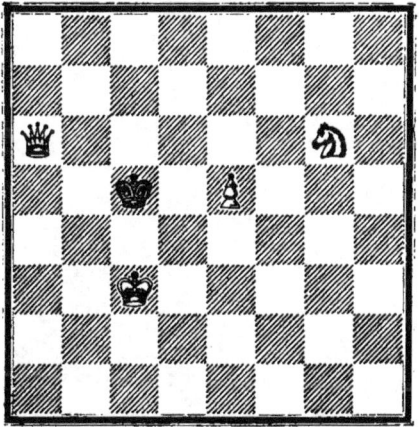

WHITE.

PROBLEM 7.
White to play and mate in three moves.

WHITE.

PROBLEM 8.
White to play and checkmate without moving his King

WHITE.

PROBLEM 9.
White to play and mate in four moves.

WHITE.

CHESS PROBLEMS.

Problem 10.
White to play and mate in three moves.

WHITE.

Problem 11.
White to play and mate in four moves.

WHITE.

Problem 12.

White to move his King alone and mate in five moves

WHITE.

SOLUTIONS TO PROBLEMS.

No. 1.

WHITE.	BLACK.
1. Q. to K. R's 4th.	If 1. K. to K's 4th.
2. Q. to K. B's 6th (checkmate.)	
	If 1. K. to Q. B's 4th
2. B. to Q. Kt's 6th (checkmate.)	
	If 1. K. to K's 6th.
2. Q. to K. B's 2d (checkmate.)	

No. 2.

WHITE.	BLACK.
1. R. to K. Kt's 8th.	If 1. B. takes R.
2. R. to Q. R's 7th (checkmate.)	
	If 1. Anything else
2. R. to Q. R's 8th (checkmate.)	

SOLUTIONS TO PROBLEMS.

No. 3.
WHITE. | BLACK.
- 8. to K. B's 7th (ch.) — 1. Kt. takes B.
- 2. Kt. to Q. B's 4th. — 2. Kt. moves.
- 3. Kt. to Q's 6th (checkmate.)

No. 4.
WHITE. | BLACK.
1. Kt. to K. Kt's 3d. — 1. K. B. takes P.
2. Kt. to K. B's 3d (ch.) — 2. K. to K. B's 5th.
3. Q. to K. R's 4th (checkmate.)

No. 5.
WHITE. | BLACK.
1. Q. to K's 6th (ch.) — 1. P. takes Q.
2. B. takes P. (ch.) — 2. K. takes B.
3. Kt. (at R's 7th) to K. Kt's 5th (ch.) — 3. Q. takes Kt.
4. Kt. to Q's 6th (checkmate.)

No. 6.
WHITE. | BLACK.
1. Kt. to K. R's 4th. — 1. K. to Q's 4th.
2. Q. to Q's 6th. (ch.) — 2. K. to K's 5th.
3. Q. to Q's 4th (checkmate.)

No. 7.
WHITE. | BLACK.
1. Kt. to K. Kt's 6th. — 1. K. to Q's 5th.
2. Q. to Q. B's 3d (ch.) — 2. K. takes P.
3. Q. to Q's 3d (checkmate.)

No. 8.
WHITE. | BLACK
1. Q. to Q's sq. (ch.) — 1. K. to Kt's 7th.
2. Q. to K's sq. — 2. K. to B's 6th.
3. Q. to Q's 2d. — 3. K. to K's 5th.
4. Q. to Q. B's 3d. — 4. K. to B's 5th.
5. Q. to Q's 3d. — 5. K. to Kt's 5th.
6. Q. to K's 3d. — 6. K. to R's 5th.
7. Q. to K. B's 3d. — 7. K. to Kt's 4th.
8. Q. to K's 4th. — 8. K. to R's 4th.
9. Q. to K. B's 4th. — 9. K. to Kt's 3d.
10. Q. to K's 5th. — 10. K. to R's 3d.
11. Q. to K. B's 5th. — 11. K. to Kt's 2d.
12. Q. to K's 6th. — 12. K. to R's sq.
13. Q. to Q's 7th. — 13. K. to Kt's sq.
14. Q. to K's 7th. — 14. K. to R's sq.
15. Q. to K. B's 8th (ch.) — 15. K. to R's 2d.
16. Q. to K. B's 6th. — 16. K. to Kt's sq.
17. Q. to K. R's 6th. — 17. K. to B's 2d.
18. Q. to Kt's 6th — 18. K. to K's 3d

WHITE	BLACK
19. Q. to B's 4th.	19. K. to K's 2d.
20. Q. to B's 5th.	20. K. to K's sq.
21. Q. to Q's 7th (ch.)	21. K. to B's sq.
22. Q. to K. R's 7th.	22. K. to K's sq.
23. Q. to K. Kt's 7th.	23. K. to Q's sq.
24. Q. to Q's 7th (checkmate.)	

No. 9.

WHITE	BLACK
1. Q. to K's 5th (ch.)	1. K. takes Q.
2. P. to Q's 4th (ch.)	2. P. takes P. in passing
3. P. takes P. (dis. ch.)	3. R. to K's 5th.
4. P. to Q's 4th (checkmate.)	

No. 10.

WHITE	BLACK
1. Kt. to K's 5th (dis. ch.)	1. K. to B's 5th (best.)
2. K. Kt's P. two.	2. K. takes R.
3. B. to Kt's 5th (checkmate.)	

No. 11.

WHITE	BLACK
1. R. to K. R's 4th.	1. B. takes Kt. (at Bl. Q's 6th.)
2. Kt. to K. Kt's 5th.	2. P. to K's 3d.
3. R. takes P. (ch.)	3. K. to K's 4th.
4. R. takes B. (disc. checkmate.)	

No. 12.

WHITE	BLACK
1. K. to K's sq.	1. K. to K's 5th
2. K. to K's 2d.	2. K. to B's 4th.
3. K. to B's 3d.	3. K. to K's 3d.
4. K. to B's 4th.	4. K. to Q's 3d.
5. K. to B's 5th (disc. ch.)	

THE END.

www.ingramcontent.com/pod-product-compliance
Lightning Source LLC
Chambersburg PA
CBHW072254130425
25082CB00010B/787